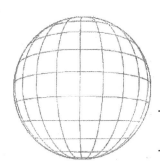

spssi

Spring 2002 Vol. 58, No. 1

Consequences of the Internet for Self and Society:
Is Social Life Being Transformed?
Issue Editors: Katelyn Y. A. McKenna and John A. Bargh

Issues in Progress
  Understanding the Harm of Hate Crime
    Robert Boeckmann and Carolyn Turpin-Petrosino
  Service Learning, Community Involvement, and Social Activism
    Arthur Stukas and Michelle Dunlap
  Aging in Society
    Toni Antonucci, Corann Okorududu, and Hiroko Akiyama
  The Residential Context of Health
    Terry Hartig and Roderick Lawrence
  Social Class and Education
    Joan M. Ostrove and Elizabeth R. Cole
  Religion as a Meaning System
    Israela Silberman
  Privacy
    Steve Margulis and Dianne Stone

Stuart Oskamp (1988–1992)
George Levinger (1984–1987)
Joseph E. McGrath (1979–1983)
Jacqueline D. Goodchilds (1974–1978)
Bertram H. Raven (1970–1973)
Joshua A. Fishman (1966–1969)
Leonard Soloman (1963)
Robert Chin (1960–1965)
John Harding (1956–1959)
M. Brewster Smith (1951–1955)
Harold H. Kelley (1949)
Ronald Lippitt (1944–1950)

Journal of Social Issues, Vol. 58, No. 1, 2002, pp. 1–8

Beyond Simple Truths: The Human-Internet Interaction

John A. Bargh*

New York University

The Internet is only 10 years old, but it has already had a great impact on the world. In its "early" days, it was both heralded as a liberating force for the spread of democracy and condemned as a grave threat to the social fabric. However, as the present articles indicate, our knowledge of the Internet across a variety of social science perspectives has now accumulated to where we have a good initial picture of how the Internet really is (or isn't) affecting social life. One theme stands out: These effects depend on how the unique qualities of Internet communication modes interact with the particular characteristics and goals of the individuals, groups, and communities using them.

The events of September 11, 2001, put many aspects of modern life in a new, stark, and poignant perspective. Among their many ramifications was to illuminate some of the positive, as well as the negative, consequences of the emergent Internet as a mode of interpersonal communication. Many of us who had friends, family, and colleagues in the downtown New York area found ourselves unable to make contact over the telephone, given the damage to vital communications switching and relay equipment. But the Internet was intact, at least enough so that e-mails were sent and received and people could stay in touch during many very dark hours. According to a Pew Foundation report (Rainie, 2001), in the 48 hours after the attack, between four and five million people turned to the Internet to make contact with loved ones and friends because they could not make contact via telephone.

Correspondence concerning this article should be addressed to John A. Bargh, Department of Psychology, New York University, 6 Washington Place, Seventh Floor, New York, NY 10003 [e-mail: john.bargh@nyu.edu]. Preparation of this article was supported in part by Public Health Service grant MH60767 and a fellowship from the Center for Advanced Study in the Behavioral Sciences, Stanford, California. I thank Grainne Fitzsimons and Katelyn McKenna for their helpful feedback on an earlier draft, and especially the authors of the articles in this issue for their contributions as well as their patience with the editorial process.

1

At the same time, the unfolding investigation into the terrorist attack has revealed that e-mail was a primary mode of communication for the network of conspirators allegedly responsible for it. The use of encryption technology made it especially difficult to decode the messages and so to gather intelligence about the movements and plans of terrorist suspects—making the Internet a much more effective means of secretive and sinister communication than the telephone or other communication modes (Kolata, 2001).

That the Internet as a mode of interpersonal communication lends itself to both beneficent and destructive uses and consequences is one theme that runs through the present issue. Although research on the social consequences of the Internet is still in its relative infancy, the issue's articles show that it has advanced beyond the initial stage of overly simplistic, "main effect" accounts. The wellsprings of these early views are clearly explicated in the article by Spears, Postmes, Lea, and Wolbert (this issue). According to their historical analysis, researchers studying the Internet from a computer science or communications orientation have been guided by the engineering concept of "communication bandwidth" and have assumed at a metatheoretical level that the reduction in social cues during Internet communication compared to the presumably richer face-to-face situation (with all of its attendant nonverbal, expressive cues) must necessarily have negative effects on social interaction. In contrast, researchers approaching the social consequences of the Internet from a social science perspective have taken a more "social deterministic" view, in which the role of personal strivings and interpersonal goals is assumed to be the sole determinant of the Internet's effects.

Thus, in the manner of the three blind men and the elephant, researchers have been prone to emphasizing the particular part of the Internet communication modality that they study as being solely responsible for its effects and consequences. As Spears et al. (this issue) point out, however, the engineering concentration on bandwidth focuses on the Internet's effect on the *quantity* of information transmitted but ignores its potential effects on the information *quality* or content (i.e., how it might alter the information being expressed) and on how that information might be perceived and interpreted by the recipient (i.e., how it might alter how the information is received). For its part, the social science focus on the individual's goals and purposes in using the Internet assumes—wrongly—that the Internet is just like any other communications medium, and that variations in communications media make no differences to outcomes.

The articles in this issue span a broad range of disciplinary perspectives on the Internet—from surveys of Internet users to experimental laboratory studies, and include interviews with Chinese business managers and American hate group members alike. Both quantitative and qualitative approaches to the question of how the Internet is affecting social life are featured. The levels of analysis range from the individual and psychological, to the interpersonal, to the group and organization, and finally to the community and governmental levels. What I found striking as a theme running throughout all of these contributions was that at every level of analysis, researchers report interactions between features of Internet use and communication on the one hand and critical features of their focal unit of analysis on the other. In other words, researchers are no longer talking about simple main effects of Internet use on people or groups or communities in general, but appear to have moved on to a more sophisticated and complex analysis.

The Person × Internet Interaction

That the particular and even unique aspects of the Internet communication situation interact with personal characteristics of the individuals involved to produce their effects on psychological and interpersonal outcomes is the conclusion reached in several of the present articles, most notably those by McKenna, Green, and Gleason (this issue) and by Kraut et al. (this issue). McKenna et al. focus on the establishment of close relationships over the Internet and show in their survey of Internet (newsgroup) users that differences in the presumed need or desire for a relationship (i.e., self-reported loneliness or social anxiety) do not directly predict who will form close Internet relationships, as the "social determinist" approach described by Spears et al. (this issue) might have predicted. Rather, effects of such interpersonal goals were entirely mediated by individual differences in preferred mode of self-expression (on-line versus face-to-face). Because the quality or nature of Internet interaction differs in important ways from face-to-face interaction, some people feel more comfortable in one domain than the other.

Kraut et al. (this issue) make a similar argument regarding the benefits of Internet use for a wide variety of measures of social and psychological well-being. Although their findings show that increases in Internet use are linked to a wide range of psychological and social benefits for all of their participants, on some outcome variables these benefits were moderated by whether the individual is an introvert or an extravert. Kraut et al. (this issue) advocate a "rich get richer" model of these social benefits, in which people who already possess relatively greater social skills (i.e., extraverts) are better able to use the Internet to meet new people and have profitable social interactions there than are those who are less socially skilled (i.e., introverts).

The Group × Internet Interaction

The "reduced cues"or "diminished bandwidth" of Internet communication compared to face-to-face settings creates an atmosphere of ambiguity. For instance, a given utterance can take on quite different meanings depending on whether it was said with a smile or not. The increased ambiguity inherent in Internet communications gives a greater role to the perceiver's or recipient's own goals, assumptions, and mindset as to how those communications are interpreted and understood (see, e.g., Higgins, 1989). Thompson and Nadler (this issue), for instance, review a decade of research on the characteristics of electronic negotiations between groups and note many traps and pitfalls that lay in wait for those who blithely treat the Internet communication situation as identical to the face-to-face setting. Among these is the e-mail sender's implicit assumption that the receiver will read each e-mail soon after it is sent, so that any delay in responding is therefore interpreted as deliberate and provocational. Here is truly a case in which the competitive nature of the intergroup negotiation relationship interacts with the "diminished bandwidth" of the Internet communication channel; the lack of trust causes the ambiguities resulting from the diminished bandwidth to be interpreted in a negative light.

It is instructive to compare this with how the same lack of cues are spun in a positive light when the goals of the interactants are different, as in the Internet relationships studied by McKenna et al. (this issue) and the "get acquainted" situations studied by Bargh, McKenna, and Fitzsimons (this issue). Here, people tend to "fill in the blanks" caused by the reduced cues on the Internet with idealized, hoped-for qualities of a best friend. Thus, the identical "diminished bandwidth" quality of the Internet produces a dramatically different outcome—idealization instead of suspicion—because of the different interpersonal goals of the interaction partners.

Another consequence of the relative anonymity afforded by Internet communication and interaction is derived from Spears et al.'s (this issue) "SIDE" model. As Spears and his coauthors argue, anonymous Internet settings do not so much "deindividuate" people, causing them to lose internal, self-related controls over their behavioral impulses, as they "depersonalize" them, making group aspects of identity relatively more salient and powerful as determinants of behavior. The consequence is that group norms become even more important guides to behavior under conditions of relatively anonymity, such as on Internet newsgroups and in chat rooms. All the more reason to be concerned about the existence of the Internet racist hate groups studied by Glaser, Dixit, and Green (this issue). Not only are people more free of the negative social consequences of publicly espousing such views when they do so under the cloak of anonymity, which can only increase the probability that they will do so, but their participation in an electronic group devoted to expressing those views will tend to incorporate that group identity into their self-concept (see McKenna & Bargh, 1998). In this way the hate group norms should be expected to become a more powerful guide to their behavior.

One other important feature of the Glaser et al. (this issue) research is how it takes advantage of the Internet to study a problem that is otherwise not easily tractable. Were it not for the cloak of anonymity afforded by the Internet chat room setting—say if they were approached by an interviewer on the street—the hate group members would be unlikely to acknowledge, much less espouse, the views they do in the chat room. This is not even to mention the difficulty of finding the members in other "real-life" venues in the first place. The article by Nosek, Banaji, and Greenwald (this issue) is a comprehensive and practical guide to doing research over the Internet and, along with detailed advice on data collection and methodologies, promotes the value of conducting social science research of any type on-line, not just studies of the effects of the Internet itself. To take just one example, concerns with the generalizability of laboratory studies of college undergraduates can be at least partly assuaged by replication via an Internet Web site, where a much wider age and demographic range of people can participate.

The Community × Internet Interaction

One major concern with the Internet is the so-called digital divide: whether the benefits of Internet use and access are being reaped only by the wealthier segments of the population, leaving the less well-off behind (i.e., "the rich get richer"). Borgida et al. (this issue) focus on this in their study of two different communities in Minnesota. What efforts, if any, were made in these two towns to have access to Internet technology penetrate to all strata of society? Borgida and his colleagues show that the history and political traditions of the particular community strongly determine whether "free-nets," or publicly provided Internet access, will be supplied to those who could not afford it otherwise. One town with a long history of providing social safety nets did set up such a free-net, whereas the other town with historically a more laissez-faire approach relied on for-profit local Internet service providers to provide its citizens with access.

As Borgida et al. (this issue) continue their study of these two communities, it will be interesting to see how the broader based Internet access of the one community affects the political participation of its citizens, relative to the other community. One of the bright hopes for the Internet for many years has been that it will facilitate the spread of democracy, both through making information more widely available to a wider range of citizens and through facilitating communication and spread of information among citizens, instead of having that information tightly controlled by governments and other power holders. Deibert (this issue) focuses on exactly this issue, in the case of the Chinese government's attempt to manage Internet use. According to his findings and analysis, the Chinese government seeks to glean the benefits (especially for commerce) of the Internet while at the same time controlling its citizens' access to outside sources of information about China and the world. The case of China is thus an important bellwether of the future, as to whether—contrary to much current belief that it is not possible—governments will be able to manage and control the effects of the Internet on their citizens.

What Are the Kids Up To?

As noted above, an individual's particular goals and motivations during the Internet interaction play a major role in how he or she will feel about the interaction partner. In a competitive atmosphere, it will be distrust and suspicion in the absence of clear evidence to the contrary; for those who really need someone to talk to, to understand them, to like them, it will be to assume, in the absence of knowledge to the contrary, the existence in the other person of all of one's ideal, hoped-for qualities. Many of us worry that this latter group of individuals often will get their hopes up too high and be disappointed, or worse, taken advantage of, by those with few scruples and more experience in the social world.

For no societal group is this concern stronger than for children and teenagers, who not only are less sophisticated and experienced in the ways of the world but are growing up with Internet communication as a normal part of everyday life, much as the telephone was to young people of the 1950s. Those two facts, when combined with the apparently naturally seductive qualities of Internet interaction (see Bargh et al., this issue), are indeed some cause for concern. They make studies of children's social use of the Internet such as that by Gross, Juvonen, and Gable (this issue) all the more important. Fortunately, what Gross and her coauthors find is that preteenagers tend to interact over the Internet with the same people they interact with to face: namely, their friends at school. Still, there are children who are not as popular and who don't have all that many friends—and so, logically, they will be more prone and vulnerable to interacting with strangers, as Gross et al. observe.

Thus, if there is one policy recommendation I'd personally want to make based on all the findings and insights contained in this issue,[1] it would be to make parents more aware of all the social interaction happening over the Internet— parents who for the most part are not nearly as computer-literate or "worldly" about cyberspace as are their children and who may not be aware of what it is their child is doing all those hours on the computer. Not that, given the findings of Gross et al., there are reasons at present to be alarmed, but it wouldn't hurt for parents in general to become better informed about all the social interaction going on over the Internet and to monitor it as they do other modes of their child's social interchange (e.g., telephone and face-to-face venues).

---

[1] And there is only this one. I share Howard, Rainie, and Jones's (in press) opinion that we don't yet know enough about the social effects of the Internet to be making strong policy recommendations; these have been made in the recent past based on research conclusions that were subsequently retracted (see Guernsey, 2001). Unless, that is, the recommendation be no regulation of the social aspects: As Spears et al. (this issue) point out, we should no more recommend regulation of Internet communication because of isolated cases of misuse than we would recommend regulation of face-to-face communication because of the occasional cases of interpersonal violence.

Internet Research: The Next Wave

Superficial aspects of Internet use—the image of the teenager alone at his or her computer terminal—have fostered the popular misconception that the Internet produces social isolation and weaker ties with family and friends (Nie & Erbring, 2000). As Nie recently argued, "When you've spent hours surfing the Internet, it is by definition something you do by yourself" (quoted in Guernsey, 2001). However, when one looks a little deeper, as do the researchers in the present issue, one draws a quite different conclusion. Use of Internet communication modes for purposes of social interaction continues to grow worldwide at a rapid rate, and as Tyler (this issue) concludes from the findings described in this issue, these interactions have much of the same impact and consequence for people as if they had taken place face to face.

And yet we have only begun the task of serious scientific research into the ways that these social interaction processes might operate differently than they do in traditional face-to-face settings. Tyler (this issue) notes further that we need less description of effects of Internet use and more theory about underlying processes, along with analysis of the critical components of communication modes, that will enable us to anticipate and predict in advance what the social effects of the next communications breakthrough will be. Major communications breakthroughs of the past, such as television, and before that the telephone, the telegraph, and the postal service, have all had profound effects on social life as well as interpersonal relations. Tyler's challenge to Internet researchers is to provide an analysis of the critical features that distinguish one domain of social interaction from the others and of how these features, separately or in combination, affect and in part determine social life. Only then will we really know what is happening out there in cyberspace—and, more importantly, why.

References

Guernsey, L. (2001, July 26). Cyberspace isn't so lonely after all. *New York Times*, p. A1.

Higgins, E. T. (1989). Knowledge accessibility and activation: Subjectivity and suffering from unconscious sources. In J. S. Uleman & J. A. Bargh (Eds.), *Unintended thought* (pp. 75–123). New York: Guilford.

Howard, P. E. N., Rainie, L., & Jones, S. (in press). Days and nights on the Internet: The impact of a diffusing technology. *American Behavioral Scientist.*

Kolata, G. (2001, September 25). When science inadvertently aids an enemy. *New York Times*, p. B1.

McKenna, K. Y. A., & Bargh, J. A. (1998). Coming out in the age of the Internet: Identity "de-marginalization" from virtual group participation. *Journal of Personality and Social Psychology, 75*, 681–694.

Nie, N. H., & Erbring, L. (2000). Internet and society: A preliminary report [On-line]. Stanford, CA: Institute for the Quantitative Study of Society. Available: www.stanford.edu/group/siqss

Rainie, L. (2001, September 15). How Americans used the Internet after the terror attack [On-line]. Washington, DC: Pew Internet & American Life Project. Available: www.pewinternet.org

JOHN A. BARGH is Professor of Psychology and Director of the Graduate Program in Social-Personality Psychology at New York University, where he has been on the faculty since receiving his PhD in Social Psychology from the University of Michigan in 1981. He is the editor of four books and the author of over 100 publications focusing mainly on the role of nonconscious influences on emotion, judgment, and social behavior. He is a recipient of the Early Career Contribution Award from the American Psychological Association and a John Simon Guggenheim Memorial Foundation fellowship.

Journal of Social Issues, Vol. 58, No. 1, 2002, pp. 9–31

Relationship Formation on the Internet: What's the Big Attraction?

Katelyn Y. A. McKenna,* **Amie S. Green, and Marci E. J. Gleason**
New York University

We hypothesized that people who can better disclose their "true" or inner self to others on the Internet than in face-to-face settings will be more likely to form close relationships on-line and will tend to bring those virtual relationships into their "real" lives. Study 1, a survey of randomly selected Internet newsgroup posters, showed that those who better express their true self over the Internet were more likely than others to have formed close on-line relationships and moved these friendships to a face-to-face basis. Study 2 revealed that the majority of these close Internet relationships were still intact 2 years later. Finally, a laboratory experiment found that undergraduates liked each other more following an Internet compared to a face-to-face initial meeting.

The Internet has become a prime venue for social interaction (D'Amico, 1998). Through e-mail, chat rooms, instant messaging, newsgroups, and other means, people are sharing aspects of their daily lives, talking about interests with like-minded others, and keeping in touch with family and friends. Social interaction has become the primary use of home computers (e.g., Moore, 2000). In the midst of all this social activity, people are forming relationships with those whom they meet on the Internet—especially those with whom they interact on a regular basis.

In many if not most ways, social interaction on the Internet resembles that in traditional, face-to-face venues (see Tyler, this issue). However, we will argue that there are some important differences. For example, there are qualities of Internet communication and interaction, such as its greater anonymity, that are known to produce greater intimacy and closeness. There are aspects of the Internet

---

Correspondence concerning this article should be addressed to Katelyn Y. A. McKenna, Department of Psychology, New York University, 6 Washington Place, Seventh Floor, New York, NY 10003 [e-mail: mckenna@psych.nyu.edu]. Preparation of this manuscript was supported in part by a Research Challenge Fund grant from New York University to McKenna.

that enable partners to get past the usual obstacles or "gates" that in traditional interaction settings often prevent potentially rewarding relationships from getting off the ground. Still other features facilitate relationship development by providing meeting places for specialized interests, so that members have important features in common from the start.

Special Qualities of Internet Communication

The Intimate Internet

Considerable research on intimate relationships has shown that both self-disclosure and partner disclosure increase the experience of intimacy in interactions (e.g., Laurenceau, Barrett, & Pietromonaco, 1998; Reis & Shaver, 1988). However, disclosing quite intimate information about oneself normally occurs only after liking and trust have been established between relationship partners. As Derlega and Chaikin (1977) posited, individuals usually do not engage in self-disclosure with one another until they are confident that they have formed a "dyadic boundary," ensuring that information disclosed by one is not leaked by the other to mutual acquaintances. Even so, such a dyadic boundary may be violated or the other member may respond negatively to the disclosure. As Pennebaker (1989) and others (e.g., Derlega, Metts, Petronio, & Margulis, 1993) have noted, there are clear dangers in disclosing personal information, such as the risk of ridicule or outright rejection by one's friends and family.

The relative anonymity of Internet interactions greatly reduces the risks of such disclosure, especially about intimate aspects of the self, because one can share one's inner beliefs and emotional reactions with much less fear of disapproval and sanction (see McKenna & Bargh, 1999, 2000). In this way, self-disclosures with on-line acquaintances are similar to the "strangers on a train" phenomenon (e.g., Rubin, 1975), in which people sometimes share quite intimate information with their anonymous seatmates. Derlega and Chaikin (1977) note that people often engage in greater self-disclosure with strangers, because a stranger does not have access to a person's social circle, and thus the dyadic boundary cannot be violated. Unlike with the stranger on a train, however, people often have repeated interactions with those they get to know on-line, so that early self-disclosure lays the foundation for a continuing, close relationship.

Getting Past the Gates

A second reason for greater self-disclosure on-line is the lack of the usual "gating features" to the establishment of any close relationship—easily discernible features such as physical appearance (attractiveness), an apparent stigma such as stuttering (McKenna & Bargh, 1999), or visible shyness or social anxiety. These gates often prevent people who are less physically attractive or socially skilled from developing relationships to the stage at which disclosure of intimate information could begin. Research has long shown the strong impact that these features have not only upon first impressions, but also in determining whether a friendship or romantic relationship will begin between two people (e.g., Hatfield & Sprecher, 1986). On the Internet such features are not initially in evidence and thus do not stop potential relationships from getting off the ground. We will return to this topic again in Study 3.

Finding Similar Others

The unique structure of the Internet allows individuals to easily find others who share specialized interests. We tend to be more attracted to others who are similar to ourselves and share our opinions (e.g., Byrne, 1971). Even within long-standing relationships, the more similar two people are, the more compatible they are, and the more likely married couples are to remain together (e.g., Byrne, 1997). However, it may be hard to find others who share one's interests in one's local area, and when people get to know one another in the traditional manner, it generally takes time to establish whether they have commonalities and to what extent. But when someone joins a newsgroup devoted to, for example, aging ferrets, he or she already knows that there is a shared base of interest with the others there. This allows the members to move quickly forward to find out what other key interests they might share and may provide a headstart to relationships.

Implications of the Distinct Qualities for Relationship Formation

It should be the case that relationships will develop closeness and intimacy significantly faster over the Internet than will relationships begun off-line, because of the greater ease of self-disclosure, as well as the founding of the relationship on more substantive bases, such as shared interests (as opposed to physical attractiveness alone). If it is the case that these relationships form on the basis of deeper and more substantive factors, one would expect not only that these relationships will become intimate quickly, but that they will be stable over time. Relationships formed on these grounds should also be able to better survive a face-to-face meeting, when gating features do come into operation.

What Is Disclosed in Self-Disclosure?

The self-relevant information that one shares with a relationship partner in the course of developing trust and intimacy is not the widely known features of one's public persona or "actual self" (Higgins, 1987), but the identity-important yet usually unexpressed aspects of oneself. What we refer to here as the "Real Me" is that version of self that a person believes he or she actually is, but is unable to or prevented from (for any of a variety of reasons) presenting to others in most situations (see Bargh, McKenna, & Fitzsimons, this issue, for more on alternative versions of self). This concept is derived directly from Carl Rogers' (1951) therapeutic notion of the "true self"—that of the client feeling "he was not being his real self . . . and felt satisfaction when he had become more truly himself" (p. 136).

The special qualities of Internet communication discussed above would be expected to have the general effect of facilitating disclosure and expression of the inner or true self, compared to face-to-face interaction, in which one's usual or "actual" self-qualities should predominate. Bargh et al. (this issue) provide evidence that Internet interaction settings do facilitate expression of the true self for the average person in an initial meeting with a stranger. Our focus here is on individual differences in the degree to which a person expresses his or her true-self concept over the Internet rather than in "real life" interaction settings. Those who do, we believe, will be more likely than others to form close and meaningful Internet relationships.

Who Will Form Strong Internet Relationships?

Logically, those individuals who are able to find similar others in traditional settings, who are able to get past the usual gating features by force of personality, attractiveness, charm, or wit, and who have the social skills needed to communicate themselves well and effectively have little need to express their true selves or "Real Me" over the Internet. The rest of us should be glad that the Internet exists. For to the extent one is commonly blocked from establishing relationships for any of the above reasons, one will have a stronger, unmet need to express his or her true self. Thus we would expect people who are lonely or are socially anxious in traditional, face-to-face interaction settings to be likely to feel better able to express their true self over the Internet and so to develop close and meaningful relationships there.

A second reason why Internet relationships should become important to the individual follows from social identity theory. Representations of external social entities, such as groups, through which the individual defines his or her identity tend to become incorporated into the self-concept (see Spears, Postmes, Lea, & Wolbert, this issue). Recent conceptualizations of the self as relational in nature (e.g., Chen & Andersen, 1999; Baldwin, 1997), in fact, also hold that one's self becomes "entangled" or defined in large part in terms of those important relationships.

Therefore, we would expect people who express and disclose their true self more over the Internet to consider the relationships they form there to be identity-important, whereas those who better express and disclose these aspects of self with those they meet off-line should tend to consider off-line, non-Internet relationships more defining of their identity (and thus more important). That is, where the person locates his or her "Real Me," on- versus off-line, should mediate whether or not he or she forms close relationships on the Internet.

Turning Virtual Relationships Into Social Realities

What will the fate of these relationships be? Will they be confined forever to cyberspace? We do not believe so. From separate lines of research on social identity, it is known that people are highly motivated to make important aspects of identity a "social reality" (Gollwitzer, 1986), through making them known to their social circle of friends and family (see Deaux, 1996; McKenna & Bargh, 1998). When one combines the principles of the social identity and the relational-self theories, a novel and potentially important hypothesis emerges about the fate of relationships formed over the Internet. If, as these theories hold, people are motivated to make important new aspects of their identity a social reality, and if—as the recent conceptions of the relational self posit—important relationships also become aspects of one's identity, then people should be motivated to make their important new relationships a social reality, that is, to bring them into their "real lives," to make them public and face to face.

Being the Real Me: A Model of Relationship Formation on the Internet

We propose that those who feel that they can better express their true selves on the Internet than they can in their non-Internet areas of life will be more likely to form close relationships with those they meet on-line. We include as two determinants of who might be more likely to locate their true selves on-line those who (1) experience social anxiety in face-to-face settings and (2) are lonely. However, there are likely several other such determinants (e.g., single working parents with little time for a social life), and by no means is it just the anxious or lonely who will form close relationships over the Internet (as our results show). Those who locate their true selves on-line, as opposed to off-line, will feel that their on-line relationships develop much more quickly than do their non-Internet relationships, these relationships will be close and meaningful, and they will be motivated to move these relationships into their face-to-face lives through a series of stages. These close relationships should also be durable and stable over time.

In order to test these predictions, we conducted two surveys and a laboratory experiment. In Study 1 we examined whether those who do locate the true self more on-line are indeed more likely to form close virtual relationships and to then integrate these relationships into their off-line lives. Study 2 examined the stability of these relationships 2 years later. Our third study is an experimental test of the role that anonymity and gating features play in the development of feelings of liking for another in on-line versus face-to-face interactions.

Study 1: The On-Line Real Me and Internet Relationship Development

Method

Sampling of newsgroups. A set of 20 Usenet newsgroups was randomly selected for this study. At the time of the study, there were approximately 16,000 newsgroups in existence. We eliminated "personals" and "penpals" newsgroups because we were interested in relationships that formed naturally from Internet interactions per se, not because the individuals were deliberately using the Internet in order to find partners. The universe of potential newsgroups was further restricted to those in which there were at least 75 posts per week and in which at least half of the posts were targeted solely to that newsgroup. This left a final population of approximately 700 newsgroups. The sample of newsgroups was randomly selected from this set in proportion to the number of newsgroups available in each of the seven major Usenet hierarchies, in order that the final sample would be representative of all Internet newsgroups. Accordingly, newsgroups were selected from each of the hierarchies. (Examples of those included are talk.politics, rec.pets.cats, comp.unix.programmer, misc.kids.health, sci.astronomy, alt.gothic.fashion, and soc.history.)

Measures. The survey contained 36 items designed to assess the relation between (a) social anxiety, (b) loneliness, (c) expression of the real self, (d) the type of relationship formed, (e) the depth of the relationship formed, and (f) behavioral actions in on-line settings (e.g., exchanging electronic mail) as well as in "real life" settings (e.g., having an affair, meeting in person). To create the indices described below, scores on each item were first separately standardized and then the mean of the items taken. Six items from Leary's (1983) Interaction Anxiousness Scale measured the respondents' level of social anxiety in face-to-face situations, along with five items from the UCLA Loneliness Scale (Russell, 1996).

Four additional questions addressed the location of the respondent's *real self*— whether the respondent felt that he or she could more easily share central aspects of identity with Internet friends than with "real life" friends or vice versa. Two items, to which the respondent answered either "yes" or "no," were: "Do you think you reveal more about yourself to people you know from the Internet than to real life (non-'Net) friends?" and "Are there things your Internet friends know about you that you cannot share with real life (non-'Net) friends?" A further two questions assessed the extent to which the respondent expressed different facets of self on the Internet than he or she did to others in real life and the extent to which a respondent's family and friends would be surprised were they to read his or her Internet e-mail and newsgroup postings. These last 2 questions were rated on 7-point scales, ranging from 1 (*not at all*) to 7 (*a great deal*).

Another question addressed the *intimacy of relationship* formed. On a 4-point scale (1 = *acquaintance*, 2 = *friend*, 3 = *very close or "best" friend*, 4 = *romantic partner*), respondents rated the closest Internet relationship they had formed to that point in time. To measure the *closeness* of the relationship formed via the Internet, 10 items were taken from Parks and Floyd's (1995) Levels of Development in On-Line Relationships Scale.

A question was included assessing the *pace* at which the respondents felt that their new on-line relationships generally develop as compared to new face-to-face relationships on a 3-point scale ranging from 1 (*typically slower*) to 3 (*typically faster*).

Relevant *behaviors* were measured in both the on-line and off-line domains. Respondents were asked to respond whether (yes or no) they had engaged in specific activities with the person they feel closest to on the Internet and the frequency of each of those activities in an average week. Items measuring on-line behaviors asked about exchanging e-mail and chatting on-line. Items measuring off-line activities concerned talking on the telephone, writing letters through the mail, and meeting one another in face-to-face situations. Additional behavioral measures included whether the respondent had ever had an affair with, or become engaged to, someone he or she had met via the Internet (yes or no).

Procedure. Over a 3-week period, questionnaires were e-mailed to every fifth poster in each newsgroup selected for the study, excluding advertisements ("spam" posts) and individuals who cross-posted to other newsgroups, until a total of 100 posters in each newsgroup had been sent a survey. In the event that the fifth poster had already been selected for the survey or that the poster did not fit the qualification for inclusion in the survey, the next (sixth) poster was selected.

Results and Discussion

Sample characteristics. Of the 2,000 surveys sent to posters, 568 were completed and returned. An additional 317 surveys were undeliverable. The response rate was thus 34%. The sample was composed of 333 females (59%) and 234 males (41%). The age of respondents ranged from 13 to 70, with the mean age being 32 years. Participants had been using the Internet for a mean of 34 months (ranging from 1 to 243 months).

Creation of indices. The items constituting the Social Anxiety index had an associated reliability coefficient (Cronbach's alpha) of .81, and the items related to the Loneliness index had a reliability coefficient for the index of .78. The associated reliability coefficient for the 4 items related to the expression of the Real Me was .83. Similarly, the 10 items involving the Closeness of the relationship possessed a reliability coefficient of .93.

In order to test the hypothesized mediational model, we conducted a structural equation modeling analysis of the relations between Social Anxiety,

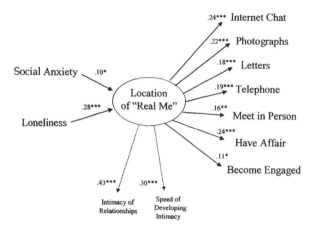

Fig. 1. Structural equation modeling analysis of the hypothesized determinants of Internet relationship formation and the transition of these relationships into real life, Study 1.
Note. Only statistically reliable paths shown. $*p < .05.$ $**p < .01.$ $***p < .001.$

Loneliness, the Real Me, Relationship Intimacy, Closeness, On-Line Behaviors, and Off-Line Behaviors. As can be seen in Figure 1, the predicted model was argely confirmed.

   Structural equation modeling analysis. First, as predicted, locating the Real Me on the Internet is significantly more likely for those who experienced higher levels of social anxiety and loneliness. Those who have a more difficult time with traditional social interactions and who feel more isolated and lonely turn to the Internet as a means of expressing facets of themselves that they are unable to express in their non-Internet lives.
   The next step of the model calls for the location of the Real Me to mediate between social anxiety and loneliness, on the one hand, and the benefits of fuller self-expression and disclosure, on the other. In support of this prediction, it can be seen in Figure 1 that the more people express facets of the self on the Internet that they cannot or do not express in other areas of life, the more likely they are to form strong attachments to those they meet on the Internet. Indeed, their on-line relationships generally develop more quickly as compared to their non-Internet relationships. They also tend to eventually bring Internet friends into their real life, through phone conversations, exchanging letters and pictures, and meeting them in person. Finally, these Internet relationships can become quite intimate, as those who feel their real selves reside on the Internet, compared to those who don't, are significantly more likely to become engaged to, or have an affair with, someone they met on the Internet. In sum, Internet acquaintanceships can and do develop into close and even intimate relationships.
   It is clear from these findings that those who participate in Internet newsgroups do tend to bring the friendships they form there into their everyday, non-Internet

lives. A full 63% of all respondents had spoken to someone they met via the Internet on the telephone, 56% had exchanged pictures of themselves, 54% had written a letter through the post, and 54% had met with an Internet friend in a face-to-face situation, tending to meet an individual an average of eight times.

Note that the lack of any reliable *direct* paths between social anxiety and loneliness, on the one hand, and relationship intimacy, closeness, and any of the off-line behaviors, on the other, further indicates the mediational role of the location of the true self. Believing that one is more one's real self on the Internet plays a crucial role in the formation of strong attachments to those one meets there and whether one brings that relationship into one's real life.

Absolute Real Me. The results just described are based upon the Real Me index as a continuous variable, with high or low scores *relative* to those of the other respondents. Thus, it is possible that all respondents had located their true self in the "real world" but simply to varying degrees, or it could be that all had located the true self on the Internet. To ensure that it is the *absolute* location of the true self—either on the Internet or in the "real world"—that matters, we recategorized respondents as locating their Real Me in an absolute sense either on-line or off-line.

The Real Me variable was redefined in terms of (1) those who locate the real self purely in the off-line domain, (2) those who locate the self equally in both the off-line and on-line domains, and (3) those for whom the real self resides purely in the on-line domain. Specifically, the Absolute Real Me variable was scored as follows: "Pure Off-Line" was defined as those who responded (a) that they did not reveal more about themselves to Internet friends than to off-line ("real-life") friends, (b) that their Internet friends did not know things about them that the respondent's off-line friends did not know, and (c) on the "not at all" side of the scale (i.e., less than 4) for *both* of the questions assessing the extent to which different facets of self were expressed mainly on the Internet. Those whom we termed "'Tweeners" were those whose responses were mixed (i.e., with a 4, with greater than 4 to some questions and less than 4 to others, with a yes to one question and a no to the other), and "Pure On-Line" was defined as the flip side of the off-liners (greater than 4s and yes to both dichotomous questions). In support of the proposed model, the results of the analyses were unchanged.

Our model also holds that whoever locates the true self on-line, regardless of anxiety and loneliness levels, will be more likely to form on-line relationships. Computing the same mediational model but including only those respondents who were *low* on both social anxiety (scoring less than 3 on 1–5 scale) and loneliness (2 or less on a 1–4 scale) yielded results consistent with that prediction. All of the significant paths in Figure 1 remained significant when the model was recomputed only for the nonanxious and nonlonely respondents, with one exception: The expression of the true self on the Internet did not lead to a significantly greater tendency to meet with Internet friends face to face or to become engaged to an

Internet partner ($ps > .20$). One reason for this may be that, with the understandable exception of those who met in order to conduct an affair, people who are not lonely in their regular lives do not feel a need to meet in real life with Internet friends. They are presumably satisfied with the relationships they have formed and the closeness they have achieved in them.

Gender differences. Although analyses controlling for gender show that the model held for members of both genders, not surprisingly there were differences in the ways that males and females assessed their Internet relationships. Previous research has shown that women more than men tend to self-disclose to others, even in casual encounters (e.g., Cozby, 1973; Jourard, 1964). Caldwell and Peplau (1982) found that women's friendships tend to be more deeply intimate than men's. Women place greater emphasis on talking and sharing emotions, whereas men tend to focus on shared activities. In terms of romantic relationships, women and men do not differ in how much they are willing to reveal to one another, but they do differ in the types of things they reveal (Rubin, Hill, Peplau & Dunkel-Schetter, 1980). These differences in the way men and women perceive and experience relationships were borne out in the present study.

Males and females equally engaged in such activities as e-mailing, meeting, exchanging pictures, writing letters, and getting together in Internet Relay Chat (IRC). Following Caldwell and Peplau's findings, females characterized the relationships they formed over the Internet as more intimate than did males (see Figure 2). Ancillary analyses showed that females described the relationships they formed as being significantly closer and deeper than did males across each of the 10 items comprising the relationship closeness index (all $ps < .01$). However,

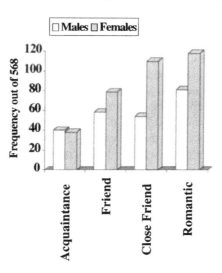

Fig. 2. The closest Internet relationships formed by males and females.

males and females involved in romantic relationships did not significantly differ across these 10 items (all $ps > .15$).

The presence-control exchange. We conducted a path analysis in order to test the sequence that an individual follows in moving a relationship from the on-line realm into that of the real world. We hypothesized that people would gradually, through a series of stages, give up the safety and control over the interaction afforded by the Internet for the greater physical reality and intimacy—but greater risk and lower personal control—of the real world. It is useful here to treat intimacy and control as commodities of a sort, in that one can trade or exchange some of one for some of the other. On e-mail, for instance, one can choose if or when to respond and do so without the pressures of real-time conversational demands; yet this greater control comes at the cost of psychological distance from the other person. In chat rooms, one gives up some control over the interaction for the greater richness of interacting in real time. Likewise, exchanging letters or telephoning requires one to give up control over details of one's identity, but one gains the greater trust and intimacy of those communication modes, as well as some degree of physical reality. Finally, interacting in person gives up all of the control advantages of the Internet in exchange for physical and psychological closeness.

Because all of the respondents reported that they had exchanged e-mail with their Internet acquaintances, the analysis was conducted beginning (as the exogenous variable) with the second most popular on-line activity, that of talking via IRC. As predicted, individuals start Internet relationships with relatively high control over the encounter and gradually relinquish that control in a series of stages (see Figure 3). It is noteworthy that there are no significant direct paths between talking via IRC (or exchanging letters) and meeting in person. The *only* significant path to meeting in person is from talking on the telephone. Thus, unless an Internet relationship progresses to the point at which the participants are talking with one another via the telephone, it is unlikely that the participants will take the final step of meeting face to face.

In summary, Study 1 strongly supported the central prediction that close and meaningful relationships do form on the Internet, as well as the proposed model of who will tend to form them and why. When people locate their true self on

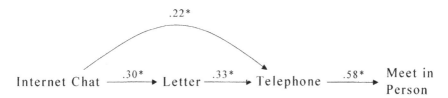

Fig. 3. Sequence of stages in exchanging control over interaction for greater intimacy in the relationship, Study 1.
$^*p < .0001$. For all paths not shown, $p > .25$.

the Internet, they presumably integrate their strong Internet relationships into their identity and self-structure and so want to make them a social reality, bringing these relationships into their real lives. Moreover, Internet relationships tend to develop closeness and intimacy more quickly than do real-life relationships. But do they last? In Study 2 we returned to these same respondents 2 years later and asked them how their Internet relationships had fared over time.

Study 2: The Temporal Stability of Internet Relationships

If, as we have argued, the bases for the formation of Internet friendships and relationships are not so much the traditional ones, such as physical attraction, but are more substantively grounded in mutual expression of true selves and discovery of common interests, then it follows that these relationships should be relatively durable and stable over time.

Method

Two years after the initial data collection, participants in Study 1 were re-contacted. A follow-up survey was e-mailed to each participant. Of the original 568 participants, 214 could no longer be reached at the original e-mail addresses. Of the 354 participants whose addresses remained valid, 145 completed and returned the survey, for a response rate of 41%.

Measures. The follow-up survey included the same measures taken 2 years earlier: social anxiety, loneliness, expression of the real self, and frequencies of on-line and off-line behaviors with the relationship partner (see Study 1). In order to reduce the time burden on the entirely volunteer participants (and so increase response rate), the questionnaire was shortened to a total of 30 items in the following manner: First, the 10 items assessing relationship closeness were omitted (these had correlated strongly with the single item assessing the intimacy of the relationship in Study 1); second, we included only the single question "I wish I had more confidence in social situations" to assess social anxiety (it had explained 81% of the variance in the social anxiety index in Study 1); thirdly and similarly, the single question, "How often do you feel that you are no longer close to anyone?" was used to assess loneliness, as it was found to explain 83% of the variance in the Study 1 loneliness index.

Measures of off-line loneliness and social anxiety were again included in the follow-up because, if socially anxious and lonely individuals are expanding their social circles through forming important relationships on the Internet and then successfully integrating them into their non-Internet lives (as Study 1 found), one would expect that this would lead to a reduction in feelings of loneliness and, perhaps, of social anxiety. It is possible that the positive reinforcement and successful formation of these on-line relationships might lead to feelings of greater self-efficacy in the traditional social domain for those with interaction anxiety (e.g., Bandura, 1977).

Therefore, several new items were added to the follow-up survey, asking respondents *directly* whether they felt that using the Internet had made them become more lonely, had made them become less lonely, or had not affected them in this way, and whether they felt that they had fewer, more, or the same number of friends since they began using the Internet. Respondents were also asked to report whether they felt that using the Internet had affected feelings of depression.

In order to discover the fate of the relationship that participants had reported to us in 1997, we included a question asking about the present status (i.e., in 1999) of that relationship. We also included a question asking whether (yes or no) the participant considered his or her Internet relationships to be as real, as important, and as close as his or her off-line relationships. We also asked participants about the number of virtual friendships they had developed in which they were able to share very personal and intimate aspects of their lives. Finally, respondents were specifically asked whether they believe they are more their true selves on the Internet or off-line on a 7-point scale from 1 (*not at all*) to 7 (*very much*); this item was included in the Real Me index.

Results and Discussion

Sample characteristics. The sample was composed of 33% male and 67% female respondents. The age of respondents ranged from 16 to 72, with the mean age being 34.5 years. Participants had been using the Internet for a mean of 63 months (with a range from 25 to 204 months).

Relationship stability. In line with our prediction, our respondents' on-line relationships remained relatively stable and durable over the 2-year period (see Table 1). Indeed, the stability of these Internet relationships compares quite favorably to that of relationships that form and endure solely in the traditional face-to-face world (see Figure 4). For example, Attridge, Berscheid, and Simpson (1995) followed 120 dating couples for 6 months and, according to the self-reports of their participants, 32% of the relationships had dissolved before the 6-month period ended. Kirkpatrick and Davis (1994) followed 354 couples in "steady or serious" dating relationships over a 3-year period; 7 months into the study 36% of the

Table 1. Fate of Relationships After Two Years

Relationship	Relationship dissolved	Became less close	Became closer and stronger	Total continuing (Columns 2 + 3)
All relationships	25%	18%	54%	75%
Acquaintanceships	33%	0%	67%	67%
Friendships	21%	21%	58%	79%
Romantic partnerships	29%	19%	52%	71%

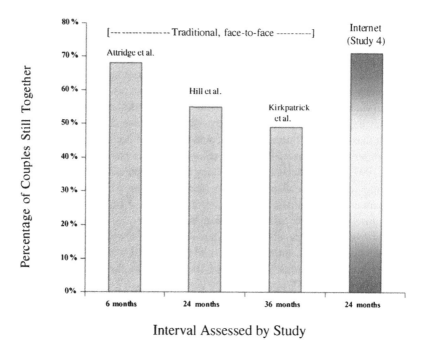

Interval Assessed by Study

Fig. 4. Comparison of relationship stability for those relationships formed in real life versus on the Internet, by time interval of duration measured in study.
Note. Full citation and description of the three comparable real-life studies in text.

couples had broken up, and at the end of the 3 years, only 49% of the couples were still together. In the classic study by Hill, Rubin, and Peplau (1976), 45% of their dating couples had ended their romantic relationships prior to the conclusion of the 2-year study.

In the present survey, 71% of the romantic relationships that had begun on the Internet in the present survey (and 75% of all reported Internet relationships) were still intact 2 years later—with the majority being reported as closer and stronger. Thus, applying the identical criterion as was used in the previous studies of dating couples (i.e., "Is the relationship continuing, yes or no?") we find that the stability of relationships initially developed on-line compares favorably to that found in studies of relationships that had initially developed face to face. Using the stricter criterion for our participants of comparing only those romantic relationships that were reported to have become closer and stronger, we find a comparable endurance rate (52%) to that found in the 2-year study of Hill et al. (1976; 55%). Also notably, 84% of our respondents reported that their on-line relationships were as real, as important, and as close as their non-Internet relationships.

Stability of Real Me index. Our 2-year follow-up survey also enabled us to assess the temporal stability of the Real Me as a personality characteristic: whether or not responses to the Real Me measure reflect a stable and reliable personality characteristic regarding an individual's ability to express his or her true self over the Internet versus face to face. Of the 34 participants who were categorized in 1997 as locating the real self absolutely on-line, none of them located the real self off-line in 1999. Of the 30 participants locating the real self solely off-line in 1997, only 3 had transferred their location of the real self to the purely on-line realm. Of the 60 "tweeners" in 1997, 50 continued to locate the self in between the two domains. Paired samples t-tests were also conducted between the individual items comprising the Real Me index at Times 1 and 2, and again no significant differences emerged (all $ps > .20$).

Social anxiety, loneliness, and depression. Relevant to the proposed model, a within-participants t-test was conducted comparing the amount of social anxiety reported in 1997 to that reported 2 years later. Results demonstrate a significant reduction in the level of social anxiety experienced by participants, $t(141) = -2.55$, $p < .01$. That is, our random sample of Internet newsgroup users were significantly less socially anxious in 1999 than they were in 1997 (i.e., after two additional years of Internet use). When asked directly to assess what effect using the Internet had on feelings of depression, only 2% of the respondents reported that it had caused them increased feelings of depression, compared to 25% for whom it had reduced feelings of depression (73% reported no effect).

A within-participants t-test also showed participants to be less lonely in 1999 than they had been in 1997, $t(141) = -5.30$, $p < .001$, and this reduction in loneliness was not qualified by differences in initial levels of loneliness. That is, both those who originally reported the lowest levels of loneliness and those who reported the highest levels of loneliness in 1997 reported equivalent reductions in loneliness in 1999. Of course, there may have been other factors besides Internet use producing such a reduction. However, when participants were also *explicitly* asked to assess the effect that using the Internet had on their feelings of loneliness, 47% reported being unaffected, 47% felt their Internet use had reduced feelings of loneliness, and only 6% reported that they felt more lonely as a result of using the Internet. The majority (68%) of participants also reported that using the Internet had increased their social circle, whereas only 3% reported having fewer friends as a result of Internet use (28% reported no change). Indeed, the average participant reported having a mean of six virtual friends with whom he or she shared intimate, personal details.

Becoming Friends on the Internet: Faster, Stronger, Deeper, Longer

We've suggested that the anonymity and lack of traditional gating features in Internet interactions are what facilitate the rapid formation of on-line friendships, as they facilitate the expression of the Real Me. We proposed that forming a friendship based initially upon mutual self-disclosure and common interests, rather than superficial features such as physical attractiveness, provides a more stable and durable basis for the relationship and enables it to survive and flourish once those "gates" do come into operation when the partners meet in person.

In support of this line of thinking, Gergen, Gergen, and Barton (1973) found that when individuals interacted in a darkened room where they could not see one another, they not only engaged in greater self-disclosure but also left the encounter liking one another more so than did those who interacted in a room that was brightly lit. Research in interpersonal attraction has shown that people like better others who are more disclosing and that, conversely, personal disclosure breeds liking by others. Collins and Miller (1994) found that not only do we like those who disclose to us and tend to like those to whom we ourselves make disclosures, but we also tend to like those who like us in return.

Interacting on the Internet is similar in some respects to interacting in a darkened room, in that one cannot see one's interaction partner, nor can one be seen. First impressions thus are formed based upon the information provided by the other person and perhaps by the positive effect of our own acts of self-disclosure, rather than upon physical features. Research has shown that it is difficult to overcome first impressions (e.g., Fiske & Taylor, 1991); one reason being that in subsequent interactions, people selectively focus upon information that is confirmatory rather than disconfirmatory of their original judgements (see Higgins & Bargh, 1987).

Whereas our first two studies confirmed our predictions that people (1) do form close, lasting relationships with those whom they meet on the Internet, (2) develop intimacy at a faster rate than in real life, and (3) successfully bring these relationships into their real lives, they do not directly test our model's assumptions about the *process* by which this happens—that is, *why* all of this occurs. Thus, we conducted a laboratory experiment to provide such a test.

Study 3: Friendship Formation in the Absence of Traditional "Gating Features"

Study 3 was designed to assess the effect that the presence (as in face-to-face interactions) versus absence (as in Internet interactions) of traditional relationship gating features (e.g., physical appearance) has on how much strangers like each other after their initial interaction. We predicted that those who met for the first time on the Internet would show greater liking for partners than would those who met face to face (Time 1). Further, it was predicted that liking for the partner would be greater for those in the Internet condition than for those in the control condition even after the final meeting (Time 2), in which participants in both conditions had met face to face and physical appearance was now operating for all pairs as a gating feature.

Method

Participants. Thirty-one male and 31 female New York University undergraduate students were recruited from the introductory psychology participant pool.

Procedure. Participants engaged in two 20-min meetings. Participants in the study were randomly assigned to one of three conditions. In the control condition, each participant interacted with his or her partner in person for both meetings. In the "IRC" condition, participants interacted first in an Internet chat room and then met face to face for the second meeting. For both the control and the IRC conditions, participants knew that they were interacting with the same person both times.

In the final, "trading places" condition, the participant interacted with one partner in person and also with a person he or she believed was a different partner over the Internet. In reality, it was the same person both times, though neither partner was aware of this. Prior to the second interaction with the ostensibly different partner, participants were instructed not to talk about their previous partner, in order to protect confidentiality. The order of meeting (Internet vs. face to face) was counterbalanced for the trading places participants. Each participant was paired with an opposite-sex partner, for a total of 10 cross-sex pairs in each of the conditions.

All participants were instructed to get acquainted with one another. After 20 min, the interaction was ended. Participants in all conditions completed a set of measures assessing the interaction and their partner and then engaged in the second interaction, following which they again assessed their partners using the same set of measures. Special care was taken during the debriefing to discover whether any participants in the trading places group suspected that they had interacted with the same person in both conditions. Data from one participant were excluded from the analyses as he suspected that he had spoken with the same partner on both occasions. No other participants in the trading places condition showed any such suspicion.

Measures. Participants rated the extent to which they liked their partner on a 14-point scale, ranging from −7 (strong dislike) to +7 (strong liking). Next, eight items taken from the Relationship Development Scale (Parks & Floyd, 1995) assessed the participants' perceptions about the quality of the interaction and the level of intimacy that had been established.

Results and Discussion

Liking for partner. An analysis of variance was conducted on partner liking scores with Communication Mode (IRC vs. face to face) as the between-participants factor and Time of Measurement (Times 1 and 2) as the

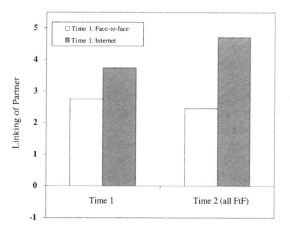

Fig. 5. Degree of liking for partner for those who met first on the Internet versus face to face, after initial meeting and also after second (face-to-face) meeting, Study 3.

within-participants factor. The main effect of Communication Mode was not reliable, $F(1, 40) = 2.27$, $p = .12$, nor was the main effect of Time, $F(1, 40) = 1.35$, $p = .25$. However, as predicted, the Communication Mode × Time interaction was reliable, $F(1, 40) = 4.98$, $p < .05$. In the IRC condition, liking for partner increased after meeting face to face, whereas liking nonsignificantly decreased for those who met continuously in person (see Figure 5).

Although the amount of liking for one's partner after 20 min of interaction (at Time 1) did not yet differ between the Internet ($M = 3.75$) and the control condition ($M = 2.75$, $t < 1$), these differences did emerge by the end of the interaction at Time 2, such that those in the Internet condition ($M = 4.70$) liked their partners significantly more than did those who met consistently face to face ($M = 2.45$), $t(38) = -2.18, p < .05$. Bargh et al. (this issue, Study 3) also found that significant differences in partner liking emerged, after a 40-min interaction, with those who interacted solely on-line liking each other more than did those who interacted solely in person.

A within-participants t-test was conducted for those in the IRC condition, comparing amount of liking at Time 1 (after interaction on IRC only) and at Time 2 (after meeting face to face). Liking increased significantly from Time 1 to Time 2, $t(20) = 1.83$, $p = .04$, one-tailed. A within-participants t-test for the control condition yielded nonsignificant results, $t(20) = 1.45, p > .10$. In other words, further face-to-face communication enhanced partner liking in the IRC condition, but not in the control group.

Also as predicted, a within-participants t-test revealed that the same person was liked substantially more when he or she interacted with a partner via the Internet ($M = 4.95$) than when the interaction took place in person, $M = 3.11$, $t(20) = 3.33$, $p < .001$. This within-participants comparison, in which the same participant provides liking ratings for both a face-to-face and an Internet inter-action partner, is a more powerful and sensitive test of our hypothesis than the between-participants comparison of the face-to-face versus IRC condition. Unlike comparisons between the face-to-face-only group and the IRC group, where lik-ing for different partners was being compared, the trading places group provides insight into how the *same pair* would like one another if they were to initially meet in one condition versus the other.

Quality of conversation. In the two experimental conditions in which partici-pants knowingly interacted with the same partner twice, the ratings of the quality of the conversation taken after the first meeting were nearly identical to those after the second meeting—that is, partners did not much alter their initial assessment after further interaction—and analyses of these ratings at Time 1 and at Time 2 produced the identical patterns of significant effects. Thus for the sake of brevity we will describe only Time 2 findings for these two conditions.

The main effect of Initial Communication Mode (first meeting face to face vs. on IRC) was not reliable ($F < 1$) but it did reliably interact with the repeated mea-sure of Conversation Quality Rating (i.e., the different items of the questionnaire), $F(5, 190) = 2.63$, $p < .02$. Inspection of the mean ratings by the two conditions revealed only one reliable difference: those participants who had met first on IRC were more likely to have told their partners what they specifically liked about them, compared to participants who met first face to face.

In the trading places condition, we compared conversation quality ratings of the "IRC partner" vs. the "face-to-face partner" (again, in reality the same person both times) using within-participants t-tests for the various questionnaire items. Two reliable differences were revealed: Participants felt they knew their IRC part-ner better than they did their face-to-face partner, $t(18) = 3.64$, $p < .001$, and they were more likely to have told their IRC than their face-to-face partner specifically what they liked about him or her, $t(18) = 2.80$, $p < .01$.

Relation between liking and conversation quality ratings. For each condition, we examined the degree to which the participant's liking of the partner was corre-lated with ratings of the quality of the conversation and how well the participant felt he or she knew the partner at the end of the meeting. According to our model, people who meet face to face base their initial liking on more superficial gating features such as physical attractiveness, and so ratings of partner liking in the control condition should be relatively unrelated to ratings of the quality of the interaction. Conversely, people who meet on the Internet, in the absence of these gating features, should show a stronger relation between the quality of the conver-sation and how well they feel they know the other person, and their overall liking ratings for that person.

In support of this prediction, there were no reliable correlations between liking for partner and any of the Conversation Quality ratings for participants in the control condition (all $rs < .16$, all $ps > .5$). In the IRC condition, however, degree of liking for the partner was significantly related to several of the items assessing the interaction experience. The more that participants in the IRC condition (a) felt certain they knew their partners, (b) felt that they could accurately predict what their partner's attitudes would be, (c) felt they had discussed a wide range of topics with their partner and moved easily from one topic to another, and (d) felt that they had been able to share intimate or personal things about themselves with the partner, the more they reported liking their partner (all $rs > .59$, $ps < .01$).

Within the trading places condition, none of the correlations between liking and the various conversation quality items was significant when the partners met face to face (all $ps > .08$). However, when these same people interacted on the Internet, there were significant correlations between degree of liking and three of the items. The more participants felt able to share intimate or personal things about themselves with the partner, the more certain they were that they knew their partner, and the more confident they were that they could accurately predict what their partner's attitudes would be, the more they liked their partner (all $rs > .47$, $ps < .05$).

In other words, when people interacted on the Internet—but not when they interacted in person—the quality of the interaction, especially the intimacy and closeness attained, determined liking. In the face-to-face meetings, the quality of the interaction did not matter to liking judgments, consistent with the notion that in face-to-face interactions it is the more superficial gating features that dominate liking and overwhelm other interpersonally important factors.

General Discussion

The three studies presented here tested the model that greater expression of one's true self on the Internet results in the rapid formation of close relationships that endure over time. Those who are socially anxious and lonely are somewhat more likely to feel that they can better express their real selves with others on the Internet than they can with those they know off-line. The close relationships that are formed on-line tend to become integrated into one's non-Internet social life in a series of stages. With each step of the process, individuals exchange more of the control they hold over their side of the interaction in return for greater intimacy.

Study 1 showed that real, deep, and meaningful relationships do form on the Internet, and Study 2 found these relationships to be stable over time. Study 3 demonstrated that when people meet on the Internet, in the absence of the gating features that are present in face-to-face situations, they like one another better than they would if they had initially met face to face. Further, this liking tends to survive a subsequent face-to-face encounter. The absence of gating features we believe to be an important reason, along with the greater self-disclosure fostered by the anonymous environment of the Internet (see also Bargh et al., this issue), for the fast development of close, stable relationships on-line documented by Studies 1 and 2. The tendency for people in general, independently of their levels of social anxiety or loneliness, to be better able to express and effectively convey important aspects of their real selves over the Internet also plays an important role in fostering on-line relationships.

A study by Kraut et al. (this issue) reports that those individuals who are gregarious and friend-rich in their off-line lives and who use the Internet more also tend to become more involved in their communities than do those who are introverted. Although introverts and extraverts alike benefited from increased Internet use, with increases in their local and distant social circles and increased face-to-face communication with family and friends, introverts who used the Internet more reported increased loneliness. The authors suggest that it may be the case that the Internet allows the friend-rich to get richer. Our studies suggest that although the friend-rich indeed appear to become richer through their on-line interactions, the friend-poor also become richer than they had been. The socially anxious and the lonely individuals who expressed their true selves on-line formed close on-line relationships and integrated them into their off-line lives, increasing their social circles and becoming less socially anxious and lonely in the process.

Our findings of decreases in loneliness and depression and increases in the size of one's social circle after 2 years of Internet use appear to conflict with the conclusions of two studies widely reported in the media. In a press release, Nie and Erbring (2000) reported results from a survey of Internet users and concluded that Internet use causes people to spend less time with family and friends. However, the full report of the study showed that this conclusion was based upon only 4.3% of the total sample. That is, over 95% of Nie and Erbring's total sample did not report spending any less time with family and friends because of use of the Internet. Moreover, even among the heaviest Internet users, 88% reported no change in amount of time spent with family and friends. It is noteworthy that Kraut et al. (this issue) report that greater levels of Internet use are associated with the average respondent's spending more, not less, time in face-to-face interactions with family and friends.

Secondly, in the original HomeNet study tracking new Internet users, Kraut et al. (1998) reported small but significant correlations between the number of hours spent on-line per week and self-reported depression and loneliness scores. From this they concluded that Internet use causes people to become more lonely and more depressed. They also found that Internet use was associated with a reduction in the size of participants' social networks. However, a 3-year follow-up survey of the same participants (Kraut et al., this issue) showed that the originally reported negative effects had disappeared, and findings from a new sample showed overall positive effects of using the Internet on social involvement and psychological well-being. Thus the overall conclusion from the complete HomeNet study is that Internet use has no harmful effects on psychological well-being and that the size of one's social circle tends to increase as one makes friends on-line—findings entirely in harmony with our own.

It is evident from all of these findings that, rather than turning to the Internet as a way of hiding from real life and from forming real relationships, individuals use it as a means not only of maintaining ties with existing family and friends but also of forming close and meaningful new relationships in a relatively nonthreatening environment. The Internet may also be helpful for those who have difficulty forging relationships in face-to-face situations because of shyness, social anxiety, or a lack of social skills. What is more, to the extent that these virtual relationships become incorporated into and thus a part of the individual's identity and "true self," they tend to be brought into the person's traditional, face-to-face, real-life circle of friends and intimates. People, it would seem, want very much to make a reality out of the important aspects of their virtual lives.

References

Attridge, M., Berscheid, E., & Simpson, J. A. (1995). Predicting relationship stability from both partners versus one. *Journal of Personality and Social Psychology, 69*, 254–268.

Baldwin, M. W. (1997). Relational schemas as a source of if-then self-inference procedures. *Review of General Psychology, 1*, 326–335.

Bandura, A. (1977). Self-efficacy: Toward a unifying theory of behavioral change. *Psychological Review, 84*, 191–215.

Byrne, D. (1971). *The attraction paradigm*. New York: Academic.

Byrne, D. (1997). An overview (and underview) of research and theory within the attraction paradigm. *Journal of Social and Personal Relationships, 14*, 417–431.

Caldwell, M. A., & Peplau, L. A. (1982). Sex differences in same-sex friendship. *Sex Roles, 8*, 721–732.

Chen, S., & Andersen, S. M. (1999). Relationships from the past in the present: Significant-other representations and transference in interpersonal life. *Advances in Experimental Social Psychology, 31*, 123–190.

Collins, N. L., & Miller, L. C. (1994). Self-disclosure and liking: A meta-analytic review. *Psychological Bulletin, 116*(3), 457–475.

Cozby, P. C. (1973). Effects of density, activity, and personality on environmental preferences. *Journal of Research in Personality, 7*, 45–60.

D'Amico, M. L. (1998, December 7). Internet has become a necessity, U.S. poll shows [On-line]. CNNinteractive. Available: http://cnn.com/tech/computing/9812/07/neednet.idg/index.htm

Deaux, K. (1996). Social identification. In E. T. Higgins & A. W. Kruglanski (Eds.), *Social psychology: Handbook of basic principles* (pp. 777–798). New York: Guilford.

Derlega, V. L., & Chaikin, A. L. (1977). Privacy and self-disclosure in social relationships. *Journal of Social Issues, 33*(3), 102–115.

Derlega, V. L., Metts, S., Petronio, S., & Margulis, S. T. (1993). *Self-disclosure*. London: Sage.

Fiske, S. T., & Taylor, S. E. (1991). *Social cognition* (2nd ed.). New York: Scott, Foresman.

Gergen, K. J., Gergen, M. M., & Barton, W. H. (1973). Deviance in the dark. *Psychology Today, 7*, 129–130.

Gollwitzer, P. M. (1986). Striving for specific identities: The social reality of self-symbolizing. In R. Baumeister (Ed.), *Public self and private self* (pp. 143–159). New York: Springer.

Hatfield, E., & Sprecher, S. (1986). *Mirror, mirror . . . The importance of looks in everyday life*. Albany, NY: State University of New York Press.

Higgins, E. T. (1987). Self-discrepancy theory. *Psychological Review, 94*, 1120–1134.

Higgins, E. T., & Bargh, J. A. (1987). Social cognition and social perception. *Annual Review of Psychology, 38*, 369–425.

Hill, C. T., Rubin, Z., & Peplau, L. A. (1976). Breakups before marriage: The end of 103 affairs. *Journal of Social Issues, 32*, 147–168.

Jourard, S. M. (1964). *The transparent self.* New York: Van Nostrand.

Kirkpatrick, L. A., & Davis, E. D. (1994). Attachment style, gender, and relationship stability: A longitudinal analysis. *Journal of Personality and Social Psychology, 66,* 502–512.

Kraut, R., Patterson, M., Lundmark, V., Kiesler, S., Mukopadhyay, T., & Scherlis, W. (1998). Internet paradox: A social technology that reduces social involvement and psychological well-being? *American Psychologist, 53,* 1017–1031.

Laurenceau, J. P., Barrett, L. F., & Pietromonaco, P. R. (1998). Intimacy as an interpersonal process: The importance of self-disclosure, partner disclosure, and perceived partner responsiveness in interpersonal exchanges. *Journal of Personality and Social Psychology, 74,* 1238–1251.

Leary, M. R. (1983). Social anxiousness: The construct and its measurement. *Journal of Personality Assessment, 47,* 66–75.

McKenna, K. Y. A., & Bargh, J. A. (1998). Coming out in the age of the Internet: Identity demarginalization through virtual group participation. *Journal of Personality and Social Psychology, 75*(3), 681–694.

McKenna, K. Y. A., & Bargh, J. A. (1999). Causes and consequences of social interaction on the Internet: A conceptual framework. *Media Psychology, 1,* 249–269.

McKenna, K. Y. A., & Bargh J. A. (2000). Plan 9 from cyberspace: The implications of the Internet for personality and social psychology. *Personality and Social Psychology Review, 4,* 57–75.

Moore, D. W. (2000, February 23). Americans say Internet makes their lives better [On-line]. *Gallup News Service.* Available: http://www.gallup.com/poll/releases/pr000223.asp

Nie, N. H., & Erbring, L. (2000). Internet and society: A preliminary report [On-line]. Stanford, CA: Institute for the Quantitative Study of Society. Available: www.stanford.edu/group/siqss

Parks, M. R., & Floyd, K. (1995). Making friends in cyberspace. *Journal of Communication, 46,* 80–97.

Pennebaker, J. W. (1989). Confession, inhibition, and disease. In L. Berkowitz (Ed.), *Advances in experimental social psychology* (Vol. 22, pp. 211–244). New York: Academic.

Reis, H. T., & Shaver, P. (1988). Intimacy as an interpersonal process. In S. Duck, D. Hay, S. E. Hobfoll, W. Ickes, & B. M. Montgomery (Eds.), *Handbook of personal relationships: Theory, research and interventions* (pp. 367–389). Chichester, UK: John Wiley & Sons.

Rogers, C. (1951). *Client-centered therapy.* Boston: Houghton-Mifflin.

Rubin, Z. (1975). Disclosing oneself to a stranger: Reciprocity and its limits. *Journal of Experimental Social Psychology, 11,* 233–260.

Rubin, Z., Hill, C. T., Peplau, L. A., & Dunkel-Schetter, C. (1980). Self-disclosure in dating couples: Sex roles and the ethic of openess. *Journal of Marriage and the Family, 42,* 305–317.

Russell, D. W. (1996). The UCLA Loneliness Scale (Version 3): Reliability, validity and factorial structure. *Journal of Personality Assessment, 66,* 20–40.

KATELYN Y. A. MCKENNA is Assistant Research Professor in the Department of Psychology at New York University. She received her BA with honors from Tulane University and her PhD from Ohio University in 1998. Her research interests focus on relationship cognition and social identity processes, especially as these unfold over the Internet.

AMIE S. GREEN is a graduate student in the Social-Personality Program in the Department of Psychology at New York University. Her research interests focus upon the role of interpersonal goals in close relationships and in interpersonal behavior among adolescents.

MARCI E. J. GLEASON is a graduate student in the Social-Personality Program in the Department of Psychology at New York University. Her research interests focus upon the role of social support for health and psychological well-being.

Journal of Social Issues, Vol. 58, No. 1, 2002, pp. 33–48

Can You See the Real Me? Activation and Expression of the "True Self" on the Internet

John A. Bargh,* Katelyn Y. A. McKenna, and Grainne M. Fitzsimons

New York University

Those who feel better able to express their "true selves" in Internet rather than face-to-face interaction settings are more likely to form close relationships with people met on the Internet (McKenna, Green, & Gleason, this issue). Building on these correlational findings from survey data, we conducted three laboratory experiments to directly test the hypothesized causal role of differential self-expression in Internet relationship formation. Experiments 1 and 2, using a reaction time task, found that for university undergraduates, the true-self concept is more accessible in memory during Internet interactions, and the actual self more accessible during face-to-face interactions. Experiment 3 confirmed that people randomly assigned to interact over the Internet (vs. face to face) were better able to express their true-self qualities to their partners.

> Can you see the real me?
> Can you? Can you?
>
> —The Who, "The Real Me" (*Quadrophenia*, 1973)

In *Life on the Screen: Identity in the Age of the Internet*, Sherry Turkle (1995) noted how the Internet, with its relative anonymity and multiple venues for social interaction, afforded individuals a kind of virtual laboratory for exploring and experimenting with different versions of self. Just as games and other forms of play afford children a relatively safe and benign way to develop social skills critically

*Correspondence concerning this article should be addressed to John A. Bargh, Department of Psychology, New York University, 6 Washington Place, Seventh Floor, New York, NY 10003 [e-mail: john.bargh@nyu.edu]. This research was supported in part by National Institute of Mental Health grant R01-MH60767 to Bargh, a New York University Research Challenge Fund grant to McKenna, and a predoctoral fellowship from the Social Sciences and Humanities Research Council of Canada to Fitzsimons. We thank Lily Hung for her assistance as experimenter and Niall Bolger for his advice concerning the data analyses.

useful for later life as an adult but without the costs and potential dangers of making mistakes, the anonymity of the Internet enables people the opportunity to take on various personas, even a different gender, and to express facets of themselves without fear of disapproval and sanctions by those in their real-life social circle.

The idea that people possess multiple senses of self, or personas, is not a new one in psychology and sociology. Both Goffman (1959) and Jung (1953) distinguished between the public self, or persona, and the individual's inner self; for Jung (1953) one's real individuality resided in the unconscious self as opposed to the conscious ego. Markus and Nurius (1986) introduced the idea of "possible selves," the potentials in terms of life growth and optional lifestyles an individual feels he or she would be able to attain if so desired. Higgins (1987) distinguished between *ideal, ought,* and *actual* self-concepts: the ideal self contains those qualities one strives someday to possess, the ought self those qualities one feels obligated to possess, and the actual self those one actually expresses to others at present.

Other than the actual self, these variations on the theme of the self-concept are all concerned with *future, potential* versions of self that do not yet exist in present time. In contrast, Turkle's (1995) vision of the Internet as a kind of social laboratory emphasized its potential for the exploration of currently possessed, alternative inner conceptions of self. This is neither a potential self nor an ideal self—it is most similar to what Carl Rogers (1951) called the *true self.*

Rogers' (1951) notion of the true self was informed by Jung's (1953) distinction between the unconscious self and its public mask, the persona. Rogers theorized that much of what happens in therapy has to do with the client feeling that "he was not being his real self, often he did not know what his real self was, and felt satisfaction when he had become more truly himself" (p. 136). For Rogers, an important feature of the process of therapy was the work towards *discovery* of the true self, so that the person could express it more freely in his or her interactions with others. The true self is thus conceptually distinct from both the ideal self or possible selves on the one hand and the actual self on the other, because Rogers (1951) viewed the true self of his clients as actually existing psychologically (i.e., a present, not a future version of self), but not fully expressed in social life (i.e., not the actual self).

If, as Turkle (1995) argued, the Internet constitutes a unique opportunity for self-expression, then we would expect a person to use it first and foremost to express those aspects of self that he or she has the strongest need to express— namely, the 'true self': those identity-important and phenomenally real aspects of self not often or easily expressed to others.

"Strangers on the Internet"

Why would the Internet be a place where the true self might be more easily expressed than in traditional, face-to-face communication venues? We suggest that one important difference between the typical Internet and typical face-to-face interaction is the Internet's ability to facilitate self-expression. There are two unique features of the Internet that are responsible for its facilitative ability in this area. First and foremost is the ability to be relatively *anonymous* in one's individual- or group-level interactions.[1] This enables one to express oneself and behave in ways not available in one's usual social sphere, both because one is free of the expectations and constraints placed on us by those who know us, and because the costs and risks of social sanctions for what we say or do are greatly reduced. If one does not conform to one's usual repertoire in that situational or relational context, one faces disapproval from one's social group (e.g., Cooley, 1902; Goffman, 1959; Rogers, 1951). Secondly, as Pennebaker (1990) and Derlega, Metts, Petronio, and Margulis (1993) have noted, in traditional face-to-face interactions there are real costs to disclosing negative or taboo aspects of oneself, even (or perhaps especially) to close friends and family. These barriers are not present outside of one's usual social sphere (Derlega & Chaikin, 1977).

In this regard Internet interactions are analogous to those one sometimes has with "strangers on a train" (Rubin, 1975) in which one opens up and self-discloses intimate details to the stranger sitting in the next seat, details that one might never have told one's colleagues at the office or even one's family and friends back home. Such self-disclosure, if (as on the Internet as opposed to the train) one has further such interactions with the same person, can lead quickly to the development of friendship. Several theorists and researchers in the area of close relationships have noted how the development of friendship is related to an increase in self-disclosure (e.g., Altman & Taylor, 1973; Derlega et al., 1993).

Moreover, disclosing the qualities and aspects of one's inner or true self has been argued to create bonds of empathy and understanding between the relationship partners. According to Derlega and Chaikin (1977), for example, "a major function of friendships and love relationships may be to validate one's self-concept by obtaining the support and understanding of the other person" (p. 110). Being able to express the true self over the Internet would thus be expected to create empathic bonds and facilitate the establishment of close relationships. Consistent with this reasoning, McKenna, Green, and Gleason (this issue) found that people who believe that they are better able to express their true self (as measured by the researchers' Real Me scale) were more likely than others to form close relationships with people met over the Internet.

Given that the special qualities of Internet interaction afford people the op- portunity to express the true self, the remaining question is whether people will be

---

[1] Anonymity is defined as "the condition of not being identifiable to the other person" (Derlega & Chaikin, 1977, p. 109). Note that by this definition, one can be relatively anonymous in certain face-to-face interactions as well, as in the "strangers on a train" phenomenon (Rubin, 1975; see below), and also relatively "nonymous" or identifiable over the Internet (as in e-mail exchanges using one's real name; e.g., John.Smith@ivy.edu).

motivated to so express it. And there are reasons to expect that people will be. For one thing, we have a real need to have others see us as we see ourselves. Swann (e.g., 1990) has shown that having a new acquaintance come to the same opinion of you that you hold yourself is a strong interpersonal motivation, often stronger than the need to have others have a positive opinion of you. Secondly, the true self, according to Rogers (1951), is composed of important aspects of one's identity that one does not often have validated as real by the significant others in one's life. Research on the motivational aspects of the self has found that people are highly motivated to make such important aspects of identity a "social reality," to have these attributes acknowledged by others so that they become authentic features of the self-concept (Baumeister, 1998; Gollwitzer, 1986). For both of these motivational reasons, if the Internet provides interaction domains that enable and facilitate expression of the true self, we should expect people to take advantage of it.

We conducted three laboratory experiments to test these predictions. First, because of the special qualities of Internet communication outlined above, an individual's true-self concept should be cognitively more accessible during an Internet interaction with a new acquaintance than in a traditional, face-to-face interaction. In the latter venue, the individual's actual-self concept will be cognitively more accessible. We test this prediction in Experiments 1 and 2 using a speeded self-judgment, reaction time methodology. Second, for the same reasons, a person should be better able to express the qualities of his or her true self to an Internet versus a face-to-face interaction partner, causing the partner to form an impression of the person that more resembles his or her true than actual self. We test this prediction in Experiment 3.

Experiment 1

We predicted that an individual's true-self concept would be more activated and accessible than his or her actual-self concept during an Internet interaction with a new acquaintance, whereas the reverse would be true during face-to-face interactions. The classic measure of the accessibility of self-concepts is the "Me/Not-Me" response task of Markus (1977). In this task, participants respond as quickly as possible as to whether each of a series of adjectives is self-descriptive, by pressing either a button labeled "Me" or another labeled "Not Me." The speed with which these responses are made is an indication of the relative accessibility, or readiness to be used, of the various concepts (see Bargh & Chartrand, 2000).

Method

Participants. Forty-six students (18 male and 28 female) enrolled in an introductory psychology course at New York University (NYU) participated in pairs for partial fulfillment of a course requirement. There were both same-sex (16) and cross-sex (7) participant pairs.

Apparatus and materials. The stimuli for the computerized reaction time task consisted of trait words presented in random order. Each word appeared in the center of the screen until the participant responded; an asterisk would then immediately appear for 1 s, followed by the next word. There were 8 practice trials and then 45 experimental trials. Thirty-five of the words were stimuli chosen from the normative likability ratings of Anderson (1968). These words were frequently encountered trait terms such as "wise" and "bossy"; half were positive and half were negative in normative valence. The remaining 10 word stimuli were the "actual-self" and "true-self" words earlier generated by the participant him- or herself. These stimuli were entered into the program by the experimenter during the experimental session; they were embedded in the longer word list so as to reduce the likelihood that the participant would notice the connection to the earlier part of the experiment.

Procedure. All sessions were conducted by the same female experimenter. Participants were greeted individually and completed the first task alone in one of two identical lab rooms. On this task, they listed the traits or other characteristics (maximum of 10 on each measure) that they believe they actually possess and express to others in social settings (the *actual self* measure) and that they possess and would like to but are not usually able to express (the *true self* measure). After a filler task, each participant then interacted with another participant, either in an Internet chat room or face to face in a lab room, for either 5 or 15 min. The purpose of varying the interaction length factor was to enable us to assess the possibility that quantitative differences in amount of information communicated between the Internet and face-to-face conditions, not qualitative differences in the communication experience, might be responsible for any obtained differences (see Walther, 1996).

In the Internet condition, the experimenter then briefly explained how to use an Internet chat room and turned on a computer monitor in the lab room, which had been set up for chat room use prior to the participant's arrival. The experimenter then left the participant alone in the room to begin interacting with the other student over the Internet. In the face-to-face condition, participants moved to a new lab room after completion of the initial measures. They were seated at a table together and were left alone in the room to interact. While participants were interacting, the experimenter entered the actual-self and true-self words generated in the self-description measure into the computers that would be used for the reaction time task.

At the end of the allotted time period (5 or 15 min), the experimenter interrupted the students' interaction and brought each into one of two soundproof computer booths, where they individually completed the reaction time self-description task. In this task, they were told that words would appear on the computer screen every few seconds; participants were instructed to press, as quickly as possible after they knew their response, the key labeled "yes" if the word described them and that labeled "no" if the word did not describe them. Upon completion of this final task, participants were individually debriefed and thanked for their participation.

Results

Preliminary analyses. The data were analyzed using a 2 (interaction mode: online or face-to-face) × 2 (interaction length: 5 or 15 min) × 2 (self-concept: actual vs. true) × 2 (participant within pair) repeated measures analysis of variance (ANOVA), with the first two factors as between-participants variables and the latter two as within-participants variables. There was no main effect of participant within pair, and it did not interact with any other variables except for an uninterpretable and theoretically uninteresting four-way interaction. Gender did not participate in any significant effects and so was excluded from further analyses.

Main analyses. Overall, participants were faster to respond to their actual-self descriptive traits than their true-self descriptions, $F(1, 19) = 16.12$, $p = .001$. As predicted, this main effect was qualified by a significant interaction between self-concept and interaction mode, $F(1, 19) = 8.65$, $p = .008$. As can be seen in Figure 1, whereas the actual self was more accessible (i.e., faster response times)

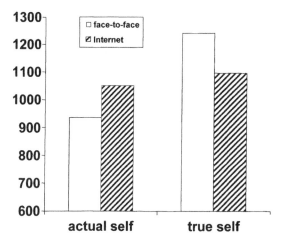

Fig. 1. Reaction times (in ms) to actual-self and true-self characteristics, by interaction venue, Experiment 1.

after face-to-face than after Internet interactions, the true self was more accessible following an initial interaction over the Internet. This effect was not moderated by interaction length ($p > .25$), so the differential activation of the true versus actual self occurred very early in the course of the interaction; moreover, the differential self-concept accessibility is attributable to qualities of the communication mode and not to the amount of information communicated during the interaction. A subsidiary analysis to assess whether the crossover interaction of self-concept activation shown in Figure 1 held equally for same-sex versus cross-sex interaction pairs revealed that whether the partners were of the same versus opposite sex made no difference in the obtained effects (all $ps > .25$).

Experiment 2

It is possible that the differential self-concept activation found in Experiment 1 was due to the anticipation of interacting either in a face-to-face or an Internet setting after being informed of this by the experimenter, rather than qualities of the interaction experience itself. For instance, knowing that one is going to interact face to face might cause one to strategically inhibit the expression of one's true self. Because such tuning or communication set effects are a real possibility (see Higgins, 1981; Zajonc, 1960), it is important to rule out this alternative if we wish to conclude that it is the Internet communication setting and interaction experience that causes the true self to become relatively more accessible. Experiment 2 was thus identical to Experiment 1 with the exceptions that (1) we did not vary the length of time participants believed they would be interacting, (2) no interaction actually took place, and (3) a control group was added, consisting of participants who were not told about any subsequent interaction.

Method

Participants. Thirty-six students (18 male and 18 female) enrolled in the NYU introductory psychology course participated in partial fulfillment of a course requirement.

Apparatus and materials. All apparatus and materials were identical to those in Experiment 1.

Procedure. The procedure was identical to that of Experiment 1, except for changes to the cover story necessary to explain why the interaction with another student was postponed until after the reaction time task. (Participants in the "no expected interaction" condition were told nothing about another student or pending interaction and completed the Me/Not-Me task after the same delay as all other participants.) Therefore, after completing the actual-self and true-self measures as described in Experiment 1, participants were told they would be interacting with another student, and those in the Internet condition were given instructions and demonstrations of how to use the chat room, exactly as in Experiment 1.

After several minutes had passed, the experimenter returned and told the participant that the other student was still working on the first task. She suggested that to save time, he or she could complete the third task before the interaction with the other student (all participants desired to do so). After completing the Me/Not-Me task, participants were fully debriefed as to the nature of the study. Three (male) participants indicated they had experienced suspicion about the existence of the partner participant, and so their data were excluded from the analyses.

Results and Discussion

A preliminary analysis revealed no reliable effects or interactions involving participant gender, and so this factor was excluded from further analyses. The data were analyzed using a 3 (type of anticipated interaction: online, face-to-face, or control) × 2 (actual-self vs. true-self content words) repeated measures ANOVA, with the first factor as a between-participants variable and the latter as a within-participants variable. The only significant effect was that participants in all conditions responded faster overall to actual-self ($M = 965$ ms) than true-self ($M = 1146$ ms) content stimuli, $F(1, 30) = 6.52, p = .016$. As expected, there was no interaction between self-concept type and anticipated communication mode, $F < 1$. Thus, when participants did not actually interact with another person over the Internet versus face to face, there was no change in activation level of their true-self versus actual-self concepts, pointing to the importance of the actual Internet interaction experience for the activation of the true-self concept. Furthermore, because the main effect held for the additional "no interaction expected" condition as well, the default case appears to be that the actual self is more accessible, typically, than the true self.

Experiment 3

Research on close relationships has identified two key ingredients necessary for their development: reciprocal *self-disclosure* of intimate personal information (e.g., Collins & Miller, 1994; Derlega et al., 1993), and the ability to present one's *desired self* and have it perceived and accepted as valid by the partner (Laurenceau, Barrett, & Pietromonaco, 1998; Murray, Holmes, & Griffin, 1996). As we have argued, the special qualities of Internet communication foster both self-disclosure and the presentation of alternative, desired versions of self. Experiment 3 tested the hypothesis that individuals would be better able to express their true selves over the Internet and have them accepted by their new interaction partner as valid, compared to those interacting face to face.

We further hypothesized that participants in the Internet interaction condition would like each other more than would those who met each other face to face, replicating the findings of McKenna et al. (this issue, Study 3). This greater degree of liking is expected for two reasons: the hypothesized greater ease of expression of the true self over the Internet, plus the likelihood that the same features of Internet communication that free one to express one's true self should also affect how one perceives one's partner. Specifically, the greater anonymity of Internet communication encompasses the fact that people lack information about each other that is usually highly influential on first impressions and liking, such as physical attractiveness, dress, and mannerisms (see, e.g., Hatfield & Sprecher, 1986). In the absence of this information, then, people should be freer to *project* hoped-for, idealized qualities onto their partners. (Importantly, however, such projection should only occur after initial liking has been established, as people will not be motivated to project wished-for features onto someone they initially dislike.) This projection of the ideal would be a second contributor to the predicted greater liking of each other by new acquaintances after an Internet versus a face-to-face meeting. In order to provide a test of the projection prediction, Experiment 3 participants also provided descriptions of their idealized friend and idealized romantic partner.

Method

Participants. Twenty male and 20 female NYU undergraduates were recruited from the introductory psychology class and received course credit for their participation.

Procedure. Participants met in cross-sex pairs for a single session of 40 min each. They were randomly assigned to either the face-to-face meeting condition or the Internet meeting condition. Prior to meeting each other, participants completed both the *actual self* measure and the *true self* measure as in Experiments 1 and 2. In addition, they also listed a maximum of five traits or characteristics that they would most like for a future romantic partner (the *ideal partner* measure) to possess, and then a maximum of five traits or characteristics that their ideal close friend (the *ideal friend* measure) would possess.

Following completion of these measures, each participant engaged in a 10 min filler task, comprised of rating the average college student on a variety of traits. Next, participants met with their assigned partner either face to face or in an Internet chat room. All participants were instructed to get acquainted and interact with their partner. After 40 min, the interaction was ended. At this point, the face-to-face participants were taken to separate rooms and the Internet participants were logged out of the chat room. All participants then rated the amount of liking they felt for their interaction partner on a 14-point scale ranging from −7 (*strong dislike*) to +7 (*strong liking*). They were then asked to list the traits and characteristics (maximum of 10) they believed their interaction partner possessed (*actual partner* measure).

Results

Self-presentation measures. Each participant's listed attributes for both the actual self and the true self were compared to the attributes listed in his or her interaction partner's ratings of him or her. The total of all synonymous matches (i.e., funny/witty) for both versions of self were coded by judges blind to the participant's gender and experimental condition. This created the Presentation of Actual Self and the Presentation of True Self measures. Intercoder reliability was 94.4%, and all differences in coding were resolved through discussion.

Projection measures. Each participant's descriptions of an ideal romantic partner and of an ideal close friend were compared to the attributes he or she ascribed to the interaction partner. As above, all synonymous matches were counted. This created the Projection of Ideal Romantic Partner and the Projection of Ideal Friend measures. Intercoder reliability was 91.7%.

Liking for partner. An independent samples t-test comparing the degree of liking at the conclusion of the interaction between those participants who talked face to face and those who spoke in an Internet chat room revealed significant differences, $t(38) = 3.01, p < .01$. Those who interacted on the Internet liked one another significantly more ($M = 5.55$) than did those who interacted in person ($M = 3.05$). This replicates the liking findings of McKenna et al. (this issue, Study 3).

Self-presentation on the Internet versus face-to-face. A one-way ANOVA was conducted on the number of self/partner matches with communication mode (Internet vs. face to face) as the between-participants factor and self-concept (actual vs. true self) as the within-participants factor. The main effect of communication mode was not reliable, $F(1, 38) = 1.62, p = .21$, nor was the main effect of self-concept, $F < 1$. However, the Communication Mode × Self-Concept interaction was reliable, $F(1, 38) = 5.05, p < .05$. As predicted, those in the Internet condition successfully presented their true selves to their partners to a significantly greater extent than did those in the face-to-face condition, whereas there were no differences in ability to present the actual-self concept (see Figure 2). Those in the face-to-face condition, on the other hand, were no more successful in conveying their true selves than their actual selves.

Projection of the ideal. Whereas expression of the true self was predicted (and found) to be a factor that facilitates initial liking between interaction partners, projection of idealized qualities onto one's partner is a mechanism hypothesized to contribute to the speedy development of Internet relationships once initial liking

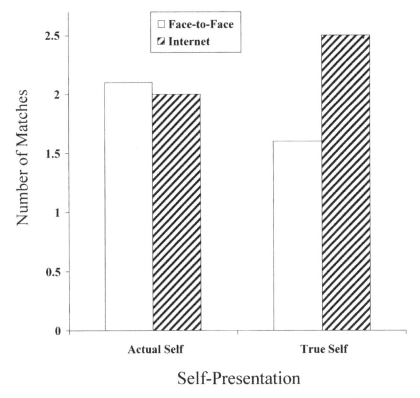

Self-Presentation

Fig. 2. Success of self-presentation over the Internet versus face to face, separately for participant's description of actual self and of true self, in terms of number of content matches with partner's free description of participant after their meeting, Experiment 3.

is established. Thus, we had predicted that such projection should occur in the Internet condition, but only for those new acquaintances one initially likes, and not for every new partner indiscriminately. Therefore, we analyzed the degree of relation between liking and these projection tendencies separately for the Internet and the face-to-face interaction conditions.

In the Internet condition, there was a significant and substantial correlation between degree of liking for a partner and the tendency to project attributes of an ideal close friend onto that partner ($r = .51$, $p < .05$). The identical correlation for the face-to-face meeting group was nonexistent ($r = -.01$). Notably, there was no relationship between liking for partner and the degree of projection of an ideal romantic partner's characteristics in either interaction condition ($r = .23$ in the Internet and $r = .14$ in the face-to-face condition). Thus, we obtained a clear tendency to project onto a liked new Internet interaction partner (but not a new face-to-face interaction partner) the qualities one hopes for in a close friendship, but not the qualities one desires in a romantic partner. In retrospect, the relative reluctance to ascribe romantic-partner qualities is understandable given the very early stage of the relationship at which we assessed the projection effect. (That projection of the ideal is dependent upon initial liking was further demonstrated by the results of an ANOVA conducted on the number of ideal/partner content matches, which revealed no general projection differences between the Internet and face-to-face conditions independently of degree of initial liking, all $Fs < 1$.)

Discussion

Experiment 3 examined two key processes hypothesized to underlie the formation and development of Internet relationships. First, consistent with predictions, participants interacting with a new acquaintance over the Internet successfully presented aspects of their true selves to their partner, as measured by the degree of match between their self-descriptions and the partner's postinteraction description of them. Participants interacting face to face were no better able to convey their desired but unexpressed selves to their partner than their actual selves. Second, also as predicted, participants interacting over the Internet projected the characteristics of their ideal close friend onto their interaction partners to the extent they liked them, whereas there was no sign of such projection between interaction partners who met face to face. We believe that both of these effects of the Internet—to foster presentation of one's true self to the other person and to allow the projection of idealized qualities onto the other—are independent contributors to the greater liking found between strangers meeting on the Internet, versus face to face.

General Discussion

Carl Rogers (1951) held that people are cognizant of the fact that they are one type of person in social settings but contain within them relatively unexpressed qualities and interpersonal abilities (e.g., being witty, bratty, aggressive) that they would like to but feel unable to present to others (i.e., the "true self"). Because of the relative anonymity of Internet communication settings, including the absence of physical "gating features" in text-based, non-face-to-face interactions, we argued that one's true self is more likely to be active during Internet than face-to-face interactions. Consistent with this prediction, Experiment 1 showed that trait content related to a participant's true self was more accessible in memory following an interaction with a stranger over the Internet, compared to after a face-to-face interaction. Experiment 2 confirmed that these effects were not due merely to the participants having an expectancy of interacting in one communication mode versus the other or strategically activating one self-concept or the other because of the anticipated communication mode.

Experiment 3 replicated the finding that people like each other better when they meet first over the Internet versus face to face (McKenna et al., this issue) and delved further into the reasons for this phenomenon. We examined the ways that individuals *present* themselves to their new partner as well as how they *project* their hoped-for qualities onto that partner. As predicted, those who interacted over the Internet were more successful than the other participants in presenting their true self to the partner, as there was a significantly better match between the partner's description of the participant and the participant's own true-self description than with his or her own actual-self description. Thus, as expected, compared to face-to-face interactions, people are better able to present, and have accepted by others, aspects of their true or inner selves over the Internet.

We also predicted and found that there was a greater tendency to project one's ideal or hoped-for partner qualities onto those whom one initially meets and likes over the Internet. There was a strong and significant correlation between liking and the degree of match between one's description of the ideal close friend and one's own description of the partner's characteristics for those who interacted over the Internet, but a near zero correlation between these measures for those who met and interacted face to face. We believe that this projection tendency over the Internet, facilitated by the absence of the traditional gating features that dominate initial liking and relationship formation, is a contributor to the establishment of close relationships over the Internet. Believing that one's partner possesses such idealized qualities also has a way of becoming a self-fulfilling prophecy; it is well-established that treating one's partner with such expectations and assumptions has the effect of producing those very behaviors and qualities (see Murray et al., 1996; Snyder, Tanke, & Berscheid, 1977; Walther, 1996).

Implications for Policy

The present findings have identified two important and unique qualities of Internet (compared to face-to-face) communication: (1) that by its very nature, it facilitates the expression and effective communication of one's true self to new acquaintances outside of one's established social network, which leads to forming relationships with them; and (2) that once those relationships are formed, features of Internet interaction facilitate the projection onto the partner of idealized qualities. In fact, these are precisely those features that previous research has determined to be critical for the formation of close, intimate relationships: Internet communication enables *self-disclosure* because of its relatively anonymous nature (e.g., Derlega et al., 1993), and it fosters *idealization* of the other in the absence of information to the contrary (e.g., Murray et al., 1996).

Like Rogers, we believe that being able to express one's true self is a positive thing; so too is forming rich and meaningful relationships with other people and expanding one's sphere of friends. At the same time, these features of Internet communication are powerful influences that should not be taken lightly. They can cause feelings of closeness and intimacy to occur at breathtaking speed (see McKenna et al., this issue), and this can be a double-edged sword. Even for people who are not currently looking for friends or romantic partners, these features of

Internet communication are likely to be seductive. Before one realizes it, one can find oneself in a friendship or intimate relationship that one wasn't looking for and that in fact causes complications and difficulty within an established social circle and home life. People in all cases—even those who are looking for new close relationships—need to distinguish the positive feelings about the relationship that are due to its Internet nature (e.g., the satisfaction of expressing the true self) from those due to the relationship itself.

Anyone (such as a well-meaning counselor or therapist) who might be considering advising his or her clients, based on the present findings, to engage in anonymous Internet interactions should provide caution and guidance as to the seductive nature of expression of the true self and the rose-colored glasses through which we tend to view our Internet partners. We worry in particular about the lonely and socially anxious, because they are the most highly motivated to find friends and romantic partners—and our Experiment 3 results show that the projection effect has a motivational basis.

Therefore, our first piece of advice to Internet users is: Take it slow. Happily, it would seem that most already do. They move their virtual close relationships through a series of smaller steps—Internet chat, telephone, initial face-to-face meeting—into their real-life social network of family and friends (McKenna et al., this issue).

And beyond keeping one's head on straight about the reasons for potentially strong feelings toward Internet relationship partners, our second piece of advice would be to make sure that any relationship is founded on shared interests, goals, and values: the factors that contribute to durable, long-lasting friendships (see McKenna & Bargh, 2000). Again, it seems that many if not most Internet users know this too: McKenna et al. (this issue) found that close Internet relationships are at least as durable as those formed face to face and (also reassuringly) that many of those who formed them were socially anxious or lonely to begin with (McKenna et al., this issue). How important it must be to lonely schoolboys or -girls to have Internet friends who like and accept them—as long as their parents pay just as much attention to their Internet friends as to their non-Internet friends (see Gross, Juvonen, and Gable, this issue).

So if a counselor, therapist, or parent adds to his or her advice that the client or child interact not just anywhere on the Internet (such as in a random chat room) but in venues in which he or she is likely to find others with similar and identity-important interests (e.g., teen idols, gourmet cooking, liberation theology), this will help found any relationship on solid ground. After all, being seduced into a rewarding, long-lasting relationship is not a bad thing.

Conclusions

In closing, we believe along with Turkle (1995) that the Internet affords a panoply of interaction domains in which alternative forms of the self can be expressed. But we would add to this that these acts of self-expression—in particular expression of one's true self—also have important consequences for establishing liking, rapport, and bonds of understanding with other people. The present findings indicate that psychological self-processes are likely to play a central role in the social life of the Internet.

References

Altman, I., & Taylor, D. A. (1973). *Social penetration: The development of interpersonal relationships.* New York: Holt, Rinehart, and Winston.

Anderson, N. H. (1968). Likableness ratings of 555 personality trait words. *Journal of Personality and Social Psychology, 9,* 272–279.

Bargh, J. A., & Chartrand, T. L. (2000). A practical guide to priming and automaticity research. In H. Reis & C. Judd (Eds.), *Handbook of research methods in social psychology* (pp. 253–285). New York: Cambridge University Press.

Baumeister, R. F. (1998). The self. In D. T. Gilbert, S. T. Fiske, & G. Lindzey (Eds.), *Handbook of social psychology* (4th ed., pp. 680–740). New York: McGraw-Hill.

Collins, N. L., & Miller, L. C. (1994). Self-disclosure and liking: A meta-analytic review. *Psychological Bulletin, 116,* 457–475.

Cooley, C. H. (1902). *Human nature and the social order.* New York: Scribners.

Derlega, V. L., & Chaikin, A. L. (1977). Privacy and self-disclosure in social relationships. *Journal of Social Issues, 33,* 102–115.

Derlega, V. L., Metts, S., Petronio, S., & Margulis, S. T. (1993). *Self-disclosure.* London: Sage.

Goffman, E. (1959). *The presentation of self in everyday life.* New York: Doubleday.

Gollwitzer, P. M. (1986). Striving for specific identities: The social reality of self-symbolizing. In R. Baumeister (Ed.), *Public self and private self* (pp. 143–159). New York: Springer.

Hatfield, E., & Sprecher, S. (1986). *Mirror, mirror: The importance of looks in everyday life.* Albany: State University of New York Press.

Higgins, E. T. (1981). The "communication game": Implications for social cognition. In E. T. Higgins, C. P. Herman, & M. P. Zanna (Eds.), *Social cognition: The Ontario Symposium* (Vol. 1, pp. 343–392). Hillsdale, NJ: Erlbaum.

Higgins, E. T. (1987). Self-discrepancy theory. *Psychological Review, 94,* 1120–1134.

Jung, C. G. (1953). *Two essays in analytical psychology* (trans. R. F. Hull). New York: Pantheon.

Laurenceau, J.-P., Barrett, L. F., & Pietromonaco, P. R. (1998). Intimacy as an interpersonal process: The importance of self-disclosure, partner disclosure, and perceived partner responsiveness in interpersonal exchanges. *Journal of Personality and Social Psychology, 74,* 1238–1251.

Markus, H. (1977). Self-schemata and processing information about the self. *Journal of Personality and Social Psychology, 35,* 63–78.

Markus, H., & Nurius, P. (1986). Possible selves. *American Psychologist, 41,* 954–969.

McKenna, K. Y. A., & Bargh, J. A. (2000). Plan 9 from cyberspace: The implications of the Internet for personality and social psychology. *Personality and Social Psychology Bulletin, 4,* 57–75.

Murray, S. L., Holmes, J. G., & Griffin, D. W. (1996). The self-fulfilling nature of positive illusions in romantic relationships: Love is blind, but prescient. *Journal of Personality and Social Psychology, 71,* 1155–1180.

Pennebaker, J. W. (1990). *Opening up: The healing power of confiding in others.* New York: Morrow.

Rogers, C. (1951). *Client-centered therapy.* Boston: Houghton-Mifflin.

Rubin, Z. (1975). Disclosing oneself to a stranger: Reciprocity and its limits. *Journal of Experimental Social Psychology, 11,* 233–260.

Snyder, M., Tanke, E. D., & Berscheid, E. (1977). Social perception and interpersonal behavior: On the self-fulfilling nature of social stereotypes. *Journal of Personality and Social Psychology, 35,* 656–666.

Swann, W. B., Jr. (1990). To be known or to be adored? The interplay of self-enhancement and self-verification. In E. T. Higgins & R. M. Sorrentino (Eds.), *Handbook of motivation and cognition* (Vol. 2, pp. 408–448). New York: Guilford.

Turkle, S. (1995). *Life on the screen: Identity in the age of the Internet.* New York: Simon & Schuster.
Walther, J. B. (1996). Computer-mediated communication: Impersonal, interpersonal, and hyperpersonal interaction. *Human Communication Research, 23,* 3–43.
Zajonc, R. B. (1960). The process of cognitive tuning in communication. *Journal of Abnormal and Social Psychology, 61,* 159–168.

JOHN A. BARGH is Professor of Psychology and Director of the Graduate Program in Social-Personality Psychology at New York University, where he has been on the faculty since receiving his PhD in Social Psychology from the University of Michigan in 1981. He is the editor of four books and the author of over 100 publications focusing mainly on the role of nonconscious influences on emotion, judgment, and social behavior. He is a recipient of the Early Career Contribution Award from the American Psychological Association and a John Simon Guggenheim Memorial Foundation fellowship.

KATELYN Y. A. MCKENNA is Assistant Research Professor in the Department of Psychology at New York University. She received her BA with honors from Tulane University and her PhD from Ohio University in 1998. Her research interests focus on relationship cognition and social identity processes, especially as these unfold over the Internet.

GRAINNE M. FITZSIMONS is a graduate student in the Social-Personality Program in the Department of Psychology at New York University. She earned her BA with honors in psychology from McGill University in 1999. Her research interests focus on the role of nonconscious motivations in close relationships and in interpersonal behavior more generally.

Journal of Social Issues, Vol. 58, No. 1, 2002, pp. 49–74

Internet Paradox Revisited

Robert Kraut,* Sara Kiesler, Bonka Boneva, Jonathon Cummings, Vicki Helgeson, and Anne Crawford
Carnegie Mellon University

Kraut et al. (1998) reported negative effects of using the Internet on social involvement and psychological well-being among new Internet users in 1995–96. We called the effects a "paradox" because participants used the Internet heavily for communication, which generally has positive effects. A 3-year follow-up of 208 of these respondents found that negative effects dissipated. We also report findings from a longitudinal survey in 1998–99 of 406 new computer and television purchasers. This sample generally experienced positive effects of using the Internet on communication, social involvement, and well-being. However, consistent with a "rich get richer" model, using the Internet predicted better outcomes for extraverts and those with more social support but worse outcomes for introverts and those with less support.

With the rapidly expanding reach of the Internet into everyday life, it is important to understand its social impact. One reason to expect significant social impact is the Internet's role in communication. From the early days of networked mainframe computers to the present, interpersonal communication has been the technology's most frequent use (Sproull & Kiesler, 1991). Over 90% of people who used the Internet during a typical day in 2000 sent or received e-mail (Pew Internet Report, 2000), far more than used any other on-line application or information source. Using e-mail leads people to spend more time on-line and discourages them from

---

*Correspondence concerning this article should be addressed to Robert Kraut, Human-Computer Interaction Institute, Carnegie Mellon University, 500 Forbes Avenue, Pittsburgh, PA 15213 [e-mail: robert.kraut@andrew.cmu.edu]. This research was funded by the National Science Foundation (Grants IRI-9408271 and 9900449). In addition, initial data collection was supported through grants from Apple Computer Inc., AT&T Research, Bell Atlantic, Bellcore, CNET, Intel Corporation, Interval Research Corporation, Hewlett Packard Corporation, Lotus Development Corporation, the Markle Foundation, the NPD Group, Nippon Telegraph and Telephone Corporation, Panasonic Technologies, the U.S. Postal Service, and US West Advanced Technologies. Tridas Mukhopadhyay and William Scherlis participated in designing and carrying out the original HomeNet studies.

49

dropping Internet service (Kraut, Mukhopadhyay, Szczypula, Kiesler, & Scherlis, 2000). Other Internet communication services are increasingly popular—instant messaging, chat rooms, multiuser games, auctions, and myriad groups comprising "virtual social capital" on the Internet (Putnam, 2000, p. 170).

If communication dominates Internet use for a majority of its users, there is good reason to expect that the Internet will have positive social impact. Communication, including contact with neighbors, friends, and family, and participation in social groups improves people's level of social support, their probability of having fulfilling personal relationships, their sense of meaning in life, their self-esteem, their commitment to social norms and to their communities, and their psychological and physical well-being (e.g., S. Cohen & Wills, 1985; Diener, Suh, Lucas, & Smith, 1999; Thoits, 1983; Williams, Ware, & Donald, 1981).

Through its use for communication, the Internet could have important positive social effects on individuals (e.g., McKenna & Bargh, 2000; McKenna, Green, & Gleason, this issue), groups and organizations (e.g., Sproull & Kiesler, 1991), communities (e.g., Borgida et al., this issue; Wellman, Quan, Witte, & Hampton, 2001), and society at large (e.g., Hiltz & Turoff, 1978). Because the Internet permits social contact across time, distance, and personal circumstances, it allows people to connect with distant as well as local family and friends, with coworkers, with business contacts, and with strangers who share similar interests. Broad social access could increase people's social involvement, as the telephone did in an earlier time (e.g., Fischer, 1992). It also could facilitate the formation of new relationships (Parks & Roberts, 1998), social identity and commitment among otherwise isolated persons (McKenna & Bargh, 1998), and participation in groups and organizations by distant or marginal members (Sproull & Kiesler, 1991).

Whether the Internet will have positive or negative social impact, however, may depend upon the quality of people's on-line relationships and upon what people give up to spend time on-line. Stronger social ties generally lead to better social outcomes than do weaker ties (e.g., Wellman & Wortley, 1990). Many writers have worried that the ease of Internet communication might encourage people to spend more time alone, talking on-line with strangers or forming superficial "drive by" relationships, at the expense of deeper discussion and companionship with friends and family (e.g., Putnam, 2000, p. 179). Further, even if people use the Internet to talk with close friends and family, these on-line discussions might displace higher quality face-to-face and telephone conversation (e.g., Cummings, Butler & Kraut, in press; Thompson & Nadler, this issue).

Research has not yet led to consensus on either the nature of social interaction on-line or its effects on social involvement and personal well-being. Some survey research indicates that on-line social relationships are weaker than off-line relationships (Parks & Roberts, 1998), that people who use e-mail regard it as less valuable than other modes of communication for maintaining social relationships (Cummings et al., in press; Kraut & Attewell, 1997), that people who use e-mail heavily have weaker social relationships than those who do not (Riphagen & Kanfer, 1997) and that people who use the Internet heavily report spending less time communicating with their families (Cole, 2000). In contrast, other survey research shows that people who use the Internet heavily report more social support and more in-person visits with family and friends than those who use it less (Pew Internet and American Life Project, 2000). Because this research has been conducted with different samples in different years, it is difficult to identify central tendencies and changes in these tendencies with time. Further, the cross-sectional nature of the research makes it impossible to distinguish self-selection (in which socially engaged and disengaged people use the Internet differently) from causation (in which use of the Internet encourages or discourages social engagement).

A longitudinal study by Kraut and his colleagues (1998) was one of the first to assess the causal direction of the relationship between Internet use and social involvement and psychological well-being. The HomeNet field trial followed 93 households in their first 12–18 months on-line. The authors had predicted that the Internet would increase users' social networks and the amount of social support to which they had access. The consequence should be that heavy Internet users would be less lonely, have better mental health, and be less harmed by the stressful life events they experienced (S. Cohen & Wills, 1985). The sample as a whole reported high well-being at the start of the study. Contrary to predictions, however, the association of Internet use with changes in the social and psychological variables showed that participants who used the Internet more heavily became less socially involved and more lonely than light users and reported an increase in depressive symptoms. These changes occurred even though participants' dominant use of the Internet was communication.

These findings were controversial. Some critics argued that because the research design did not include a control group without access to the Internet, external events or statistical regression could have been responsible for participants' declines in social involvement and psychological well-being (e.g., Gross, Juvonen, & Gable, this issue; Shapiro, 1999). However, these factors would have affected heavy and light Internet users similarly, so they could not account for the differences in outcomes between them.

A more pertinent problem noted in the original HomeNet report is the unknown generalizability of the results over people and time. The participants in the original study were an opportunity sample of families in Pittsburgh. In 1995 and 1996, when they began the study, they initially had higher community involvement and more social ties than the population at large. In addition, they had little experience on-line, and few of their family and friends had Internet access. One possibility is that using the Internet disrupted this group's existing social relationships. Had the study begun with a more socially deprived sample or more recently, when more of the population was on-line, the group's use of the Internet for social interaction might have led to more positive effects. In addition, some critics questioned the particular measures of social involvement and well-being deployed in this study (e.g., Shapiro, 1999).

The present article addresses these issues of generalizability through a follow-up of the original HomeNet sample and a new longitudinal study. The rationale for both studies is similar. If use of the Internet changes the amount and type of interpersonal communication people engage in and the connections they have to their friends, family, and communities, then it should also influence a variety of psychological outcomes, including their emotions, self-esteem, depressive symptoms, and reactions to stressors (e.g., S. Cohen & Wills, 1985; Diener et al., 1999; Thoits, 1983; Williams et al., 1981). The follow-up study examined the longer-term impact of Internet use on those in the original HomeNet sample, providing a second look at a group for whom initial Internet use had poor effects. It retained the outcome measures collected in the original HomeNet study.

A second study followed a new sample in the Pittsburgh area, from 1998 and 1999. It compared an explicit control group of those who had recently purchased a television set with those who had recently purchased a computer. It examined the impact of the Internet on a broader variety of social and psychological outcome measures than did the original HomeNet study. The goal was not to make differentiated predictions for each measure, but to see if using the Internet had similar consequences across a variety of measures of social involvement and psychological well-being. The sample was sufficiently large to permit an analysis of the impact of individual differences in personality and social resources on Internet usage and outcomes. In particular, the research examined whether using the Internet had different consequences for people differing in extraversion and in social support. As discussed further in the introduction to Study 2, people differing in extraversion and social support are likely use the Internet in different ways. In addition, they are likely to have different social resources available in their off-line lives, which could change the benefits they might gain from social resources they acquire on-line.

Study 1: Follow-Up to the Original HomeNet Sample

The data for the follow-up study are from 208 members of 93 Pittsburgh families to whom we provided a computer and access to the Internet in 1995 or 1996. The families were recruited through four high school journalism programs and four community development organizations in eight Pittsburgh neighborhoods. The sample was more demographically diverse than was typical of Internet users at the time. Details of the sampling and research protocol are described in Kraut, Scherlis, Mukhopadhyay, Manning, and Kiesler (1996).

The analyses of social impact reported in Kraut et al. (1998) were drawn from Internet usage records and from surveys given just before participants began the study and again in May 1997. Server software recorded participants' use of the

Internet—hours on-line, e-mail volume, and Web sites visited per week. The surveys included four measures of social involvement (time spent in family communication, size of local social network, size of distant social network, and perceived social support; S. Cohen, Mermelstein, Kamarck, & Hoberman, 1984), and three well-established measures of psychological well-being: the UCLA Loneliness Scale (Russell, Peplau, & Cutrona, 1980), the Daily Life Hassles Scale, a measure of daily-life stress (Kanner, Coyne, Schaefer, & Lazarus, 1981), and the Center for Epidemiological Studies' Depression Scale (CES-D; Radloff, 1977). It included the demographic characteristics of age, gender, household income, and race as control variables, because there is evidence that these factors influence both the amount of Internet use and its social and psychological outcomes (e.g., Magnus, Diener, Fujita, & Payot, 1993; Von Dras & Siegler, 1997). We also included the personality trait of extraversion (Bendig, 1962) as a control variable, because extraversion is often associated with well-being (Diener et al., 1999) and may also influence the way people use the Internet. However, the sample was too small to examine statistical interactions involving the extraversion measure. See Table 1 for basic statistics and other information about these variables.

Kraut et al. (1998) used a regression analysis of the effect of hours of Internet use on social involvement and psychological well-being in 1997 (Time 2), controlling for scores on these outcome measures at the pretest (Time 1) and the demographic and personality control variables. The follow-up study reexamined the impact of use of the Internet by adding a third survey, administered in February 1998 (Time 3). For about half the participants, the final survey came nearly 3 years after they first used the Internet; for the other half, the final survey came nearly 2 years later.

Method

All longitudinal research faces the potential of participant attrition. Our research was especially vulnerable because we had not planned initially to follow the participants for more than 1 year. Many of the high school students in the original sample graduated and moved to college. Further, technology changed rapidly during this period, and some participants changed Internet providers, ending our ability to monitor their Internet use. Of the 335 people who qualified for participation in the original study, 261 returned a pretest survey at Time 1 (78%), 227 returned a survey at Time 2 (68%), and 154 returned a survey at Time 3 (46%). Because this research is fundamentally about changes in social and psychological outcomes, we limit analysis to 208 participants who completed a minimum of two out of three surveys.

We used a longitudinal panel design to examine the variables that influenced changes in social involvement and psychological well-being from Time 1 to Time 2 and from Time 2 to Time 3. The measure of Internet use is the average hours per

Table 1. Descriptive Statistics for Variables in Studies 1 and 2

	Study 1			Study 2			
Variable	Mean	SD	N	Alpha	Mean	SD	N
Adult[a]	.66	.48	208	NA	.88	.32	446
Male[a]	.42	.50	208	NA	.47	.50	446
White[a]	.72	.45	208	NA	.92	.27	438
Income[b]	5.53	1.27	197	NA	4.91	1.55	443
Education[c]				NA	4.06	1.23	446
Computer sample[a]				NA	.72	.45	446
Extraversion[g]	3.54	.77	204	.80	3.22	.65	389
Social support[g]	4.02	.57	206	.81	3.80	.54	389
Internet use[h]	.72	.76	206	.86	.00	.78	406
Local circle (log)[d]	3.01	.81	206	NA	2.56	.79	375
Distant circle (log)[e]	3.01	1.15	206	NA	2.21	1.05	361
Family communication (log)[f]	4.31	.78	193	NA	4.10	1.63	389
Face-to-face communication[h]				.55	−.01	1.00	406
Phone communication[g]				.83	4.69	1.15	387
Closeness near friends[g]				NA	3.54	.76	434
Closeness distant friends[g]				NA	2.94	1.10	286
Community involvement[g]				.70	2.83	.75	390
Stay in Pittsburgh[g]				NA	3.69	1.38	388
Trust[g]				.74	3.17	.83	391
Anomie[g]				.57	2.66	.63	391
Stress[j]	.24	.17	208	.88	.22	.14	382
Loneliness[g]	1.93	.68	204	.75	2.10	.66	389
Depression[i]	.65	.40	205	.88	.53	.47	389
Negative affect[g]				.88	1.67	.64	390
Positive affect[g]				.88	3.49	.72	388
Time pressure[g]				.82	3.02	.76	390
Self-esteem[g]				.85	3.70	.62	389
Computer skill[g]				.90	3.26	.93	389
US knowledge[k]				.41	.71	.33	388
Local knowledge[k]				.34	.68	.26	388

Note: All variables are coded so that higher numbers indicate more of the variable. NA = not available. [a]Dichotomous variable (0/1). [b]Six categories, from under $10,000 to over $75,000. [c]Six categories, from less than 11th grade to graduate-level work. [d]Truncated at 60 and logged. [e]Truncated at 100 and logged. [f]Sum of minutes communicating with other household members, logged. [g]5-point Likert response scale, with endpoints 1 and 5, where 5 is highest score. [h]Hours per week using the Internet (logged) in Study 1; mean of standardized variables in study. [i]4-point Likert scale, with endpoints 0 and 3, where 3 is highest score. [j]Mean of dichotomous response scales (0/1). [k]Proportion correct on multiple choice questions.

week a participant spent on-line between any two surveys, according to automated usage records (i.e., weekly use between Times 1 and 2 and between Times 2 and 3). Because this variable was highly skewed, we used a log transformation. When assessing the impact of Internet use on social involvement and psychological well-being at one time, we statistically controlled for the prior level of social involvement and psychological well-being, by including the lagged dependent variable as a control variable in the model. Since this analysis controls for participants' demographic characteristics and the lagged outcome, one can interpret the coefficients associated with Internet use as the effect of Internet use on changes in these outcomes (J. Cohen & Cohen, 1983, pp. 417–422). (For example, when examining the effect of Internet use on loneliness at Times 2 and 3, we included the lagged variable for loneliness at Times 1 and 2, respectively, in the model to control for the effects of prior loneliness on Internet use and on subsequent loneliness.)

As demographic control variables, we included adult status (0 if age ≤ 18; 1 if age > 18), gender (0 = female; 1 = male), race (0 = non-White; 1 = White) and household income. Because teens use the Internet substantially more than adults and in different ways (Kraut et al., 1998), we included the Generation × Internet Use interaction to determine whether the Internet had similar effects on both generations. Because the personality trait of extraversion is likely to influence social involvement, Bendig's (1962) measure of extraversion was included as a control variable when we were predicting social support and the size of local and distant social circles. Because daily-life stress is a risk factor for psychological depression, we included Kanner et al.'s (1981) hassles scale as a control variable when predicting depressive symptoms.

The analyses were conducted using the xtreg procedure in Stata (StataCorp, 2001) for cross-sectional time series analyses with independent variables modeled as a fixed effect and participant modeled as a random effect. For the dependent measures listed in Table 2, the basic model is

$$
\begin{aligned}
\text{Dependent Variable}_{T_n} = {} & \text{Intercept} + \text{Demographic Characteristics}_{T_1} \\
& + \text{Time Period} + \text{Dependent Variable}_{T_{n-1}} \\
& + \text{Control Variables}_{T_n} + \text{Log Internet Hours}_{T_{n-1}} \\
& + \text{Log Internet Hours}_{T_{n-1}} \times \text{Time Period} \\
& + \text{Log Internet Hours}_{T_{n-1}} \times \text{Generation}_{T_1}.
\end{aligned}
$$

In the model Dependent Variable$_{T_n}$ is a measure of social involvement or psychological well-being at the end of the second or third time period and Dependent Variable$_{T_{n-1}}$ represents the same measure administered in the previous time period. The analyses of particular interest are the main effects of Internet use on subsequent measures of social involvement and psychological well-being and the statistical interactions of Internet use and time period on these outcomes. The main effect of Internet use assesses the cumulative impact of Internet use over the two or three years of the study, and the interaction of Internet use with time period assesses whether this impact is the same in the early period (previously reported in Kraut et al., 1998) and in the more recent period.

Results

Table 2 shows results from the analyses. Kraut et al. (1998) showed Internet use was associated with declines in family communication and in the number of people

Table 2. Analysis of the Original HomeNet Study After 3 Years

Independent variables	Social support[a] beta	SE	p	Local social circle[b] beta	SE	p	Distant social circle[c] beta	SE	p	Family communication (log)[d] beta	SE	p	Stress[e] beta	SE	p	Depression[f] beta	SE	p	Loneliness[g] beta	SE	p
Intercept	0.00	0.04		3.76	3.37		8.85	6.74		-0.03	0.05		0.01	0.01		-0.01	0.03		0.03	0.04	
Adult (0 = teen; 1 = adult)	-0.13	0.09		-19.37	7.41	**	-49.02	14.70	***	0.34	0.11	**	0.00	0.02		-0.14	0.06	*	0.04	0.09	
Male (0 = female; 1 = male)	-0.16	0.08	*	-2.74	6.89		6.57	13.70		-0.08	0.10		0.00	0.02		0.02	0.05		0.27	0.08	**
Household income	0.00	0.00		-0.20	0.15		0.14	0.29		0.00	0.00		0.00	0.00	*	0.00	0.00		0.00	0.00	
White (0 = other; 1 = White)	0.15	0.09		-8.26	8.23		-6.74	16.38		0.11	0.13		0.04	0.02	†	-0.14	0.07	*	-0.22	0.10	*
Time period[h]	0.10	0.06		0.97	2.52		-4.04	4.66		-0.34	0.10	***	0.06	0.01	***	0.01	0.04		0.12	0.06	†
Stress[e]																0.61	0.17	***			
Extraversion[i]	0.07	0.05		1.04	2.74		-5.28	5.21		0.37	0.08	***	0.54	0.06	***	0.18	0.06	***	0.44	0.05	***
Lagged dependent variable[j]	0.45	0.07	***	0.21	0.06	***	0.33	0.10	***	0.05	0.07		0.03	0.01	*	-0.01	0.03		0.00	0.05	
Internet hours (log)	0.02	0.05		-1.15	3.29		-5.14	6.27		0.16	0.12		-0.01	0.02		-0.13	0.05	*	-0.21	0.08	**
Internet × Period	0.10	0.08		-0.37	3.06		2.88	5.62		-0.02	0.13		0.04	0.02	†	-0.08	0.06		-0.09	0.10	
Internet × Adult	0.06	0.09		5.44	6.08		7.52	11.57													
n	189			189			187			177			195			187			186		
R^2	0.29			0.26			0.17			0.15			0.46			0.20			0.36		

Note. Variables were centered before analyses. $n = 208$.

[a]Cohen, Mermelstein, Kamarck, & Hoberman, 1984. [b]Number kept up with monthly, living in the Pittsburgh area. [c]Number kept up with annually, living outside of the Pittsburgh area. [d]Log of the minutes communicating per day. [e]Kanner, Coyne, Schaefer, & Lazarus, 1981. [f]Radloff, 1977. [g]Russell, Peplau, & Cutrona, 1980. [h]Period 1 is 12–18 months, from 1995 or 1996 to 1997, and period 2 is from the first posttest in 1997 to the second posttest in 1998. [i]Bendig, 1962. [j]Dependent variable measured approximately 12–18 months previously.

† $p < .10$. * $p < .05$. ** $p < .01$. *** $p < .001$.

in participants' local and distant social circles, and with increases in loneliness, depressive symptoms, and daily-life stress. Of these effects, Internet use over the longer period tested in the current analyses was associated only with increases in stress. Two significant Internet Use × Time Period interactions suggest that Internet use had different effects early and late in respondents' use of the Internet. In particular, depressive symptoms significantly increased with Internet use during the first period but significantly declined with Internet use during the second period (for the interaction, $p < .05$). Loneliness significantly increased with Internet use during the first period but was not associated with Internet use during the second period (for the interaction, $p < .01$). Whether these differences in results over time reflect participants' learning how to use the Internet as they gain more experience or whether they reflect changes in the Internet itself over this period is a topic we will return to in the Discussion.

Because teenagers use the Internet more than their parents and because teens and adults differed on several of the outcomes reported in Table 2, we tested the differential effects of Internet use with age. There was only one marginally significant interaction: Adults' stress increased more than teens' stress with more Internet use ($p < .10$).

Study 2: A Longitudinal Study of Computer and Television Purchasers

Study 2 is a replication of the original HomeNet research design in a sample of households that had recently purchased new home technology: either a computer or TV. We added controls to the design and new measures. First, we attempted to manipulate Internet use to create a true experiment, with participants randomly assigned to condition. We recruited households who recently bought a new home computer and randomly offered half free Internet service; households in the control condition received an equivalent amount of money ($225) to participate. Unfortunately, this experimental procedure failed when, by the end of 12 months, 83% of the control households obtained Internet access on their own (versus 95% of the experimental households who took advantage of free Internet service). Because this attempt to conduct a true experiment failed, we combined the groups for analyses of the effects of using the Internet.

Another design change was to add a comparison group: recent purchasers of a new television set. Study 1 had only compared heavier and lighter users of the Internet, all of whom had access to it. The addition of a television purchaser comparison group in Study 2 (of whom just 29% obtained Internet access after 12 months) provided a sample that was unlikely to use the Internet and helped to rule out explanations of change based on external events. In analyses of the effects of Internet use, we included participants from the television purchaser group but controlled for sample selection bias by creating a dummy variable indicating whether participants were recruited for buying a television or computer.

We also increased the number of dependent variables to examine the generalizability of the effects of using the Internet across outcomes and measures. The original study contained four measures of personal social involvement and three of psychological well-being. We added measures of personal social involvement (spending time with family and friends, use of the telephone, perceived closeness to a random sample from the respondents' social networks). In response to Putnam's (2000) concerns that the Internet might undercut community participation as well as interpersonal contact, we added measures of involvement with and attitudes toward the community at large. To measure psychological well-being, we added scales measuring the experience of negative and positive affect, perceived time pressure, and self-esteem. Because the Internet is a source of information as well as social contact, we added knowledge tests and a scale to measure computing skill. To test whether the distance-minimizing properties of the Internet blur traditional distinctions between geographically close and distant regions, our measures of social involvement and knowledge differentiated between these, for example, asking separately about local and distant social circles and about knowledge of the Pittsburgh region and broader areas.

Finally, we extended the HomeNet study conceptually by examining the differential effects of individual differences in extraversion and perceived social support on the effects of Internet use. Extraversion is the tendency to like people, to be outgoing, and to enjoy social interaction; it is a highly stable personality trait, predictive of social support, social integration, well-being, and positive life events (e.g., Magnus et al., 1993; Von Dras & Siegler, 1997). The perception of social support refers to feelings that others are available to provide comfort, esteem, assistance, and information or advice; perceived social support buffers the effects of stress (e.g., Cohen, 1988).

We offer two opposing models of the relationship between extraversion and social support and Internet use. A "rich get richer" model predicts that those who are highly sociable and have existing social support will get more social benefit from using the Internet. Highly sociable people may reach out to others on the Internet and be especially likely to use the Internet for communication. Those who already have social support can use the Internet to reinforce ties with those in their support networks. If so, these groups would gain more social involvement and well-being from using the Internet than those who are introverted or have limited networks. They can gain these benefits both by adding members to their social networks and by strengthening existing ties.

By contrast, a "social compensation" model predicts that those who are introverted or lack social support would profit most from using the Internet. People with fewer social resources could use the new communication opportunities on-line to form connections with people and obtain supportive communications and useful information otherwise missing locally (see McKenna & Bargh, 1998). At the same time, for those who already have satisfactory relationships, using the Internet might interfere with their real-world relationships if they swap strong real-world ties for weaker ones on-line. Analogous to the finding that cancer patients with emotionally supportive spouses can be harmed by participating in peer-discussion support groups (Helgeson, Cohen, Schulz, & Yasko, 2000), it is possible that people with strong local relationships might turn away from family and friends if they used the Internet for social interaction.

Method

Sample. We recruited participants through advertisements placed in local newspapers, soliciting for a study of household technology people who purchased a new computer or new television within the previous 6 months. We obtained agreement from all adults and children in the family above age 10 to complete surveys. Half of the computer purchaser households were randomly offered free Internet access to participate in the study; the other participants were offered payments to complete surveys. After the initial telephone contact, we mailed consent forms and pretest surveys with return envelopes. Unlike the procedures used in Study 1, we did not encourage Internet use or provide technology support.

Measures. We administered surveys three times during the study, in February 1998, 6 months later (August 1998), and 1 year later (February 1999). Because we had automated measures of Internet usage only for the group randomly given Internet access, our main independent variable is an index of self-reported Internet use (e.g., "I use the World Wide Web very frequently"; "Time per day spent using e-mail"; "Frequency per month of using a computer at home"; the full text of unpublished measures is available at http://HomeNet.hcii.cs.cmu.edu/progress/research. html). Within the group randomly given Internet access, the Pearson correlations between the self-report index of Internet use and the automated count of the number of sessions logged into the Internet in the 8 weeks surrounding the questionnaires was moderate, $r(112) = .55$ at Time 2 and $r(104) = .42$ at Time 3. These correlations reflect moderate validity of the self-report measure, although they are far from perfect because there is error both in the self-reports and in the server data (e.g., the usage records do not include Internet use at work and include cases in which one family member uses another's account).

We used self-report measures to assess demographic characteristics of the participants and measures from the original HomeNet study, including perceived social support (S. Cohen et al., 1984), size of local and distant social circles, and time talking with other family members. We used the same measure of extraversion (Bendig, 1962). We added new measures of anomie (Srole, 1956), trust in people (Rosenberg, 1957, revised from Survey Research Center, 1969), community involvement (adapted from Mowday, Steers, & Porter's [1979] measure of organizational commitment; e.g., I spend a lot of time participating in community activities; I feel part of the community in Pittsburgh), and intentions to stay in the Pittsburgh area (Even if I had a chance to move to another city, I would very much want to stay in the Pittsburgh area). We also assessed respondents' relationships with specific family and friends by asking them "How close do you feel?" to five individuals living in the Pittsburgh area and five living outside of the area who were closest to them in age. Participants described closeness to each nominee on 5-point Likert scales.

To assess well-being, we again used the CES-D to measure depressive symptoms (Radloff, 1977), the Daily Life Hassles Scale (Kanner et al., 1981), and the UCLA Loneliness Scale (Russell et al., 1980) from the original HomeNet study. We added measures of self-esteem (Heatherton & Polivy, 1991), positive and negative affect (Watson, Clark, & Tellegen, 1988), perceived time pressure (adapted from Kraut & Attewell, 1997) and physical health (scale from the SF-36 short form, health survey; Ware, Snow, Kosinski, & Gandek, 1993).

Finally, because the Internet is a source of information as well as communication, we added measures of knowledge. We included a self-report measure of skill using computers, expanded from the original HomeNet study (e.g., I am very skilled at using computers; I don't know much about using computers [reverse-scored]). We also added a test of knowledge, including multiple choice items on national current events, Pittsburgh current events, and general knowledge from a high school equivalency test (Research & Education Association, 1996). The knowledge test contained different items at different time periods.

Analyses. Data come from 216 households. Of the 446 individuals who were eligible to be in the sample, 96% completed survey 1, 83% completed survey 2 and 83.2% completed survey 3. Analyses are based on 406 respondents (91% of the original sample) who completed at least two surveys. The analyses were similar to those for Study 1. We used Stata's xtreg procedure, with participant as a random effect (StataCorp, 2001), to analyze the panel design. In the Study 2 models, social involvement, well-being, and knowledge outcomes at the second and third time periods were regressed on self-reported Internet use during those periods, controlling for demographic characteristics and the lagged dependent variables. The models control for whether the respondent came from the television purchaser or computer purchaser subsample and whether the data for the dependent variables were collected at the second or third time period. To test whether levels of extraversion and social support moderated the effects of using the Internet, we included the main effects for the Bendig (1962) measure of extraversion and S. Cohen et al.'s (1984) measure of social support and the interaction of these variables with Internet use. We included adult status, gender, race, education, and household income as demographic controls. Because teenagers use the Internet quite differently from adults, we also included the interaction of generation with Internet use.

Results

Table 2 shows scale reliabilities and descriptive statistics for variables in the sample, averaged over the three time periods. A table of correlations is available at http://HomeNet.hcii.cs.cmu.edu/progress/research.html

Effects on interpersonal and community social involvement. Models testing the effects of using the Internet on interpersonal communication and community involvement are shown in Tables 3 and 4, respectively. The main effects of Internet use on these measures of social involvement were generally positive. As Table 3 shows, participants who used the Internet more had larger increases in the sizes of their local social circle ($p < .01$) and distant social circle ($p < .01$) and their face-to-face interaction with friends and family increased ($p < .05$). As Table 4 shows, they also reported becoming more involved in community activities ($p < .10$) and felt greater trust in people ($p < .05$). The only significant reversal to the positive trend is that those who used the Internet more became less committed to living in the Pittsburgh area ($p < .05$).

The interaction with extraversion shows that the association of Internet use with changes in community involvement was positive for extraverts and negative for introverts. Figure 1a illustrates these effects. Holding constant respondents' prior community involvement, extraverts who used the Internet extensively reported more community involvement than those who rarely used it; on the other

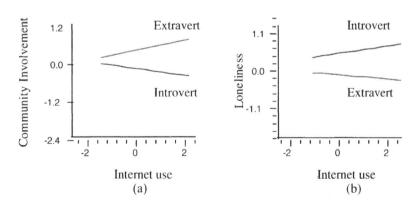

Fig. 1. Interaction of Internet use and extraversion with community involvement and loneliness.

Note. Plots show the effects on community involvement and loneliness of Internet use for people differing in extraversion. Plots show predictions from the models reported in Tables 4 and 5 as Internet use and extraversion move through the range appearing in the sample. Internet use varied from 1.12 standard deviation units less than the mean to 2.54 standard deviation units greater than the mean. The "Introvert" line represents the most introverted respondent, with an extraversion score -2.12 units below the mean, corresponding to a value of 1.10 on the original 5-point Bendig (1962) Extraversion Scale. The "Extravert" line represents the most extraverted respondent, with a score 1.78 units greater than the mean, corresponding to a value of 5 on the original scale.

Table 3. Predicting Interpersonal Social Involvement as a Function of Use of the Internet Over Time and Individual Difference Variables, Study 2

Independent variables	Social support[a]			Local social circle (log)[b]			Distant social circle (log)[c]			Family communication (log)[d]			Face-to-face communication[e]			Phone communication[e]			Closeness to local friends[e]			Closeness to distant friends[e]		
	beta	SE	p	beta	SE	p	beta	SE	p	beta	SE	p	beta	SE	p	beta	SE	p	beta	SE	p	beta	SE	p
Intercept	-0.01	0.02		-0.02	0.03		0.01	0.04		0.29	0.01	***	0.02	0.03		-0.02	0.03		-0.01	0.06		-0.01	0.04	
Adult (0 = teen; 1 = adult)	0.18	0.05	***	-0.04	0.10		0.31	0.12	*	0.00	0.03		-0.55	0.11	***	0.12	0.10		0.27	0.17		0.15	0.16	
Male (0 = female; 1 = male)	-0.09	0.03	**	0.03	0.06		-0.08	0.07		-0.01	0.02		-0.19	0.07	**	-0.30	0.07	***	-0.29	0.12	*	-0.02	0.09	
Household income	0.15	0.06	*	0.37	0.12	**	0.28	0.15	†	-0.03	0.04		-0.11	0.13		-0.04	0.13		-0.41	0.25	†	-0.16	0.20	
White (0 = other; 1 = White)	0.02	0.01	*	-0.01	0.02		0.01	0.03		-0.01	0.01		-0.01	0.02		0.03	0.02		-0.09	0.04	*	0.01	0.03	
Education	0.01	0.01		0.00	0.03		0.06	0.03	†	0.00	0.01		-0.04	0.03		-0.02	0.03		0.00	0.05		-0.01	0.04	
Computer sample (0 = no; 1 = yes)	0.02	0.04		0.12	0.07		0.07	0.09		-0.01	0.02		-0.22	0.08	**	-0.03	0.08		-0.10	0.13		-0.10	0.10	
Time period (0 = 1st 6 months; 1 = 2nd 6 months)	0.01	0.02		-0.05	0.04		-0.12	0.05	*	0.00	0.01		0.03	0.05		0.08	0.04	†	0.00	0.00		-0.04	0.06	
Lagged dependent variable	0.53	0.03	***	0.33	0.04	***	0.46	0.03	***	3.86	0.04	***	0.28	0.03	***	0.50	0.03	***	0.99	0.00	***	0.50	0.04	***
Extraversion[f]	0.15	0.03	***	0.09	0.05	*	0.09	0.06		0.02	0.01		0.14	0.05	**	0.16	0.05	**	0.00	0.00		0.01	0.07	
Social support[a]				0.17	0.05	***	0.13	0.07	†	0.04	0.02	*	0.28	0.07	***	0.11	0.06	†	0.00	0.00		0.30	0.08	***
Internet use[c]	-0.01	0.02		0.12	0.04	**	0.15	0.05	**	0.00	0.01		0.09	0.04	*	0.05	0.04		0.00	0.00		0.07	0.06	
Internet × Extraversion	0.01	0.03		0.02	0.06		-0.05	0.07		-0.01	0.02		-0.02	0.07		0.10	0.06		0.00	0.00		0.01	0.08	
Internet × Support				0.01	0.07		0.02	0.09		0.05	0.02	**	-0.11	0.08		-0.08	0.07		0.00	0.00		0.15	0.10	
Internet × Adult	-0.11	0.06	†	-0.13	0.11		-0.02	0.15		-0.06	0.03	†	0.30	0.13	*	0.04	0.12		0.00	0.00		0.35	0.18	*
n	406			385			365			373			406			391			351			285		
R^2	.51			.42			.47			.95			.31			.51			.16			.44		

Note. Variables were centered before analyses.

[a] Cohen, Mermelstein, Kamarck, & Hoberman, 1984. [b] Number kept up with monthly, living in the Pittsburgh area. [c] Number kept up with annually, living outside of the Pittsburgh area. [d] Minutes communicating per day. [e] See Table 2. [f] Bendig, 1962.

† $p < .10$. * $p < .05$. ** $p < .01$. *** $p < .001$.

Table 4. Predicting Community Social Involvement as a Function of Use of the Internet Over Time and Individual Difference Variables, Study 2

Independent variables	Community involvement[a]			Stay in Pittsburgh[a]			Trust[b]			Anomie[c]		
	beta	SE	p	beta	SE	p	beta	SE	p	beta	SE	p
Intercept	0.00	0.02		-0.02	0.04		-0.01	0.02		0.00	0.02	
Adult (0 = teen; 1 = adult)	0.11	0.07		-0.01	0.14		0.30	0.08	***	-0.24	0.06	***
Male (0 = female; 1 = male)	-0.09	0.04	*	0.11	0.08		-0.01	0.05		0.07	0.04	*
Household income	-0.10	0.09		0.47	0.18	**	0.22	0.10	*	-0.12	0.08	
White (0 = other; 1 = White)	-0.05	0.02	**	-0.06	0.03	*	-0.02	0.02		-0.03	0.01	†
Education	0.05	0.02	**	0.01	0.04		0.04	0.02		-0.03	0.02	*
Computer sample (0 = no;1 = yes)	0.09	0.05	†	0.11	0.10		0.07	0.06	†	-0.07	0.05	
Time period (0 = 1st 6 months; 1 = 2nd 6 months)	0.01	0.04		-0.07	0.06		-0.01	0.04		0.04	0.03	
Lagged dependent variable	0.51	0.03	***	0.55	0.03	***	0.51	0.03	***	0.43	0.03	***
Extraversion[d]	0.17	0.04	***	0.13	0.07	*	0.07	0.04	†	-0.06	0.03	†
Social support[e]	0.17	0.04	***	0.19	0.08	*	0.21	0.05	***	-0.16	0.04	***
Internet use[d]	0.05	0.03	†	-0.13	0.06	*	0.07	0.03	*	-0.01	0.03	
Internet × Extraversion	0.10	0.05	*	0.09	0.09		0.00	0.05		-0.01	0.04	
Internet × Support	0.02	0.05		-0.08	0.10		0.02	0.06		0.02	0.05	
Internet × Adult	-0.01	0.09		0.10	0.17		-0.12	0.10		-0.04	0.08	
n	403			402			405			405		
R^2	.50			.49			.48			.47		

Note. Variables were centered before analyses.
[a] See Table 2. [b] Srole, 1956. [c] Rosenberg, 1957. [d] Bendig, 1962. [e] Cohen, Mermelstein, Kamarck, & Hoberman, 1984.
† $p < .10$. * $p < .05$. ** $p < .01$. *** $p < .001$.

hand, introverts who used the Internet extensively reported less community involvement than those who rarely used it. Interactions of Internet use with social support show that Internet use was associated with larger increases in family communication for those who initially had more social support. Each of these interaction effects supports the "rich get richer" hypothesis.

Finally, interactions of age with Internet use suggest different positive effects for adults and teens. Teens, as compared with adults, increased their social support and family communication with more Internet use, whereas adults increased their face-to-face interaction with family and friends and their closeness to distant relatives and friends with more Internet use.

Effects on psychological and physical well-being. Table 5 shows the effects of Internet use on psychological well-being. These results are mixed, showing that, overall, both stress and positive affect increased with Internet use. The several interactions of Internet use with extraversion indicate that Internet use was associated with better outcomes for extraverts and worse outcomes for introverts. In particular, extraverts who used the Internet more reported increased well-being, including decreased levels of loneliness, decreased negative affect, decreased time pressure, and increased self-esteem. In contrast, these same variables showed declines in well-being for introverts. Figure 1b illustrates these effects. Holding constant prior loneliness, extraverts who used the Internet extensively were less lonely than those who rarely used it, whereas introverts who used the Internet extensively were more lonely than those who rarely used it. There were no interactions with social support or with age and no effects on measures of physical health (not shown in the table).

Effects on skill and knowledge. Table 6 shows the effects of Internet use on self-reported computer skill and multiple choice tests of knowledge. Computer skill increased with more Internet use ($p < .001$); this increase was larger among those with more social support ($p < .05$). General knowledge (not shown in the table) and knowledge of national current events did not change with Internet use. In contrast, those who used the Internet more became less knowledgeable about the local Pittsburgh area ($p < .05$).

Different uses of the Internet. Because the way people choose to use the Internet could strongly influence its effects, we asked participants to report how often they used the Internet for various purposes. We conducted an exploratory factor analysis of these items to create four scales reflecting different uses of the Internet: (a) for communication with friends and family; (b) for acquiring information for school, work, news, and other instrumental purposes such as shopping; (c) for entertainment, such as playing games, downloading music, and escape; and (d) for meeting new people and socializing in chat rooms. These uses of the Internet were moderately interrelated (mean $r = .51$). Using the Internet for communication

Table 5. Predicting Psychological Well-Being as a Function of Use of the Internet Over Time and Individual Difference Variables. Study 2

Independent variables	Stress[a] beta	SE	p	Loneliness[b] beta	SE	p	Depression[c] beta	SE	p	Negative affect[d] beta	SE	p	Positive affect[d] beta	SE	p	Time pressure[e] beta	SE	p	Self-esteem[f] beta	SE	p
Intercept	0.00	0.00		0.00	0.02		0.01	0.01		0.01	0.02		0.00	0.02		0.00	0.02		-0.01	0.02	
Adult (0 = teen; 1 = adult)	0.04	0.02	**	0.08	0.06		0.01	0.05		-0.12	0.07	†	0.05	0.08		0.23	0.09	**	0.06	0.05	
Male (0 = female; 1 = male)	-0.01	0.01		-0.01	0.03		0.02	0.03		-0.02	0.04		0.07	0.05		-0.18	0.05	***	0.11	0.03	***
Household income	0.00	0.02		-0.10	0.07		0.01	0.06		-0.03	0.09		-0.15	0.09	†	0.12	0.10		-0.01	0.07	
White (0 = other; 1 = White)	0.00	0.00		-0.01	0.01		-0.02	0.01		-0.03	0.02	*	0.02	0.02		0.03	0.02		0.01	0.01	
Education	0.01	0.00		0.01	0.02		-0.01	0.01		0.03	0.02		0.00	0.02		-0.02	0.02		-0.01	0.01	
Computer sample (0 = no; 1 = yes)	-0.02	0.01	†	-0.06	0.04	†	-0.03	0.04	†	-0.08	0.05		-0.02	0.06		-0.03	0.06		0.07	0.04	†
Time period(0 = 1st 6 months; 1 = 2nd 6 months)	0.01	0.01		-0.04	0.03		-0.04	0.02	†	-0.04	0.03		0.07	0.03	*	-0.06	0.04	†	0.03	0.02	
Lagged dependent variable	0.54	0.03	***	0.27	0.03	***	0.48	0.03	***	0.39	0.03	***	0.32	0.03	***	0.41	0.03	***	0.58	0.03	***
Extraversion	0.00	0.01	*	-0.21	0.03	***	0.03	0.02		0.01	0.04		0.09	0.04	*	-0.15	0.04	***	0.05	0.03	†
Social support	-0.02	0.01	*	-0.59	0.04	***	-0.21	0.03	***	-0.23	0.04	***	0.41	0.05	***	-0.12	0.05	*	0.28	0.03	***
Internet use	0.01	0.01		0.03	0.02		0.01	0.02		0.04	0.03		0.14	0.03	***	0.05	0.03		0.02	0.02	
Internet × Extraversion	-0.01	0.01		-0.08	0.03	*	-0.05	0.03		-0.12	0.04	**	0.04	0.05		-0.14	0.05	**	0.09	0.03	**
Internet × Support	0.01	0.01		0.01	0.04		0.01	0.04		-0.08	0.05		-0.08	0.06		0.06	0.06		0.04	0.04	
Internet × Adult	-0.02	0.02		-0.10	0.07		-0.09	0.06		-0.13	0.09		0.10	0.09		-0.06	0.10		0.01	0.07	
n	398			406			405			405			405			406			406		
R^2	.51			.66			.48			.40			.43			.42			.63		

Note. Variables were centered before analyses.
[a] Kanner, Coyne, Schaefer, & Lazarus, 1981. [b] Russell, Peplau, & Cutrona, 1980. [c] Radloff, 1977. [d] Watson, Clark, & Tellegen, 1988. [e] Adapted from Kraut & Attewell, 1997. [f] Heatherton & Polivy, 1991.
† $p < .10$. * $p < .05$. ** $p < .01$. *** $p < .001$.

Table 6. Predicting Knowledge as a Function of Use of the Internet Over Time and Individual Difference Variables, Study 2

Independent variables	Computer skill			U.S. knowledge			Local knowledge		
	beta	SE	p	beta	SE	p	beta	SE	p
Intercept	0.02	0.02		0.00	0.01		0.00	0.01	
Adult (0 = teen; 1 = adult)	-0.11	0.07		0.18	0.04	***	0.13	0.03	***
Male (0 = female; 1 = male)	0.05	0.04		0.04	0.02	†	0.04	0.02	*
Household income	-0.01	0.08		0.09	0.04	*	0.06	0.04	
White (0 = other; 1 = White)	-0.01	0.02		0.00	0.01		0.00	0.01	
Education	0.03	0.02		0.03	0.01	***	0.03	0.01	***
Computer sample (0 = no; 1 = yes)	-0.10	0.05	†	0.01	0.03		0.02	0.02	
Time period (0 = 1st 6 months; 1 = 2nd 6 months)	0.04	0.03		-0.04	0.02	*	-0.09	0.01	***
Lagged dependent variable	0.65	0.03	***	0.22	0.04	***	0.11	0.04	**
Extraversion	0.02	0.03		-0.02	0.02		0.00	0.01	
Social support	0.03	0.04		0.05	0.02	*	0.01	0.02	
Internet use	0.31	0.03	***	0.00	0.01		-0.03	0.01	*
Internet × Extraversion	-0.02	0.04		0.01	0.02		0.03	0.02	
Internet × Support	0.10	0.05	*	0.00	0.03		0.00	0.02	
Internet × Adult	0.14	0.08		-0.01	0.04		0.01	0.04	
n	400			403			403		
R^2	.71			.15			.15		

Note. Variables were centered before analyses.

† $p < .10$. * $p < .05$. ** $p < .01$. *** $p < .001$.

with family and friends ($r = .69$) and for information ($r = .62$) had the highest association with the Internet use index reported in Table 2, followed by use for entertainment ($r = .51$) and meeting new people ($r = .38$). Those with more extraversion were more likely than those with less extraversion to use the Internet to keep up with friends and family ($r = .10, p < .05$) and to meet new people on-line and frequent chat rooms ($r = .12, p < .05$), but the associations were weak. Those with stronger initial social support were less likely than those with weaker support to use the Internet to meet new people or use chat rooms on-line ($r = -.11, p < .05$) or for entertainment ($r = -.14, p < .05$). Adults were less likely than teens to use the Internet for meeting new people ($r = -.41, p < .001$) and for entertainment ($r = -.29, p < .001$).

To test whether particular ways of using the Internet were more beneficial than others, we conducted a mediation analysis by adding the measures of specific Internet use to the models in Tables 3–6. These additions did not significantly affect the interactions between overall Internet use and extraversion or social support.

Discussion

The original HomeNet sample began using the Internet in 1995 or 1996. Our follow-up of participants remaining in the sample in 1998 showed that most of the negative outcomes initially associated with use of the Internet dissipated, except for its association with increased stress. The statistical interactions of loneliness and depressive symptoms with time period suggest that use of the Internet led to negative outcomes during the first phase of the study and more positive outcomes later.

In Study 2, conducted from 1998 to 1999, more use of the Internet was associated with positive outcomes over a broad range of dependent variables measuring social involvement and psychological well-being: local and distant social circles, face-to-face communication, community involvement, trust in people, positive affect, and unsurprisingly, computer skill. On the other hand, heavier Internet use was again associated with increases in stress. In addition, it was associated with declines in local knowledge and declines in the desire to live in the local area, suggesting lowered commitment to the local area.

Having more social resources amplified the benefits that people got from using the Internet on several dependent variables. Among extraverts, using the Internet was associated with increases in community involvement and self-esteem and declines in loneliness, negative affect, and time pressure; it was associated with the reverse for introverts. Similarly, among people with more rather than less social support, using the Internet was associated with more family communication and greater increases in computer skill. Adults and teens gained somewhat different benefits from Internet use, with adults more likely to increase their face-to-face interactions locally and their closeness to geographically distant relatives and friends.

What accounts for the differences between the original HomeNet research, showing generally negative consequences of using the Internet, and the follow-ups, showing generally positive consequences? Maturation of participants between the early and late phases of Study 1, differences in samples between Studies 1 and 2, and changes in the Internet itself are all potential explanations for this shift in results. Although our research cannot definitely choose among these explanations, a change in the nature of the Internet is the most parsimonious explanation.

Maturation of participants and changes in the way they used the Internet could potentially account for the shift in results between the early and later phases of Study 1. For example, as the novelty of using the Internet wore off, participants may have jettisoned unrewarding Internet activities and increased their use of more personally rewarding ones. However, the first phase of Study 1, with its negative outcomes, occurred during participants' first year on-line. Study 2, with its positive outcomes, also occurred during a 1-year period, when most participants were new to the Internet. Thus, although maturation could account for differences between the early and late phases of Study 1, it cannot account for differences between Studies 1 and 2.

Participants in Studies 1 and 2 came from separate opportunity samples. These sample differences make comparisons between the two studies problematic and could potentially account for differences in results between them. For example, the original sample included a larger proportion of teens and minorities. Although teenagers and adults gained somewhat different benefits from using the Internet, teenagers did not fare worse overall than adults from using the Internet. Similarly, supplementary analyses (not shown in Tables 3–6) do not reveal racial differences in outcomes that can account for difference between the two studies. Participants in Study 1 had more social support and were more extraverted than those in Study 2, probably because they were recruited from families with organizational member-ships. However, the statistical interactions with extraversion and social support reported in Study 2 would lead one to expect that outcomes would be more posi-tive in Study 1 than Study 2, but this was not the case. Although other unmeasured differences in the samples might account for the differences in results between Study 1 and Study 2, differences in age, race, and social resources do not appear to do so.

The similarity of findings comparing the early and later phases of Study 1 and comparing Studies 1 and 2 suggests that changes in the Internet environment itself might be more important to understanding the observed effects than maturation or differences between samples. Simply put, the Internet may have become a more hospitable place over time. From 1995 to 1998, the number of Americans with access to the Internet at home more than quadrupled. As a result, many more of participants' close family and friends were likely to have obtained Internet access. Similarly, the services offered on-line changed over this period, increasing the ease with which people could communicate with their strong ties. For example, new communication services, such as America Online's instant messaging, allow users to subscribe to a list of family and friends and be notified when members of their "buddy lists" come on-line. In addition to these changes to the on-line social environment, over the span of this research, the Internet provided a richer supply of information, with more news, health, financial, hobby, work, community, and consumer information available. It began to support financial and commercial transactions. Together, these changes could have promoted better integration of participants' on-line behavior with the rest of their lives.

Our finding from Study 2 that extraverts and those with more support benefited more from their Internet use is consistent with this idea. That is, the Internet may be more beneficial to individuals to the extent they can leverage its opportunities to enhance their everyday social lives. Those who are already effective in using social resources in the world are likely to be well positioned to take advantage of a powerful new technology like the Internet.

Research shows that people can form strong social bonds on-line and that relationships formed on-line can carry over to the off-line world (e.g., Parks & Roberts, 1998; McKenna et al., this issue). However, research also suggests that strong relationships developed on-line are comparatively rare. Most studies show that people use the Internet more to keep up with relationships formed off-line than to form new ones on-line (e.g., Kraut et al., 1996; Pew Internet and American Life Project, 2000). In addition, on-line relationships are weaker on average than those formed and maintained off-line (e.g., Cummings et al., in press; Gross et al., this issue). Gross et al. (this issue) also report that adolescents who feel socially anxious and/or lonely are especially likely to communicate on-line with people with whom they do not feel close. Thus one would expect that a diet filled with on-line relationships would be harmful to the social and psychological health of Internet users. Fortunately, people don't seem to use the Internet this way. Rather they mingle their on-line and off-line worlds, using the Internet to keep up with people from their off-line lives and calling and visiting people they initially met on-line (Kraut et al., 1996; McKenna et al., this issue).

Although the impact of using the Internet across the two studies was generally positive, some negative outcomes remained. Across both studies, as people used the Internet more, they reported increases in daily life stress and hassles. Supplementary analyses did not identify any single stressor that occurred more frequently with Internet use, even though the cumulative increase with Internet use was statistically significant. One explanation is that the time spent on-line leaves less for a wide range of other activities and that this time drought may lead to a generalized perception of stress.

In addition to increases in stress, heavier Internet use was also associated with declining commitment to living in the local area and less knowledge about it. These declines may come about because the Internet makes available an abundance of on-line information (and social relationships) outside of the local area. Unlike regional newspapers, for example, the Internet makes news about distant cities as accessible as news about one's hometown.

The mechanisms by which the Internet has its impact on social involvement and psychological well-being remain unclear. One possibility is that the effects of using the Internet depend upon what people do on-line. For example, one might expect that interpersonal communication with friends and family would have more beneficial effects than using the Internet for downloading music, playing computer games, or communicating with strangers. Another possibility is that all uses of the Internet are equivalent in this regard and that the important factor is not how people use the Internet, but what they give up to spend time on-line. Thus the effects of using the Internet might be very different if it substitutes for time spent watching television than if it substitutes for time spent conversing with close friends. No research to date, however, including our own, can distinguish between these two possibilities. Our own attempts to identify the unique effects of using the Internet for different functions were unsuccessful. Self-report measures may be too insensitive to track true differences in use.

Understanding the mechanisms for the Internet's impact is essential for informing private, commercial, and public policy decisions. People need better information to know whether to ration their time on-line or to decide which uses of the Internet are in their long-term interests. As experience with television suggests, enjoyable uses of new technology may be harmful in the long term (e.g., Huston et al., 1992; Putnam, 2000). Service providers need to decide what applications to offer on-line. Schools and libraries need to decide whether to offer e-mail and chat capabilities along with their information-oriented services.

Experiments are a standard way to assess the impact of an intervention. Although laboratory experiments can identify short-term consequences of Internet use, they are too limited to illuminate how the Internet affects slowly emerging phenomena, such as social relationships, community commitment, or psychological well-being (Rabby & Walther, in press). Unfortunately, it is probably too late in the evolution of the Internet to carry out true long-term experiments, at least in North America. We tried to conduct such an experiment on Internet use for Study 2, but in less than 12 months, 83% of the households in the control group had acquired Internet access on their own.

Nonetheless, researchers should continue to attempt to discern how using the Internet is affecting people's lives with the best designs possible. Although cross-sectional designs are most common in research on the impact of the Internet (e.g., Cole, 2000; Parks & Roberts, 1998; Pew Internet & American Life Project, 2000; Riphagen & Kanfer, 1997), they cannot distinguish preexisting differences among people who use the Internet from consequences of using it. Therefore, we believe longitudinal designs are essential to understanding the effects of Internet use and the differences in these effects as the Internet changes. In addition, we need better and more detailed descriptions of how people spend their time, both on-line and off, to relate these detailed descriptions to changes in important domains of life. The diary measures used by Gross et al. (this issue) are a step in this direction.

References

Bendig, A. W. (1962). The Pittsburgh scales of social extraversion, introversion and emotionality. *Journal of Psychology, 53*, 199–209.

Cohen, J., & Cohen, P. (1983). *Applied multiple regression/correlation analysis for the behavioral sciences.* Hillsdale, NJ: Erlbaum.

Cohen, S. (1988). Perceived stress in a probability sample of the United States. In S. Spacapan and S. Oskamp (Eds.), *The social psychology of health* (pp. 31–67). Thousand Oaks, CA: Sage.

Cohen, S., Mermelstein, R., Kamarck, T., & Hoberman, H. (1984). Measuring the functional components of social support. In I. G. Sarason & B. R. Sarason (Eds.), *Social support: Theory, research and applications* (pp. 73–94). The Hague, Holland: Martinus Nijhoff.

Cohen, S., & Wills, T. A. (1985). Stress, social support, and the buffering hypothesis. *Psychological Bulletin, 98*, 310–357.

Cole, J. (2000). Surveying the digital future: The UCLA Internet report [On-line, retrieved November 17, 2000]. Available: http://WWW.CCP.UCLA.EDU/pages/internet-report.asp

Cummings, J., Butler, B., & Kraut, R. (in press). The quality of online social relationships. *Communications of the ACM.*

Diener, E., Suh, E. M., Lucas, R. E., & Smith, H. (1999). Subjective well-being: Three decades of progress. *Psychological Bulletin, 125*, 276–302.

Fischer, C. S. (1992). *America calling.* Berkeley and Los Angeles: University of California Press.

Heatherton, T. F., & Polivy, J. (1991). Development and validation of a scale for measuring state self-esteem. *Journal of Personality and Social Psychology, 60*, 895–910.

Helgeson, V. S., Cohen, S., Schulz, R., & Yasko, J. (2000). Group support interventions for people with cancer: Who benefits from what? *Health Psychology, 19*, 107–114.

Hiltz, S. R., & Turoff, M. (1978). *Network nation: Human communication via computer.* Reading, MA: Addison Wesley.

Huston, A. C., Donnerstein, E., Fairchild, H., Feshbach, N. D., Katz, P. A., Murray, J. P., Rubinstein, E. A., Wilcox, B., & Zuckerman, D. (1992). *Big world, small screen: The role of television in American society.* Lincoln, NE: University of Nebraska Press.

Kanner, A. D., Coyne, J. C., Schaefer, C., & Lazarus, R. S. (1981). Comparisons of two modes of stress measurement: Daily hassles and uplifts versus major life events. *Journal of Behavioral Medicine, 4*, 1–39.

Kiesler, S., Lundmark, V., Zdaniuk, B., Kraut, R., Scherlis, W., & Mukhopadhyay, T. (2000). Troubles with the Internet: The dynamics of help at home. *Human-Computer Interaction, 15*(4), 223–352.

Kraut, R. E., & Attewell, P. (1997). Media use in a global corporation: Electronic mail and organizational knowledge. In S. Kiesler (Ed.), *Culture of the Internet* (pp. 323–342). Mahwah, NJ: Erlbaum.

Kraut, R. E., Mukhopadhyay, T., Szczypula, J., Kiesler, S., & Scherlis, B. (2000). Information and communication: Alternative uses of the Internet in households. *Information Systems Research, 10*, 287–303.

Kraut, R. E., Patterson, M., Lundmark, V., Kiesler, S., Mukhopadhyay, T., & Scherlis, W. (1998). Internet paradox: A social technology that reduces social involvement and psychological well-being? *American Psychologist, 53*(9), 1017–1032.

Kraut, R. E., Scherlis, W., Mukhopadhyay, T., Manning, J., & Kiesler, S. (1996). The HomeNet field trial of residential Internet services. *Communications of the ACM, 39*, 55–63.

Magnus, K., Diener, E., Fujita, F., & Payot, W. (1993). Extraversion and neuroticism as predictors of objective life events: A longitudinal analysis. *Journal of Personality & Social Psychology, 65*, 1046–1053.

McKenna, K. Y. A., & Bargh, J. A. (1998). Coming out in the age of the Internet: Identity "de-marginalization" through virtual group participation. *Journal of Personality and Social Psychology, 75,* 681–694.

McKenna, K. Y. A., & Bargh, J. A. (2000). Plan 9 from cyberspace: The implications of the Internet for personality and social psychology. *Personality and Social Psychology Review, 4,* 57–75.

Mowday, R., Steers, R., & Porter, L. (1979). The measurement of organizational commitment. *Journal of Vocational Behavior, 14,* 224–227.

Parks, M., & Roberts, L. (1998). Making MOOsic: The development of personal relationships on line and a comparison to their off-line counterparts. *Journal of Social and Personal Relationships, 15,* 517–537.

The Pew Internet & American Life Project. (2000, May 10). Tracking online life: How women use the Internet to cultivate relationships with family and friends [On-line, retrieved May 15, 2000]. Available: http://www.pewinternet.org/reports/

Putnam, R. D. (2000). *Bowling alone.* New York: Simon & Schuster.

Rabby, M., & Walther, J. B. (in press). Computer-mediated communication impacts on relationship formation and maintenance. In D. Canary & M. Dainton (Eds.), *Maintaining relationships through communication: Relational, contextual, and cultural variations.* Mahwah, NJ: Erlbaum.

Radloff, L. (1977). The CES-D Scale: A self-report depression scale for research in the general population. *Applied Psychological Measurement, 1,* 385–401.

Research & Education Association. (1996). The best test preparation for the GED (General Educational Development). Piscataway, NJ: Author.

Riphagen, J., & Kanfer, A. (1997). How does e-mail affect our lives? [On-line, retrieved October 15, 1999]. Champaign-Urbana, IL: National Center for Supercomputing Applications. Available: http://www.ncsa.uiuc.edu/edu/trg/e-mail/index.html

Rosenberg, M., with Suchman, E. A., & Goldsone, R. K. (1957). *Occupations and values.* Glencoe, IL: Free Press.

Russell, D., Peplau, L., & Cutrona, C. (1980). The revised UCLA Loneliness Scale: Concurrent and discriminant validity evidence. *Journal of Personality and Social Psychology, 39*(3), 472–480.

Shapiro, J. S. (1999). Loneliness: Paradox or artifact? *American Psychologist, 54*(9), 782–783.

Sproull, L., & Kiesler, S. (1991). *Connections: New ways of working in the networked organization.* Cambridge, MA: MIT Press.

Srole, L. (1956). Social integration and certain corollaries. *American Sociological Review, 21,* 709–716.

StataCorp. (2001). Stata Statistical Software: Release 7.0. College Station, TX: Stata Corporation.

Survey Research Center. (1969). *1964 election study.* Ann Arbor, MI: University of Michigan, Inter-University Consortium for Political Research.

Thoits, P. (1983). Multiple identities and psychological well-being: A reformulation and test of the social isolation hypothesis. *American Sociological Review, 48,* 174–187.

Von Dras, D. D., & Siegler, I. C. (1997). Stability in extraversion and aspects of social support at midlife. *Journal of Personality & Social Psychology, 72,* 233–241.

Ware, J. E., Snow, K. K., Kosinski, M., & Gandek, B. (1993). *SF-36 Health Survey: Manual and interpretation guide.* Boston: Nimrod.

Watson, D., Clark, L. A., & Tellegen, A. (1988). Development and validation of brief measures of positive and negative affect: The PANAS scales. *Journal of Personality and Social Psychology, 54,* 1063–1070.

Wellman, B., Quan, A., Witte, J., & Hampton, K. (2001). Does the Internet increase, decrease or supplement social capital? Social networks, participation, and community commitment. *American Behavioral Scientist, 45,* 436–455.

Wellman, B., & Wortley, S. (1990). Different strokes for different folks: Community ties and social support. *American Journal of Sociology, 96*(3), 558–588.

Williams, A. W., Ware, J. E., & Donald, C. A. (1981). A model of mental health, life events, and social supports applicable to general populations. *Journal of Health and Social Behavior, 22,* 324–333.

ROBERT KRAUT is Herbert Simon Professor of Human-Computer Interaction at Carnegie Mellon University. He holds a PhD in social psychology from Yale

University and has worked as a research scientist at AT&T Bell Laboratories and Bell Communications Research and as a faculty member at University of Pennsylvania and Cornell University. He has broad interests in the design and impact of information technology. He has conducted empirical research on office automation and employment quality, technology and home-based employment, the communication needs of collaborating scientists, the design of information technology for small-group intellectual work, and the impact of national information networks on organizations and families.

SARA KIESLER is Professor of Human-Computer Interaction at Carnegie Mellon University. She holds a PhD in psychology from Ohio State University. Her research examines social aspects of technology and technological change, especially computer communication and human-computer interaction. Her projects currently span topics in human-robot interaction, use of information technology in cars, home technology, impact of the Internet, electronic communities and groups, and distributed and multidisciplinary work groups or organizations.

BONKA BONEVA is a postdoctoral fellow in the Human-Computer Interaction Institute at Carnegie Mellon University. She received a PhD in sociology from the University of Sofia and has done doctoral work in psychology at the University of Pittsburgh. She has previously worked at the Bulgarian Academy of Sciences, the University of Sofia, Northwestern University, and the University of Pittsburgh. Her research and publications include work on personality factors in international and internal migration, reconstructing social identities under new sociocultural conditions, and theoretical and methodological issues of power motivation. Recently, she has been studying the impact of gender in computer-mediated communication.

JONATHON N. CUMMINGS is a postdoctoral fellow in the Human-Computer Interaction Institute at Carnegie Mellon University, from which he received his PhD in organization science. He earned his BA in psychology from the University of Michigan and his AM in social psychology from Harvard University. He is currently interested in the social impact of Internet use in households and the workplace, interaction processes and performance consequences of distributed work, and statistical analyses and visualization tools for understanding social networks.

VICKI HELGESON is an Associate Professor of Psychology at Carnegie Mellon University. She received her PhD in experimental social psychology from the University of Denver and completed a postdoctoral fellowship in health psychology at the University of California at Los Angeles. Her research interests focus on the intersections of gender, relationships, and health. She has conducted a number of longitudinal studies that focus on how people adjust to chronic illness, including breast cancer, heart disease, prostate cancer, and diabetes. Much of this work has been supported by the National Institutes of Health.

ANNE M. CRAWFORD is a postdoctoral fellow in the Human-Computer Interaction Institute at Carnegie Mellon University involved with longitudinal research on the impact of computers, Internet, and other technologies on social relationships and family interaction. Previously, she was Senior Data Analyst for the Pittsburgh Youth Study at the University of Pittsburgh Medical Center and Health System for a longitudinal study of substance use and delinquency among adolescent males. She was data analyst for the HIV and Alcohol Prevention Project at the University of Kentucky in 1998–99. She received her PhD in social psychology from the University of Kentucky in 1998.

Journal of Social Issues, Vol. 58, No. 1, 2002, pp. 75–90

Internet Use and Well-Being in Adolescence

Elisheva F. Gross,* **Jaana Juvonen, and Shelly L. Gable**

University of California, Los Angeles

Previous research suggests that Internet use may be associated with decreases in well-being among adolescents. However, there has been little investigation of the relationship between well-being and social aspects of Internet use. In the present study, 130 7th graders from a middle-class public school in California completed dispositional measures of well-being, and on three subsequent evenings they responded to questions regarding their Internet use (including detailed logs of instant messages) and daily well-being. Time spent on-line was not associated with dispositional or daily well-being. However, as suggested by intimacy theory, the closeness of instant message communication partners was associated with daily social anxiety and loneliness in school, above and beyond the contribution of dispositional measures.

As Internet use among teenagers has grown exponentially in the last 10 years (Becker, 2000), so has concern over its effect on their psychological well-being. Of over 1,000 U.S. parents surveyed in 1999, almost two thirds expressed concern that "going on-line too often may lead children to become isolated from other people," whereas 40% endorsed the belief that "children who spend too much time on the Internet develop antisocial behavior" (Turow, 1999).

Such apprehensions are not simply the fears of overprotective parents; they received initial empirical support from the first major study of the Internet's psychological impact. A longitudinal investigation of first-time Internet users known as the HomeNet study (Kraut et al., 1998) reported that using the Internet for as little as 3 hr weekly led to increased levels of depression and reductions in social

---

Correspondence concerning this article should be addressed to Elisheva F. Gross, Department of Psychology, University of California, 1285 Franz Hall, Los Angeles, CA 90095-1563 [e-mail: egross@ucla.edu]. This research was undertaken with the financial support of a Jacob K. Javits Graduate Fellowship and a research grant from the UCLA Psychology Department to the first author. Portions of this article were presented at the biennial meeting of the Society for Research in Child Development, Minneapolis, Minnesota, April 2001. We are grateful to Grace Chien, Kristina Cutura, Lorain Wang, and May Yip for collecting and entering data.

support over the course of 2 years. Results showed teenagers to be the population most vulnerable to these negative effects. Kraut and colleagues speculated that adolescents' heavy usage of the Internet for on-line communication led them to forsake critical bonds with local friends and family for weak relations with strangers.

In considering the application of Kraut and colleagues' findings to adolescents, two concerns in particular should be noted. First, because the HomeNet sample did not include a non-Internet-using control group, we cannot determine how much of the downward trend in participants' well-being was due to their Internet use or to the unfortunate but steady decline in perceived social support and overall contentment *typically* reported by youth as they proceed through adolescence (Larson, 1999). Second, the Kraut et al. study (like most studies of youth Internet use, e.g., Roberts, Foehr, Rideout, & Brodie, 1999) did not gather detailed accounts of on-line social activity (i.e., with whom and about what Internet users were communicating). Given the importance of supportive peer relationships to healthy adolescent development (for a review, see Hartup, 1996), we argue that an understanding of the relation between youth Internet use and psychological well-being requires a consideration of *with whom* adolescents communicate on-line.

Well-Being and Close Relationships

The need to form and maintain strong interpersonal bonds has been described as a fundamental need (Baumeister & Leary, 1995) and one that is critical to healthy development (e.g., Sullivan, 1953). Research on young adults has found that feeling close and connected to others on a daily basis is associated with higher daily well-being, and in particular, feeling understood and appreciated and sharing pleasant interactions are especially strong predictors of well-being (Reis, Sheldon, Gable, Roscoe, & Ryan, 2000). As outlined by Reis and Shaver (1988), intimacy is developed and sustained through social exchanges with responsive others (e.g., pleasant interactions and feeling understood). Intimacy emerges as an expectation for peer relationships in late childhood or early adolescence (Buhrmester & Furman, 1987; Sullivan, 1953), and the expectations and meanings of friendships remain constant throughout adolescence and adulthood. Thus close and meaningful interactions with peers are likely to be at least as important to adolescent well-being as they are to adult well-being. Indeed, research affirms that close peer relationships contribute positively to adolescent self-esteem and well-being, whereas peer relationship problems such as peer rejection and a lack of close friends are among the strongest predictors of depression and negative self-views (see Hartup, 1996). From the perspective of intimacy theory (Reis & Shaver, 1988), Internet use could undermine *or* foster well-being, depending on whether it supplants (as suggested by Kraut et al., 1998) or expands opportunities for meaningful, daily contact with close peers.

Adolescent Internet Use

Two advances in the use of the Internet are important to our understanding of the nature of on-line relationships and social exchanges. First, new technologies have been developed to further facilitate synchronous on-line interaction with known others. One such feature, instant messages (IMs), allows users to be informed when friends are on-line and to chat with them through text windows that appear on the screens of the two parties involved. Because of its dyadic, real-time, and private format, the IM is structurally and functionally comparable to other important and pervasive forms of social interaction in adolescence: "hanging out" face to face and talking on the phone. Indeed, a recent study by the Pew Internet and American Life Project (2001) indicates that for a fifth of American teenage Internet users, instant messaging (IMing) has become the primary means of contacting friends. Second, with more youth (particularly from middle- and upper-income households) accessing the Internet from home than ever before, teens are increasingly likely to find their close friends on-line. Thus, youth need not necessarily forsake their school-based relationships when they log on; the Internet can now be both a space in which to interact with distant associates and strangers and a supplemental medium for communication with one's established, off-line peer network.

The Present Study

We present findings from a study on adolescents' daily Internet use and psychological adjustment, with a specific focus on IMing. Participants in this research completed three daily reports of their overall well-being, socially specific adjustment (loneliness and social anxiety in school), and after-school activity, including Internet use. Dispositional measures of these variables were also collected in participants' classrooms prior to the daily reporting. Given the tendency for psychological well-being (Reis et al., 2000) and loneliness (Larson, 1999) to fluctuate within and across days as a function of social contact, we expected that daily indicators of well-being would be especially important to consider.

Analyses will be presented in two parts: descriptive and correlational. First, distinct forms of Internet use will be explored in the context of both overall time on-line and time in non-Internet activities. The second set of results will be devoted to the investigation of associations among on-line activity and well-being. It is proposed that with the increasing ease and speed of on-line communication with friends, adolescents' psychological well-being is not associated with how much time they spend either on the Internet or in specific on-line domains. Rather, we predict that socially specific aspects of psychological adjustment—loneliness and social anxiety with school peers—are related to the closeness of relationships with on-line communication partners. In order to enable the collection of detailed communication variables, we focus on the characteristics of discrete, dyadic IM exchanges. Specifically, we test the prediction that adolescents who report lower levels of loneliness and social anxiety, relative to their peers, would be more likely to IM with people to whom they felt close. In addition, we expected the daily indicators of loneliness and social anxiety to improve predictions of partner closeness beyond the contributions of trait indicators. Given the centrality of motives for and content of self-relevant disclosure to the process of intimacy (Reis & Shaver, 1988), we also explored the associations among well-being and IM motives and topics. Finally, in light of previously reported gender differences in early adolescents' verbal intimacy with friends (Papini, Farmer, Clark, Micka, & Barnett, 1990) and Internet use (see Becker, 2000), we took gender into account in our analyses.

Method

Demographic data (age, gender, ethnicity), background information on Internet use (e.g., on-line tenure, parental rules regarding Internet use, shared phone access, and speed of Internet connectivity), and dispositional measures of psychological adjustment (depression, social anxiety, and loneliness) were collected from participants in school. For the same night as the data were collected (8–14 hr later) and for two consecutive nights thereafter, participants provided daily reports on three general sets of variables: specific on-line activities, general after-school activity, and psychological adjustment.

Participants

To allow us to examine an adolescent peer context in which Internet use is widespread, we sampled from a relatively homogenous mid- to high-socioeconomic-status community. All seventh-grade students were recruited from one public middle school in Southern California. Parental consent was received for 33% of boys and 47% of girls recruited ($p < .001$), resulting in 49 male and 81 female participants. The participants ranged in age from 11 to 13 years of age, with the majority aged 12 ($M = 12.11$, $SD = .40$). Of the 120 participants who reported their ethnicity, 59.2% identified themselves as European American, 17.5% as Asian American, 10% as being of mixed heritage, 5.8% as Latino/a, 1.7% as African American, and 5.8% as other.

Procedure

To encourage Internet users and nonusers alike to participate in the study and to reduce the likelihood of reactivity, the study was explained during a class and in a letter to parents as research "investigating how adolescents feel about themselves and their peers and how they spend their time after school, including on the

Internet." All participants first completed a confidential self-report questionnaire in class. Participants were then directed to complete the daily report just before going to sleep each night. To encourage timely and complete participation, researchers visited each classroom daily during the course of the study to collect the previous night's and distribute that night's log. Each time participants returned a daily report complete and on time, they were rewarded by the researchers with a piece of candy and a lottery ticket for two movie passes to be raffled in their classroom after the study.

A total of 17 participants did not complete any nightly logs, resulting in 113 participants reporting a total of 275 days, an average of 2.12 of 3 possible days per person. Girls were more compliant, on average completing more logs than boys ($Ms = 2.41, 1.63, p = .001$). There was no significant difference in either psychological measures or levels of typical Internet use between participants who submitted at least one versus no daily reports.

One-Time Measures

Typical after-school activity. To enable comparisons of our data with other studies of Internet use (i.e., America Online/Roper Starch, 1999), participants were asked to estimate how much time they spend "on a typical day" using the Internet at home. In addition, in order to situate Internet use in the context of daily after-school activity, five other types of after-school activity were assessed: homework, organized activity (e.g., sports team, club, lesson), hanging out with friends, talking on the phone, and watching television. Next to each activity, participants marked one of five alternatives (*none, 30 minutes or less, 1 hour, 2–3 hours, 4 hours or more*) to indicate daily engagement.

Loneliness. Nine items from the 30-item UCLA Loneliness Scale, Version 3 (Russell, 1996) were used to assess global feelings of isolation. The words "in school" were added to each item to enable assessment in this specific setting. On 5-point scales ($1 = not at all true for me, 5 = all the time true for me$), participants responded to such questions as "How often do you feel left out at school?" Higher scores indicate greater levels of loneliness.

Social anxiety. Global social anxiety was measured using the generalized social anxiety subscale of the Social Anxiety Scale for Adolescents (SAD-G) devised by La Greca and Lopez (1998). This instrument assesses adolescents' subjective experience of generalized social avoidance, inhibition, and distress. Participants rated each of four descriptive self-statements (e.g., "I feel shy even with people I know very well") on a 5-point scale. Higher scores indicate increased levels of social anxiety.

Friendship. A quantitative measure of friendship (number of close friends at school) was included to provide construct validity for the measures of school-based loneliness and social anxiety, as well as to serve as a proxy for the size of social circle assessment used in the HomeNet study (Kraut et al., 1998).

Depressed mood. The 10-item short form of the Child Depression Inventory (CDI; Kovacs, 1992) was administered with eight filler items. For each item, participants selected one of three statements that was "most true" for them *in the past two weeks* (e.g., "(a) Things bother me once in a while, (b) Things often bother me, or (c) Things bother me all the time.") A higher index score indicates greater levels of depressed mood.

Daily Measures

Our primary aim in using a dual-survey approach at this preliminary stage of investigation was to verify participants' in-school global self-reports of peer-related adjustment and after-school behavior with daily reports of their behaviors across three weekdays. Therefore, daily scores across the three days were combined as a mean, despite the potential loss of key information regarding within-person variability (see Reis & Gable, 2000).

Daily after-school activity. Participants were asked to estimate how much time they spent that day on the six after-school activities mentioned above. In addition, eight categories of on-line activity were listed: e-mail, games, multiuser dimensions (MUDs), message boards, list-servs/newsgroups, chat rooms, IMs, and Web or America Online (AOL) sites. Next to each activity, participants rated engagement using the 5-point time scale (*none* to *4 hours or more*) described above.

Characteristics of on-line communication. In order to balance our interest in the details of interaction with our concern for participant attrition and fatigue, the log required participants to provide more extensive information for only their single lengthiest IM interaction that day, as follows: relational identity of IM partner (stranger, acquaintance, friend, best friend, girlfriend/boyfriend, or family member); origin of contact with partner (on-line, off-line in school or off-line outside of school); duration of relationship (six possible categories, from *this is the first time we've met* to *over 2 years*); gender of partner; relative age of partner; their own motives for IMing; and topics discussed. Participants were asked to indicate how much they discussed each of 13 communication topics ranging from less intimate (e.g., politics, schoolwork/college, sports) to more intimate topics (e.g., gossip, boyfriend/girlfriend stuff, friends). Topics were selected based on observations of public teen chat conversations and feedback from pilot participants.

Loneliness. A daily index of loneliness was developed from the UCLA Loneliness Scale. Seven items from the dispositional measure were used. Participants indicated the degree to which each statement was true for them "today at school."

Social anxiety. LaGreca and Lopez's (1988) SAD-G scale was adapted for use as a daily measure, with each of four items assessing how participants felt at school that day.

Subjective well-being. The Student's Life Satisfaction Scale (SLSS; Huebner, 1991) was adapted for use a daily assessment of student's global life satisfaction (cf., depression) beyond such specific domains as peer relations at school. Participants rated their agreement on a 5-point scale ($1 = strongly\ disagree$ to $5 = strongly\ agree$) for each of seven statements according to how they felt that day (e.g., "My life was just right today"). Higher scores indicate greater daily subjective well-being.

Psychometric Properties of the Adjustment Variables

All standardized psychological scales employed demonstrated acceptable internal consistency and congruence with distributions and correlates of normative adolescent populations, as reported by scale authors (see Table 1 for all internal consistency reliability coefficients). To establish construct validity, we computed correlations between the dispositional and aggregated daily measures of social functioning (see Table 1). These correlations were moderate to strong, ranging

Table 1. Correlations Among Psychological Adjustment Variables and Instant Message Partner Closeness

Variables	Mean	SD	α	1	2	3	4	5	6
Dispositional adjustment measures									
1. Number of close friends in school	3.44	1.0							
2. Depression	2.76	3.1	.83						
3. Loneliness	19.54	6.5	.84	−.380***	.523***				
4. Social anxiety	6.87	2.8	.79	−.331***	.493***	.560***			
Daily adjustment measures									
5. Daily subjective well-being	26.38	5.8	.89		−.510***	−.437***	−.361***		
6. Loneliness	13.51	5.1	.83	−.411***	.494***	.609***	.355***	−.560***	
7. Social anxiety	6.17	2.7	.74	−.322**	.474***	.479***	.511***	−.440***	.748***

Note: All nonsignificant ($p > .01$) correlations were omitted. Cronbach's alpha internal reliability statistics are in the column labeled α. Reliabilities for daily adjustment measures represent averages of the daily alphas.
** $p = .001$. *** $p = .0001$.

from $r = .51$ for social anxiety to $r = .61$ for loneliness. Also, it should be noted that the correlations between dispositional and daily measures of psychological well-being were similar across all three days, suggesting a lack of bias stemming from the collection of dispositional and Day 1 measures on the same day. No effects of gender or ethnicity were observed on any psychological measures.

Results

Internet Usage in the Context of Adolescents' After-School Time

Using the traditional response format of how often participants use the Internet, the in-school survey revealed that 90% of participants use the Internet "occasionally" or "regularly" at home. Similarly, 84% of respondents reported that they go on-line on a "typical day." Consistent with these figures, 70% of participants ($n = 110$) reported at least one Internet session during the 3 days of our study. On a given single day, however, between 40% and 57% of participants ($n = 76-99$) reported that they did *not* go on-line. Thus, global questions seemed to bias usage estimates to be somewhat higher (14–21%) than those reported in daily logs. In order to portray an average daily assessment, all activities and psychological measures were averaged across days for all participants.

On average, the Internet consumed less of participants' daily after-school time than any of the other five activities measured. Participants reported over 1 hr in organized activities (e.g., clubs, lessons; $M = 62.35$ min, $SD = 57.4$) and watching television ($M = 62.99$, $SD = 56.6$), and more than 2 hr doing homework ($M = 129.60$, $SD = 60.4$). Average daily time on-line ($M = 46.6$ min, $SD = 59.7$) most closely approximated time spent on the phone ($M = 64.31$, $SD = 115.1$) and with friends ($M = 70.18$, $SD = 70.0$).

As shown in Figure 1, on average, participants devoted the majority of their daily time on-line to three domains: IMing ($M = 28.85$ min, $SD = 42.4$), visiting Web sites and "surfing the Web" ($M = 24.45$, $SD = 33.6$), and e-mail ($M = 20.38$, $SD = 24.3$). No significant gender differences in levels of overall or specific types of Internet usage were revealed by t-tests, after excluding the 5 boys (of $n = 113$) who comprised the long tail (95th percentile) of high daily game activity (i.e., 75 min or more of on-line game play per day). It should be noted that the average sum of time spent in specific domains far surpassed average daily overall time participants reported spending on the Internet, suggesting that participants commonly engaged in simultaneous activity, or "multitasking."

Characteristics of IMs

Participants reported exchanging IMs with an average of 2.68 ($SD = 1.83$) different people per day. Additional data were collected about participants' longest

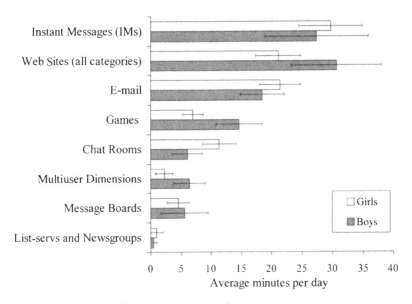

Fig. 1. Average daily time (+*SE*) spent on-line by domain.

IM interaction each day. The median interaction duration was 30 min, and 54% of participants who reported IMing (*n* = 43) indicated that they communicated with the person "every day" or "almost every day." An additional 14% reported weekly contact with the IM partner. In contrast, only 7% of instant messengers stated that the reported interaction was the first IM they had ever exchanged with that particular person.

IM motives and topics. Participants' motives for and topics of IM communication convey the social and personal nature of participants' interactions. The topics most commonly reported by both boys and girls were friends (58%), gossip (51%), and "boyfriend/girlfriend stuff" (50%). The most widely reported motive for IMing was "to hang out with a friend," endorsed by 92% of instant messengers (*n* = 43), and nearly three fourths of instant messengers reported IMing because they were bored (74%).

IM partners. Consistent with our expectations, participants' relationships with IM partners (*n* = 86) were described, on average, as relatively long-standing friendships with peers first met in school. Most IM partners (86%) were reported to be "about the same age" (i.e., less than 2 years older or younger) as the participant, whereas the remaining 14% were described as 2 or more years older. Just over half (54%) of reported IM interactions occurred in same-sex dyads. Of the partners, 88% were first met off-line, predominantly at school (67%). Only 12% of partners were first encountered on-line. Sixty-five percent of participants reported knowing their IM partner for more than a year, and 35% had known their partner for more than 2 years. No participants reported knowing their partner for less than a week.

To be able to describe the closeness of participants' relationships with IM partners, partner type was ordered on the dimension of closeness. First, we excluded three low-frequency categories (boyfriend/girlfriend, family member, other) because the closeness of these relationships varies considerably among young adolescents (cf. Brown, 1999). Second, we represented the remaining categories as a 4-point closeness scale ($1 = stranger$, $2 = acquaintance$, $3 = friend$, and $4 = best$ $friend$). Third, we averaged closeness of the communication partner across days. Reported closeness of the relationship with primary IM partners was fairly consistent across the three days (Cronbach's $\alpha = 68$) and reflected participants' tendency to communicate with friends ($M = 3.10$, $SD = 0.8$). Examination of cross-tabulations of IM partner closeness and origin of the relationship (i.e., off-line vs. on-line) showed that the vast majority of friends and all best friends were initially met *off-line*. The few strangers with whom participants communicated were largely met on-line (five out of six). Closeness differed neither by gender nor by tenure on-line.

Internet Usage and Psychological Adjustment

Overall usage levels. Consistent with our predictions, time on-line—overall or in specific domains (e.g., chat, games)—was not correlated with psychological adjustment. In addition, analysis of variance comparisons among groups of Internet users of varying levels of tenure (e.g., 0–6 months vs. 2 years or more using the Internet) yielded no significant differences on any psychological measures.

Predicting closeness of relationship with IM partner from daily adjustment. Pearson correlations between IM partner closeness and all psychological measures (controlling for effects of gender, average daily time on-line and average daily time on IMs) yielded significant associations with daily levels of loneliness, $r(38) = -.43$, $p = .01$, and social anxiety, $r(38) = -.40$, $p = .01$, suggesting that participants who felt relatively socially anxious and/or lonely in school *on a daily basis* were more likely to communicate in IMs with people with whom they did not have a close affiliation.

Hierarchical multiple regressions were performed to test the multivariate model: the contribution of average daily social anxiety to the average closeness of IM partners. It should be noted that because the data reported here are correlational, inferences cannot be made regarding the direction of causality; that is, our data cannot distinguish whether problematic peer relations cause individuals to seek out unfamiliar communication partners on-line, or, conversely, if on-line communication with a close friend from school is responsible for improved comfort and connectedness in school. In spite of this limitation, the temporal sequencing of the data collection (i.e., daytime feelings in school precede nighttime Internet use) requires that we frame the association between school adjustment and on-line communication in terms of the former predicting the latter.

To take into account the potential influence of gender and the possibility that time spent on-line might increase the likelihood of friends also being on-line, we entered gender and the average daily total time on-line as first and second steps in the regression, respectively.[1] To control for the influence of dispositional social anxiety, the initial global assessments obtained at school on the first day were then entered into the equation. We were thus able to examine whether daily average social anxiety would add substantially to an explanation of partner closeness beyond that provided by the global measure. The daily measure of social anxiety significantly predicted closeness of IM partner, $\beta = .45$, $p < .02$, adding 13% to the total variance explained by the model, $\Delta R^2 = .13$, $p < .02$.

Similarly, daily and dispositional loneliness were entered as successive third and fourth steps in a hierarchical regression predicting average closeness of IM partner. As predicted, daily loneliness predicted an additional 8% of the total variance, $\Delta R^2 = .08$, $p < .06$, $\beta = -.41$, $p < .06$ (i.e., above and beyond the contribution of dispositional anxiety). In predicting the closeness of IM partners, then, daily loneliness and daily anxiety are important. Teens who, on average, reported feeling more daily loneliness and/or social anxiety in school were more likely to communicate with a stranger than with a friend or close friend after school. To provide discriminant evidence for our claim that IM partner characteristics were associated with socially specific rather than overall well-being, correlations were computed between closeness and both dispositional (CDI) and daily (SLSS) global well-being. Associations were nonsignificant, indicating that general feelings of life contentment or dissatisfaction could not predict the closeness of participants' IM partners.

Exploratory analyses: IM motives and topics. Consistent with the pattern of our main findings, exploratory analyses revealed that time spent discussing certain social topics was associated with interpersonal adjustment. Specifically, participants who reported feeling lonely in school both in general and on a daily basis were less likely to talk about friends when IMing, $r(23) = -.47$, $p = .01$, and $r(23) = -.43$, $p = .01$, respectively. Similarly, participants with higher dispositional social anxiety were less likely than their more comfortable peers to discuss romantic topics, $r(36) = -.44$, $p = .01$.

---

[1] On-line tenure and constraints on phone and Internet usage (i.e., parental rules, shared phone access, speed of Internet connectivity) were not significantly associated with any of the predictor or outcome variables and were therefore excluded from subsequent regression analyses.

Examination of participants' motives for IMing also supports the hypothesis that on-line communication serves distinct functions for adolescents experiencing peer-related distress. Although the most commonly reported motive for IMing was to "hang out with a friend," the motive "to avoid being alone" was unique in demonstrating significant associations with psychological adjustment. Daily average social anxiety was significantly and positively correlated with solitude avoidance, $r(35) = .55$, $p = .0001$. In addition, youth reporting fewer close friends in school were significantly more likely to report IMing to avoid being alone, $r(35) = -.53$, $p = .001$.

Discussion

The aim of the present study was twofold: first, to examine more closely what adolescents were doing on-line, and second, to examine whether distinctions among on-line activities and communication partners allow us to better understand the relation between Internet use and well-being.

In spite of the growing role of on-line communication in the lives of young people, even regular Internet users in our sample continued to spend most of their after-school time on traditional activities, many of which involved peer interaction (e.g., participating in clubs or sports, hanging out with friends, talking on the phone). Moreover, on-line communication appears to be similar in several ways to traditional means of youth social interaction (Brown, 1999): it occurred largely in private settings (i.e., e-mail and IMs) with friends who were also part of participants' daily, off-line (e.g., school) lives. In addition, on-line communication was reported to be mainly devoted to ordinary yet intimate topics (e.g., friends, gossip) and motivated by a desire for companionship.

Given that participants reported spending much of their on-line time engaged in interactions with close others, the null association between time spent on-line and psychological well-being is not surprising. According to intimacy theory (Reis & Shaver, 1988), such interactions should be *positively* related to well-being. Likewise, on-line usage by specific domain (e.g., downloading music, chatting) were not associated with well-being. Indeed, the very meaning of time spent in individual on-line domains may be complicated by the prevalence of on-line multitasking among participants. In future research, event-contingent reports, in which participants keep a log of on-line activities when they occur, may be more sensitive to such distinctive and potentially important context of use (Reis & Gable, 2000).

As expected, *whom adolescents communicated with on-line* was found to predict peer-related psychological well-being. Although most social interaction through IMs occurred between friends known from off-line, the closeness of participants' relationships with IM partners was predicted by daily social functioning. Specifically, participants who reported feeling lonely or socially anxious in school on a daily basis were more likely to communicate through IMs with people they did not know well (i.e., strangers vs. friends).

These findings suggest that when they feel connected and comfortable with school-based peers, early adolescents use the Internet to seek out additional opportunities to interact with them. In the case of chronic or even temporary feelings of social discomfort or detachment, however, adolescents may use the Internet to avoid being alone, and, in doing so, turn to people disconnected from their daily life.

But do Internet-based relations provide anxious and lonely youth with the intimacy and companionship that are missing in their off-line lives? Alternatively, because these youth are more likely to communicate with strangers, are they more vulnerable to on-line predators? These questions await future research. In our sample, the closeness of participants' relationships with their IM partners was significantly associated with the relationship's origin, meaning that there were few cases of close friendships developed on-line. Given the growing evidence that close relationships can and do originate on the Internet, especially for individuals experiencing difficulty in their off-line social life (see McKenna & Bargh, 2000), we suspect that their absence in the present sample may be at least in part the result of our sample's limited size and frequency of lonely individuals. Future investigations of larger school-based samples and including older adolescents and greater numbers of marginalized youth will provide additional insight on this phenomenon among youth.

In contrast to previously reported gender differences in both levels and types of on-line communication (America Online/Roper Starch, 1999; Kraut et al., 1998), boys and girls in the present study reported equivalent levels and characteristics of interpersonal communication not only on the Internet, but also on the telephone. The present findings indicate a need for further research on early adolescent girls' and boys' communication with friends, on and off the Internet.

In addition, future studies should compare younger and older youth. We would expect changes in social Internet use to mirror developmental changes in intimacy and friendship patterns. For example, with age, teenagers report spending more time in person with an opposite-sex peer (e.g., Brown, 1999; Furman, Brown, & Feiring, 1999); they may also be increasing their *on-line* cross-sex communication. Alternatively, early adolescents may communicate with members of the opposite sex sooner, if the Internet provides a safe space for this otherwise daunting social contact. Interestingly, in the current sample, 46% of IM interactions occurred in cross-sex dyads.

Finally, although in the present sample parental rules regarding Internet usage were not found to be influential, further research is needed on the family context of use, particularly in light of the differing depictions of parental on-line monitoring offered by youth and their parents (Pew Internet and American Life Project, 2001).

Two limitations to the present research should be noted. First, the majority of participants were European American, middle to upper-middle class, and, according to even the most recent data (e.g., Becker, 2000), considerably more experienced and engaged with the Internet than the average American seventh grader. Although our findings on the distribution of psychological adjustment variables and general Internet usage patterns are consistent with various community and national probability samples, future studies will benefit from drawing upon diverse youth populations. We may find different patterns of on-line behavior or different relations between on-line behavior and well-being in contexts in which the majority of Internet users' peers do not (yet) have on-line access at home. Perhaps this can account for discrepant findings of studies conducted at different stages of the exponential growth of home Internet access.

A second limitation stems from the number of daily logs on which participants reported Internet use. We attempted to address compliance issues by limiting the complexity of the nightly logs, administering a raffle for participants, and visiting classrooms daily. Nevertheless, there were still incidents of noncompliance and a number of logs completed on days that participants simply did not use the Internet. Future research can expand the duration of sample days to overcome this limitation to maximize the many benefits of obtaining daily reports of Internet use and well-being.

Conclusions

The findings presented here suggest that McKenna and Bargh's (2000) claim that "there is no simple main effect of the Internet on the average person" (p. 59) applies to the case of early adolescents. Our results are not inconsistent with their and others' evidence that the Internet may serve distinct functions for socially anxious and lonely individuals. At the same time, we find that normatively adjusted adolescents use the Internet as yet another tool in their communications repertoire. This finding conveys a very different picture from that provided by early studies and media reports on adolescent Internet use. We have argued that advances in communications technology and the continuing growth in youth Internet access may help to explain the discrepancy across studies (e.g., early and more recent investigations) and samples (e.g., of adults vs. teenagers). This said, continuing research is needed to further examine the functions and potential long-term effects of the many distinct and rapidly evolving uses of the Internet. In conducting such research, researchers are urged to take into account the social and developmental context of adolescents' daily lives.

References

America Online/Roper Starch. (1999). *Youth cyberstudy* (Roper no. CNT 154). New York: Roper Starch Worldwide.
Baumeister, R., & Leary, M. R. (1995). The need to belong: Desire for interpersonal attachments as a fundamental human motivation. *Psychological Bulletin, 117*, 497–529.

Becker, H. J. (2000). Who's wired and who's not: Children's access to and use of computer technology. *Future of Children, 10*, 44–75.

Brown, B. B. (1999). Measuring the peer environment of adolescents. In S. L. Friedman & T. D. Wachs (Eds.), *Measuring environment across the life span: Emerging methods and concepts* (pp. 59–90). Washington, DC: American Psychological Association.

Buhrmester, D., & Furman, W. (1987). The development of companionship and intimacy. *Child Development, 58*, 1101–1113.

Furman, W., Brown, B. B., & Feiring, C. (Eds.). (1999). *The development of romantic relationships in adolescence.* New York: Cambridge University Press.

Hartup, W. W. (1996). The company they keep: Friendships and their developmental significance. *Child Development, 67*, 1–13.

Huebner, E. S. (1991). Correlates of life satisfaction in children. *School Psychology Quarterly, 6*, 103–111.

Kovacs, M. (1992). *Children's Depression Inventory.* North Tonawanda, NY: Multi-Health Systems.

Kraut, R., Patterson, M., Lundmark, V., Kiesler, S., Mukopadhyay, T., & Scherlis, W. (1998). Internet paradox: A social technology that reduces social involvement and psychological well-being? *American Psychologist, 53*, 1017–1031.

La Greca, A. M., & Lopez, N. (1998). Social anxiety among adolescents: Linkages with peer relations and friendships. *Journal of Abnormal Child Psychology, 26*, 83–94.

Larson, R. W. (1999). The uses of loneliness in adolescence. In K. J. Rotenberg & S. Hymel (Eds.), *Loneliness in childhood and adolescence* (pp. 244–262). New York: Cambridge University Press.

McKenna, K. Y. A., & Bargh, J. A. (2000). Plan 9 from cyberspace: The implications of the Internet for personality and social psychology. *Personality and Social Psychology Review, 4*, 57–75.

Papini, D. R., Farmer, F. F., Clark, S. M., Micka, J. C., & Barnett, J. K. (1990). Early adolescent age and gender differences in patterns of emotional self-disclosure to parents and friends. *Adolescence, 25*, 959–976.

Pew Internet and American Life Project. (2001). *Teenage life online: The rise of the instant message generation and the Internet's impact on friendships and family relationships* [On-line, retrieved July 19, 2001]. Available: http://www.pewinternet.org/reports/pdfs/PIP_Teens_Report.pdf

Reis, H. T., & Gable, S. L. (2000). Event-sampling and other methods for studying everyday experience. In H. T. Reis & C. M. Judd (Eds.), *Handbook of research methods in social and personality psychology* (pp. 190–222). New York: Cambridge University Press.

Reis, H. T., & Shaver, P. (1988). Intimacy as an interpersonal process. In S. Duck (Ed.), *Handbook of personal relationships* (pp. 367–389). Chichester, UK: Wiley.

Reis, H. T., & Sheldon, K. M., Gable, S. L., Roscoe, J., & Ryan, R. M. (2000). Daily well-being: The role of autonomy, competence, and relatedness. *Personality and Social Psychology Bulletin, 26*, 419–435.

Roberts, D. F., Foehr, U. G., Rideout, V. J., & Brodie, M. (1999). *Kids and media at the new millennium: A comprehensive national analysis of children's media use.* Menlo Park, CA: Kaiser Family Foundation.

Russell, D. W. (1996). UCLA Loneliness Scale (Version 3): Reliability, validity, and factor structure. *Journal of Personality Assessment, 66*, 20–40.

Sullivan, H. S. (1953). *The interpersonal theory of psychiatry.* New York: Norton.

Turow, J. (1999, May 4). The Internet and the family: The view from the family, the view from the press [On-line, retrieved July 19, 2001]. The Annenberg Public Policy Center of the University of Pennsylvania. Available: http://www.appcpenn.org/internet/family/rep27.pdf

ELISHEVA F. GROSS is a doctoral student at the University of California, Los Angeles. After earning her bachelor's degree at Yale University in 1995, she developed and directed new media projects in nonprofit community organizations dedicated to developing communication, technical, and creative skills among youth from diverse backgrounds. Her current research focuses on adolescent social cognitive development as a function of social and cultural context.

JAANA JUVONEN is a Behavioral Scientist at RAND and an Adjunct Associate Professor in the Psychology Department at the University of California, Los Angeles. Her area of expertise is in early adolescent peer relationships and psychosocial adjustment. She has coedited two books: *Social Motivation: Understanding Children's School Adjustment* (1996) and *Peer Harassment in School: The Plight of the Vulnerable and Victimized* (2001).

SHELLEY L. GABLE received her PhD in social and personality psychology from the University of Rochester. She is currently an Assistant Professor of Psychology at the University of California, Los Angeles, where she conducts research on motivation, close relationships, daily well-being, and appetitive social processes.

Journal of Social Issues, Vol. 58, No. 1, 2002, pp. 91–107

When Are Net Effects Gross Products? The Power of Influence and the Influence of Power in Computer-Mediated Communication

Russell Spears*
University of Amsterdam

Tom Postmes
University of Exeter

Martin Lea
Manchester University

Anka Wolbert
University of Amsterdam

The rush to judgment about the social effects of the new communications media has branded them as positive and negative in equal measure. Alienation from "real world" relationships coupled with a lack of social regulation within the medium is balanced by liberation from the influences, inequalities, and identities to which people are subjected in face-to-face interaction. We argue that such general conclusions may in fact be turned upside down and propose that these media may actually strengthen social bonds but also reinforce power inequalities. Reviewing evidence of our research with university students, employing the social identity model of deindividuation effects, we show how these technologies can often be more "social," and socially regulated, than face-to-face interaction.

* Correspondence concerning this article should be addressed to Russell Spears, Social Psychology Program, University of Amsterdam, Roetersstraat 15, 1018 WB Amsterdam, The Netherlands [e-mail: Sp_Spears@macmail.psy.uva.nl]. We would like to thank the editors, John Bargh and Katelyn McKenna, and Irene Frieze for their encouragement and patience. Portions of the research reported here supported by the Economic and Social Research Council (Virtual Society? Program), United Kingdom, by The Royal Dutch Academy of Sciences, The Netherlands, and by the Kurt Lewin Institute.

Researchers of computer-mediated communication, the Internet, and information communication technologies (ICTs) in general have pointed to a range of social costs and benefits of these new media. Identified costs include alienation from social relations in the "real world." Social benefits include the liberation of users from social influences and inequalities to which people are exposed in face-to-face interaction (group pressure, power relations) and freedom from the restrictions of our everyday identities. In other words, these communication technologies can be seen as setting up sometimes unwanted barriers *with* everyday life and also as eliminating unwanted boundaries *from* everyday life. We provide a theoretical and empirical critique of both of these assumptions, arguing that in important respects these characterizations may often be the wrong way round.

The Internet and ICTs have been accused of having a range of harmful social effects (hence net effects as "gross products"). For example, the influential HomeNet study suggests that the Internet leads us to neglect the "strong ties" of our everyday lives (e.g., Kraut et al., 1998). The Internet can become addictive, and social contact often falls below the standards set by face-to-face interaction, producing frustration and flaming and diverting us from our immediate social responsibilities. In short, concerns of social cohesion and social conduct have put these new media in the dock. We propose that this verdict is premature. Already doubts are being expressed as to whether the Internet is damaging to existing social relationships (see McKenna & Bargh, 2000). In this article we also question whether being ensconced on the Internet really is as damaging to social conduct and character as some theorists and popularizers have supposed.

The article's second main theme moves us from the social to the political realm. Much has been made of the power of computer-mediated communication (CMC) and the Internet as technologies of democratization and even liberation. Researchers have pointed to the equalizing nature of communication (e.g., Kiesler & Sproull, 1992) as well as to the possibilities of freeing ourselves from restrictive or even stigmatized identities (e.g., Turkle, 1995). Although we do not deny these possibilities, when we examine how ICTs are actually used and by whom, the picture is somewhat less rosy. Although hierarchies have sometimes become flatter within the organization, there is little evidence that power has become less centralized. Moreover, these media continue to be characterized by the relative social exclusion of disadvantaged groups both from the technology and within it (e.g., Thomas & Wyatt, in press). We do not have all the answers to these apparent paradoxes, but we can point to some processes by which power relations are reinforced as well as transcended.

Our theoretical critique examines the assumptions embedded in social psychological and communications theories that have fostered the two dominant themes identified above. Many current theoretical approaches have their roots in the engineering concept of communication bandwidth (Spears, Lea, & Postmes, 2001), proposing that limiting information exchange can have deleterious effects on social communication. The implications for the social effects of technology follow directly ("technological determinism"). They are positive where social influences are obstacles for individual performance (as in the realm of Group Decision Support Systems, where determinist perspectives have tended to be utopian). The social effects are negative where social influence regulates behavior and keeps it in check (where dystopian views prevail). Underlying both of these visions is the assumption that face-to-face interaction is more truly, richly "social" than interaction in cyberspace. Consequently the ICTs are held to lack qualities of truly social interaction.

As we will argue below, the assumptions are more clear-cut than is justified by the empirical support they receive. There is little compelling evidence that the "social nature" of CMC can be determined in such a direct manner from technical efficiency, whether this is cast in terms of social presence, of information richness, or of reduced social cues. For example, research suggests that in some contexts, the use of ICTs stimulates antinormative behavior, whereas in other contexts behavior is *more* normative and social influence stronger (Spears, Lea, & Postmes, 2001). Likewise, contradictory results have emerged for status equalization (Schofield, 1999; Spears & Lea, 1994; Straus, 1997; Weisband, Schneider, & Connolly, 1995), social cohesion and attraction (Lea, Spears, & De Groot, 2001; Walther, 1996), and decision quality (Chun & Park, 1998; Postmes & Lea, 2000).

It is important not to underestimate the importance of information-based perspectives, however. Their assumptions are widely shared, and as a consequence we find these conceptions are applied to a broad range of social effects. In response some theorists have dismissed *all* perspectives that claim to identify the ways in which technology can produce social consequences, concluding that technological determinism is too limited to explain the rich interaction between technological and social influences. This theoretical response has fueled an equally one-sided countermovement that assumes that technologies are principally constructed by their social uses ("social determinism"; see Spears, Postmes, Wolbert, Lea, & Rogers, 2000, for a review).

Taking a more interactionist approach, we try to plot a course between both forms of determinism, arguing that many of the same social psychological processes and principles apply in virtual communication as in face-to-face interaction and that the social dimension can actually be enhanced in certain ways by these media. The empirical part of the article elaborates this point by presenting experimental evidence from our own research program using the social identity model of deindividuation effects (SIDE; Reicher, Spears, & Postmes, 1995; Spears & Lea, 1994).

A SIDE Look at Anonymity in CMC

The two themes outlined above, that CMC is less social and that it can also be liberating, formed for us a focus for questioning some of the assumptions and conclusions of established approaches to communication in virtual environments. The current vision seemed to us overstated if not wrong. First, the assumption that computer communication was less social or socially regulated than face-to-face communication is questionable and depends to a considerable degree on how "social" is defined. Second, we were also wary of the more positive views of the Internet as a political liberator where social differences might be left behind at will. We address these social and political themes in turn.

The idea that interaction via computers is less social or socially regulated follows from restricted-bandwidth principles in communication theory and from restricted definitions of self and social interaction in social psychology. From the perspective of social identity theory and its sister theory, self-categorization theory (Tajfel & Turner, 1986; Turner, 1985), there are important group dimensions to self and social interaction. In these terms, the group is not just an external entity or collection of individuals with which we interact, but it is also internal and identity defining. Similarly "social" interaction is not just a question of interpersonal interaction between individuals: In (inter)group situations, social interaction implicates individuals acting as members of groups or social categories.

These broader definitions of self and situation open the way to a redefinition of social interaction and communication that does not necessarily depend on the quantity or even the quality of information transfer. The social properties of communication do not have to rely exclusively (if at all) on what is transmitted "down the wire"; the social dimensions of self may already be partly determined by how the communicators define themselves beforehand. We have argued that information restrictions of the medium may actually privilege more "social" levels of self-definition (as groups and categories; Spears & Lea, 1994). This is because cues to category membership may be both discrete (simple cues) and either discreet (subtly communicated, sometimes in language style) or easily discerned (because they reflect shared and sometimes chronically salient features). The individuating cues associated with personal identity are by contrast potentially infinite, complex, and much more abundant in the broader bandwidth medium of face-to-face communication.

This is one cornerstone of the SIDE model. We have argued that the visual anonymity characteristic of computer-based communication can have important social psychological effects (albeit ones determined by the interaction of identity with context rather than being generic). Similar phenomena have been studied by deindividuation theorists investigating the consequences of anonymity in crowds (e.g., Diener, 1980; Zimbardo, 1969; see Postmes & Spears, 1998). Deindividuation theory proposes that behavior becomes socially deregulated under conditions of anonymity and group immersion, as a result of reduced self-awareness (e.g., Diener, 1980; Prentice-Dunn & Rogers, 1989; Zimbardo, 1969). This notion has been imported by researchers of CMC to explain antisocial behavior, much as it has been applied to crowd behavior.

However, our conclusions are quite different from those of deindividuation theory. Although we do not dispute many of the effects obtained in this literature, we do contest the explanation of them as resulting from social (or self-) deregulation. On the contrary we argue, in line with social identity accounts of collective behavior (Reicher, 1987), that "deindividuation effects" are highly socially regulated because anonymity can increase the salience and impact of contextually relevant group identities ("depersonalization" rather than deindividuation; deindividuation is by definition socially deregulated, whereas depersonalization reflects the operation of social identities; see, e.g., Postmes & Spears, 1998; Spears, Postmes, Lea, & Watt, 2001). To this extent we argue that self-definition and social behavior in anonymous interaction not only is as social as in face-to-face interaction, but insofar as it may enhance the impact of group identities, it may be more so. Although this claim is controversial, it is supported by a meta-analysis of the deindividuation literature (Postmes & Spears, 1998). There is actually no strong evidence for counternormative behavior under conditions of anonymity and much stronger evidence of conformity to local norms that could be inferred from the context or group identity (although of course these local group norms will often be in conflict with more general standards of conduct; see Postmes & Spears, 1998). The implication is that if ICTs create deindividuating conditions, behavior can be highly socially regulated in these media.

We have referred to the effect of anonymity on identity salience as the cognitive dimension of SIDE because it influences the accessibility of contextually relevant identities. This dimension of the SIDE model is also defined as cognitive in order to distinguish it from the *strategic* dimension of the SIDE model (Reicher et al., 1995; Spears & Lea, 1994). The strategic dimension refers to the actual expression of behavior that is associated with contextually salient identities *but that takes into account social constraints on behavior*. For example, accountability to a powerful outgroup may lead members of the ingroup to suppress behaviors that are consistent with their identity but that transgress outgroup norms and could be punished (Reicher & Levine, 1994a). Conversely the presence of ingroup members may give the groups the collective strength to express behaviors that might otherwise be punished (Reicher & Levine, 1994b), as well as strengthening accountability to ingroup norms (Barreto & Ellemers, 2000). Self-presentation here is not just a question of individual impression management but crucially depends on the identity that is salient and the relation to the (powerful) audience. As we shall see a number of important features of ICTs come into play when we are considering this strategic dimension (e.g., the ability to dissimulate and play with identity).

To summarize, the SIDE model consists of two dimensions, relating to self-categorization (cognitive) and self-expression (strategic), and analyzes the conditions that facilitate or impede these. This framework has helped us to account for the richness and variety of effects in CMC while not losing sight of the underlying social psychological process. We now proceed to present empirical evidence, mostly from our own research program, to back up our claims that the new computer-based communications media do not escape either the power of the social or social power. That is, we argue that social influence, rather than being filtered out, can be even stronger in CMC compared to face to face, and similarly that power differentials, rather than being diluted, can be magnified.

The Cognitive SIDE: Anonymity Makes Us More
(Not Less) Socially Responsive

One of the direct predictions of the SIDE model outlined above is that the impact of group influence and social norms should be strengthened in anonymous CMC, at least to the extent that these norms are salient. What is the evidence for this? In the first study testing this hypothesis, we manipulated the salience of group identity versus personal identity in a sample of 1st-year psychology students at the University of Manchester (Spears, Lea, & Lee, 1990). In the group identity salient condition we described the study as focusing interest on the communication styles of psychology students as a group (and indicated that we were not interested in participants as individuals), whereas in the personal identity salient condition we described the study as focusing on individual differences in communication styles. Moreover, half the groups communicated via terminals in separate rooms, rendering the participants visually anonymous. For the other half, communication occurred in the same room so that people could see each other (they also communicated via computer in order to control for any effects of this medium).

We also provided feedback about the (progressive) student norm relating to the discussion topics (pretested on a previous cohort of psychology students at University of Manchester). Following the self-categorization explanation of group polarization (Turner, 1985; Wetherell, 1987), we expected groups to polarize in the direction of the student norms when group identity was salient. Crucially, we expected this effect to be stronger under conditions of anonymity, as this should increase the salience of this group identity. We found that identity salience and anonymity interacted to produce strongest polarization in the direction of the group norm in the condition in which group identity of the psychology students had been made salient and in which they were isolated and thus visually anonymous. Norm-directed polarization was actually eliminated and reversed in the condition in which personal identity was salient and participants isolated and anonymous, suggesting that people tried to differentiate themselves from the group when the individual identity was salient.

These results confirm that social influence is, somewhat paradoxically, strongest under conditions of isolation and anonymity, provided that group identity is salient. However, not all theorists agree that group polarization results from group conformity. Although Kiesler and her associates had already found evidence of enhanced group polarization in CMC (e.g., Siegel, Dubrovsky, Kiesler, & McGuire, 1986), in line with the reduced social cues model, these researchers had interpreted this phenomenon as reflecting *less* normative influence within the group (see Wetherell, 1987, for a review of theories of group polarization).

To address this we used another paradigm to assess the effects of social influence in a more subtle way. In this study, 1st-year psychology students at the University of Amsterdam participated in a study concerned with communication via computers (Postmes, Spears, Sakhel, & De Groot, 2001). Before the communication phase of the experiment, however, we used a surreptitious priming procedure (a scrambled sentence task) to cue either a prosocial or an efficiency norm that would be relevant to the subsequent group discussion. The efficiency norm was designed to activate principles associated with cost-effectiveness, task focus, and so on (words relating to this theme were embedded in the scrambled sentences). The prosocial norm was designed to activate principles more associated with a person-centered and caring approach to social problems. Group identity was made salient by means of joint participation on a collective task, and participants were either anonymous or made identifiable by means of scanned photos. They then discussed a problem in which they had to propose a policy solution for a hospital crisis. The dependent variable was whether groups proposed solutions more focused on patient care (prosocial solutions) or more focused on the efficient management of the hospital (efficiency-oriented solutions). As predicted, groups conformed more to the norm that had been primed under conditions of anonymity.

A further study showed that the norm primed in two group members transferred to two *neutrally* primed members during discussion, but only in anonymous groups. Moreover, this effect strengthened over time, and group influence was mediated by the enhanced salience and identification with the group caused by anonymity. This study thus confirmed that a truly social group influence process causes the influence and conformity.

One disadvantage of such experimental studies is that the contexts are not always naturalistic and they occur in short time frames in groups of minimal meaning and involvement (Walther, 1995). In further research we traced computer groups that formed naturally as part of a course and examined norm formation over time (Postmes, Spears, & Lea, 2000). In line with our claim that computer communication is highly normatively regulated, a network analysis showed that conformity to the locally defined group norms increased over time, that norms distinguished between groups, and that communication outside the group (with the course instructor) was governed by quite different norms.

This study also provided evidence that "flaming" behavior was also normatively regulated and could often be seen as reflecting intimacy rather than antagonism within the group. Such behavior has typically been defined, often a priori, as aggressive and antinormative and interpreted within the deindividuation/reduced social cues framework. However, in practice, behavior that counts as flaming has often been something of a mixed bag of responses that do not always necessarily reflect the aggression and disinhibition associated with this concept. Moreover, research often fails to make comparisons for the baseline frequency of similar patterns of behavior in other communications media, including face to face. One central weakness of many reports of flaming in the literature is that coding schemes often take comments at face value or out of context with little evidence of the intention to cause offense and paying lip service to the specific nature of the relation between communicators, which can change the meaning of the behavior. Many behaviors superficially coded as flaming can thus reflect more ironic, hyperbolic, or playful forms of communication rather than being aggressive. Our research revealed many instances of "flames" that a more decontextualized analysis might misrecognize as offensive. Narrative and meta-analytic reviews of the literature also confirm that flaming may reflect the operation of local norms that vary widely between newsgroups, Web sites, and intranet cultures (Lea, O'Shea, Fung & Spears, 1992; Walther, Anderson, & Park, 1994). Having said this, the anonymity with respect to the target of communication in CMC can permit more daring forms of communication (see "Strategic Constraints and Possibilities in Cyberspace," below).

Computer communication, especially as employed in organizational environments, is often viewed as a rather cold and rational task-oriented medium, to be contrasted with the more socially "warm" face-to-face communication (e.g., Walther, 1997; see Lea, 1991). As the research described above shows, however, we would argue that social warmth is more likely to be a property of the group and its norms than a generic feature of the medium. The SIDE model predicts not only that the social norms may have greater sway, but also that the anonymity of the medium may intensify a range of group processes including attraction to the group.

We tested this prediction in a further study in which students from the University of Manchester participated (Lea et al., 2001). We used path analysis to show that anonymity functions to increase group-based self-categorization, which in turn increases attraction to the group (consistent with principles of self-categorization theory). Self-categorization in terms of the group also increased stereotyping of *others* in terms of the group, which again resulted in enhanced group attraction through a second path. The tendency of anonymity to increase group effects (in this case group attraction) by making salient a common ingroup identity captures the cognitive dimension of the SIDE model relating to the salience of (group) self-definition. This research also showed that alternative predictions that anonymity generically increases task focus and reduces group attraction (e.g., Walther, 1997) received no support.

Further research with university students from the University of Amsterdam and University of Manchester confirms that individual anonymity can lead to more gender stereotyping and behavior when gender identity is salient (Postmes

& Spears, 2000), more self-stereotyping in terms of gender stereotypes (Brouwer, Kawakami, Rojahn, & Postmes, 1997), and greater intergroup differentiation (Postmes, Spears, & Lea, in press; Watt, Lea, & Spears, in press). All these effects are consistent with the cognitive dimension of SIDE, indicating enhanced group salience and depersonalization under conditions of anonymity (but see Spears, Lea, & Postmes, 2001, for important caveats).

To summarize, the evidence presented so far is that the anonymity associated with CMC, far from undermining the social dimension to self and behavior, can strengthen its very basis. When combined with category salience, it can intensify group-based effects such as group polarization, conformity to group norms, social attraction, stereotyping, self-stereotyping, and intergroup differentiation. Evidence that depersonalizing conditions can accentuate status and power differences for gender categories (Postmes & Spears, 2000) is also in keeping with the argument that social boundaries can be strengthened in CMC (see also Postmes, Spears, & Lea, 1998; Spears & Lea, 1994; and below).

Strategic Constraints and Possibilities in Cyberspace: Power, Playing, Politics

In the previous section we considered the effects on self-definition and consequent behavior flowing from the "cognitive" effects of anonymity. We now consider how intentions and behavior deriving from salient identities might be constrained or facilitated in computer communication environments by the technological features characteristic of these media. Once again, anonymity plays an important role here. It means that we can choose to play out roles in ways that suit our audiences and agendas and even play completely different people (people from different categories). The "play" element (Suler, 2000; Turkle, 1995) is not just playful but can also reflect serious concerns: it may be strategic, part of "power play." Such strategic concerns move us from the social dimensions of the Internet to consider issues of power. This will often implicate us as members of (more or less powerful) groups or categories, although power and accountability can also be important in interpersonal communication contexts.

ICTs are in many respects presented as technologies of liberation and equalization and much lauded for these imputed attributes. For example, in the organizational contexts of computer use, CMC has been proposed to transcend many status differentials (e.g., Kiesler & Sproull, 1992). The argument is that anonymity provides a protection from the consequences of speaking out of turn (there is no turn taking in CMC) while blocking cues to status that might intimidate and keep us in our place. In terms of the Internet, liberation takes on even broader form, starting with the freedom to choose identity and one's audience and transcend the restrictions of locality. Virtual communities provide new sources of solidarity and empowerment (Rheingold, 1993; Wellman & Gulia, 1999).

There is at least one other side to the story to qualify the utopian vision. In an earlier effort to inject some counterargument into this characterization we proposed that CMC and the Internet shared some properties with the "panopticon" (Spears & Lea, 1994), a correctional institution devised by the 19th-century philosopher Jeremy Bentham that relied on centralized surveillance as a more subtle form of control than direct coercion. The anonymity and isolation associated with CMC and the Internet reproduce key panoptic properties. Moreover, the informationalization of these technologies makes it almost impossible to avoid leaving traces of social or economic activity. Implied surveillance is another key feature of the panopticon (Gandy, 1993; Zuboff, 1988; see Deibert, this issue).

The analogy is imperfect, because CMC and the Internet are of course also (relatively flat and free-flowing) communication networks that contrast with the centralized communication channel of the panopticon, and people may often at least assume they have privacy and security. However, the point is to alert us to the possibility that these media can also be seen as domains in which power and status may still operate, often in quite subtle ways. Many of the features characteristic of CMC and the Internet are double-edged in that although they may allow us to transcend power relations, they can also function to reinforce them. On the one hand the Internet allows us not only to disseminate information widely but also to target people of like mind and interest that might otherwise be inaccessible or invisible (McKenna & Bargh, 1998) and facilitate the coordination of group action and social support (Deibert, this issue). On the disempowering side the Internet can also disperse and isolate people, leaving them less aware of the collective identities that give them strength and giving them less power to resist collectively (Castells, 1996).

We now consider social psychological evidence of this Janus-faced character of computer communication in relation to power. The basic strategic principle of the SIDE model is that people take into account the audience and its power of sanction or reward (in the case of the outgroup) and even judgments of approval or opprobrium (in the case of the ingroup). When we are anonymous to a powerful authority or outgroup, this makes power less of an issue, and the fact that anonymous communication can lead to more equal contributions has already been well documented. However, caution is in order. First, much research suggests that cues to group identity are not eliminated in computer communication. For example, evidence indicates that gender is recognizable in text-based language use (Savicki, Kelley, & Oesterreich, 1999; Thomson & Murachver, 2001). This is likely to be equally true of other social categories, such as class and ethnicity, that have distinctive codes (Burkhalter, 1999). When these cues do seep through, status and group differences can persist and even be accentuated (Herring, 1994; Hollingshead, 1996; Postmes et al., 1998; Spears & Lea, 1994; Straus, 1997; Weisband et al., 1995). These power effects are consistent with the cognitive dimension of SIDE.

Research using the SIDE model suggests that the isolation associated with CMC may be disempowering compared to the copresence of face-to-face communication and may reduce the likelihood of contesting and resisting powerful outgroups (Reicher & Levine, 1994b). However, the copresence of other ingroup members not only provides a physical means of support, it also allows the *communication* of support. The communication channels provided by CMC therefore also present a means to communicate social support that might facilitate collective resistance despite isolation. We investigated this issue by adapting the paradigm used by Reicher and Levine (1994a). In this paradigm, undergraduate participants respond to questions about study and recreation. Behaviors that are normative for students and acceptable to the staff (e.g., partying) are distinguished from items that are normative but punishable (e.g., copying essays). Students are normally reluctant to endorse punishable items when accountable to the staff outgroup but are more likely to do so in the copresence of fellow ingroup members (Reicher & Levine, 1994b).

The question we addressed was whether computer communication could function as a channel of support in a similar way. In one study employing 1st-year psychology students at the University of Amsterdam as participants, we used a variant of this paradigm in which we asked about attitudes toward the exploitation of students for compulsory participation in experiments (the Amsterdam students as a group were against the high course credit requirement). In this case the experimenter formed the powerful outgroup member to whom participants were accountable. During a computer communication phase, participants thought that they were anonymously exchanging their views on this topic with fellow students but received false feedback endorsing the student norm criticizing their exploitation (held constant). Crucially we manipulated the degree of support the fellow students would be prepared to give in a later phase of the study in which they were supposed to discuss this topic with the experimenter. As predicted, participants were more likely to voice their criticism later in a questionnaire identifiable to the experimenter when they had previously received peer support during the computer communication phase.

In a further program of research we have investigated how people actually change their identity to manipulate the audience even more explicitly. In this research we were interested in how people might adopt a different gender identity ("gender bending") to serve personal or political agendas. Cases of men adopting female identities to exploit the trust deriving from this identity for greater access or intimacy are now well documented (e.g., Lea & Spears, 1995; Van Gelder, 1985). This is an example of a powerful group exploiting the identity manipulation potential afforded by the Internet; male harassment, whether disguised by identity or not, forms a recurring problem on the Net. Despite the image of the Internet as a liberating technology and its steadily increasing use by women, it remains relatively male-dominated in terms of culture and control (e.g., Herring, 1994;

Millar, 1998; Postmes et al., 1998; Spears & Lea, 1994; Thomas & Wyatt, in press). Partly because of this, women may be increasingly inclined to assume male or neutral identities to avoid unwanted attention or to be taken seriously (Wolbert, 2000).

We investigated this experimentally by setting up a study in which male and female participants (students at the University of Amsterdam) thought that they would engage in discussion in an Internet chat room on one of a range of topics. These topics were pretested to reflect domains in which males were ex-pected to have more knowledge and expertise (e.g., cars, investment) and those in which women were stereotypically more knowledgeable (emotions, relation-ships). Participants were informed that one of the topics listed would be randomly chosen for discussion. In the meantime they were asked to choose between a range of avatars (pictorial icons that would represent them in the chat room) for each particular discussion topic. We found that male participants generally chose male or neutral avatars and that this was not moderated by the discussion topic. However, whereas women chose female-gendered avatars for the female topics, they switched to neutral or male avatars for the male topics (Wolbert, 2000). We also replicated this general pattern in research where we used Web sites pretested for their technical versus socioemotional content: Women were more likely to shift their identities to more neutral or masculine avatars for the technical sites.

At one level this can be seen as a strategy of empowerment: Dissimulation gets around the fact that women may be ignored or not taken seriously if they maintain their true gender identity. However, at a more group level this may function to make women even *less visible* on the Web than they actually are, especially in masculine domains (a self-fulfilling prophecy). Moreover, if women are more able to influence men in this "guys guise," it may work only so long as they do not blow their gender cover (i.e., so long as they reinforce male ways!). If these identities start to percolate into our everyday relations this would represent a further ironic "e-masculation" of women and female identity. In short the adaptive individual strategy might paradoxically turn out to be counterproductive at the group level. This reminds us that power can often operate in very subtle ways and that the powerless may be implicated in their own oppression by the very same features of the technology that can be presented as liberating (Spears & Lea, 1994).

To summarize, although the anonymity associated with CMC and the Internet produce opportunities for dissimulation and identity play, it is not always clear that these possibilities translate into shifts in the balance of power, either in cy-berspace or outside. Moreover, at the level of self-definition, anonymity can some-times reinforce power relations by strengthening the social identities that constitute them.

Conclusions and Policy Implications

We have tried to challenge some of the prevailing assumptions that have followed the new communications technologies onto the scene and have sometimes overstayed their welcome. There is a compelling temptation with any new technologies (or anything new) to make something akin to a "fundamental attribution error" and ascribe effects to generic properties of the medium rather than to the social contexts of use. Some of the bizarre predictions that accompanied other new technologies from the steam engine to the telephone remind us that hype and moral panics are not new either. If technological determinism is the Scylla here, however, social determinism forms an equally problematic Charybdis. Social factors do not trump technological features nor vice versa. We need to appreciate *how* the two interact without privileging either (Spears & Lea, 1994). These social processes are probably more different in degree than in kind from similar social processes that occur in face-to-face interaction. A central plank of our argument has been that the isolation and anonymity in cyberspace do not make the process any less social and that the outcome can be even more social in a number of ways. This also applies to power relations and other forms of social difference. Although ICTs can sometimes make cues to power or status disappear, such cues are often simple and powerful enough to get through.

What are the specific policy implications of this analysis? Although space limitations preclude a detailed overview (but see Spears et al., 2000), we can draw a number of general lessons. A first point is that because it is difficult to generalize in any meaningful way about *generic* effects, this makes it equally difficult to legislate about a technology the effects of which are so clearly embedded in social practices and norms. In this sense it is probably as important to focus on the normative contents of technology use as on the technology itself. This is understandably an area in which governments have rightly been reluctant to intervene (unless activity is deemed criminal). After all, no one would advocate legislating for face-to-face interaction, because this is a medium in which interpersonal violence can occur. If we take this message of social regulation seriously, what happens when one gets into these media is probably of less concern than the issue of being excluded by them. The digital divide is probably a bigger problem than any social isolation or division arising from life (partially) on-line, and governments need to prevent this gap from widening.

The power of CMC and the Internet to accentuate social regulation means that policymakers should consider not just individual rights and freedoms, but also those associated with social categories and communities. As we saw from the gender example, what might be liberating from an individual perspective might not have this effect at the level of the group, and policymakers need to ensure that individual freedoms do not necessarily come at the expense of collective inequalities, either in terms of access or *quality* of use. Policymakers need to take a critical view of the power of these media to equalize or liberate and appreciate the subtle ways in which they may also reinforce existing identities, power relations, and politics. For example, the possibility of e-voting may represent a liberation at one level, but being able to vote from the comfort of one's home not only presupposes a home, it may also prime individual identities and interests more than when the journey to the polling booth takes one through disadvantaged inner-city areas. The possibilities offered by the new media bring new powers for those with criminal intent (fraud, stalking, and pedophilia are presented with new channels of exploitation) but also potential means of surveillance and law enforcement.

The complexity of the issues should be no excuse for paralysis in terms of policy. On the contrary, the lesson is that the policy implications require a context-specific analysis that is socially as well as technologically grounded and therefore one that demands the inputs of social scientists. Awareness of the specific effects of these technologies, the power to intensify social effects and social differences, is therefore important if we are develop policy and the policing of these technologies. Whether policymakers choose to emphasize panoptic power or democratizing potential is a political question, but one that needs to be informed by the effects the technology can have in interaction with social factors.

References

Barreto, M., & Ellemers, N. (2000). You can't always do what you want: Social identity and self-presentational determinants of the choice to work for a low status group. *Personality and Social Psychology Bulletin, 26*, 891–906.

Brouwer, J., Kawakami, K., Rojahn, K., & Postmes, T. (1997). De effecten van de (on)zichtbaarheid van sekse als categorie op zelfstereotyping [The effects of (in)visibility of sex as category on self-stereotyping]. *Fundamentele Sociale Psychologie, 11*, 150–157.

Burkhalter, B. (1999). Reading race online: Discovering racial identity in Usenet discussions. In P. Kollock & A. Smith (Eds.), *Communities in cyberspace*. London: Routledge.

Castells, M. (1996). *The information age: Economy society and culture: Vol. 1. The network society.* Oxford: Blackwell.

Chun, K. J., & Park, H. K. (1998). Examining the conflicting results of GDSS research. *Information and Management, 33*, 313–325.

Diener, E. (1980). Deindividuation: The absence of self-awareness and self-regulation in group members. In P. Paulus (Ed.), *The psychology of group influence.* (pp. 209–242). Hillsdale, NJ: Erlbaum.

Gandy, O. H., Jr. (1993). *The panoptic sort: A political economy of personal information.* Oxford: Westview.

Herring, S. (1994). Gender differences in computer-mediated communication: Bringing familiar baggage to a new frontier [On-line]. *Electronic Journal of Communication / Revue Electronique de Communication, 3*. Available: http://www.cios.org/www/ejc/v3n293.htm

Hollingshead, A. B. (1996). Information suppression and status persistence in group decision making: The effects of communication media. *Human Communication Research, 23*, 193–219.

Kiesler, S., & Sproull, L. (1992). Group decision making and communication technology. *Organizational Behavior and Human Decision Processes, 52*, 96–123.

Kraut, R., Patterson, M., Lundmark, V., Kiesler, S., Mukopadhyay, T., & Scherlis, W. (1998). Internet paradox: A social technology that reduces social involvement and psychological well-being? *American Psychologist, 53*, 1017–1031.

Lea, M. (1991). Rationalist assumptions in cross-media comparisons of computer-mediated communication. *Behaviour & Information Technology, 10,* 153–172.

Lea, M., O'Shea, T., Fung, P., & Spears, R. (1992). "Flaming" in computer-mediated communication: Observations, explanations, implications. In M. Lea (Ed.), *Contexts of computer-mediated communication* (pp. 30–65). Hemel Hempstead, England: Harvester Wheatsheaf.

Lea, M., & Spears, R. (1995). Love at first byte? Building personal relationships over computer networks. In J. T. Wood and S. Duck (Eds.), *Understudied relationships: Off the beaten track* (pp. 197–233). Thousand Oaks, CA: Sage.

Lea, M., Spears, R., & De Groot, D. (2001). Knowing me, knowing you: Effects of visual anonymity on stereotyping and attraction in computer-mediated groups.*Personality and Social Psychology Bulletin, 27,* 526–537.

McKenna, K. Y. A., & Bargh, J. A. (1998). Coming out in the age of the Internet: Identity "de-marginalization" through virtual group participation. *Journal of Personality and Social Psychology, 75,* 681–694.

McKenna, K. Y. A., & Bargh, J. A. (2000). Plan 9 from cyberspace: The implications of the Internet for personality and social psychology. *Personality and Social Psychology Review, 4,* 57–75.

Millar, M. (1998). *Cracking the gender code: Who rules the wired world?* Toronto: Second Story.

Postmes, T., & Lea, M. (2000). Social processes and group decision making: Anonymity in group decision support systems. *Ergonomics, 43,* 1152–1274.

Postmes, T., & Spears, R. (1998). Deindividuation and anti-normative behavior: A meta-analysis. *Psychological Bulletin, 123,* 238–259.

Postmes, T., & Spears, R. (2000). *Contextual moderators of gender differences: Behavior and stereotyping in computer-mediated groups.* Manuscript submitted for publication.

Postmes, T., Spears, R., & Lea, M. (1998). Breaching or building social boundaries? SIDE-effects of computer-mediated communication. *Communication Research, 25,* 689–715.

Postmes, T., Spears, R., & Lea, M. (2000). The formation of group norms in computer-mediated communication. *Human Communication Research, 26,* 341–371.

Postmes, T., Spears, R., & Lea, M. (in press). The effects of anonymity in intergroup discussion: Bipolarization in computer-mediated groups. *Group Dynamics.*

Postmes, T., Spears, R., Sakhel, K., & de Groot, D. (2001). Social influence in computer-mediated groups: The effects of anonymity on social behavior. *Personality and Social Psychology Bulletin, 27,* 1243–1254.

Prentice-Dunn, S., & Rogers, R. W. (1989). Deindividuation and the self-regulation of behavior. In P. B. Paulus (Ed.), *The psychology of group influence* (2nd ed., pp. 86–109). Hillsdale, NJ: Erlbaum.

Reicher, S. D. (1987). Crowd behaviour as social action. In J. C. Turner, M. A. Hogg, P. J. Oakes, S. D. Reicher, & M. S. Wetherell (Eds.), *Rediscovering the social group: A self-categorization theory* (pp. 171–202). Oxford: Basil Blackwell.

Reicher, S. D., & Levine, M. (1994a). Deindividuation, power relations between groups and the expression of social identity: The effects of visibility to the out-group. *British Journal of Social Psychology, 33,* 145–164.

Reicher, S. D., & Levine, M. (1994b). On the consequences of deindividuation manipulations for the strategic considerations of self: Identifiability and the presentation of social identity. *European Journal of Social Psychology, 24,* 511–524.

Reicher, S. D., Spears, R., & Postmes, T. (1995). A social identity model of deindividuation phenomena. *European Review of Social Psychology, 6,* 161–198.

Rheingold, H. (1993). *The virtual community: Homesteading on the electronic frontier.* Reading, MA: Addison-Wesley.

Savicki, V., Kelley, M., & Oesterreich, E. (1999). Judgments of gender in computer-mediated communication. *Computers in Human Behavior, 15,* 185–194.

Schofield, J. W. (1999, October). *The Internet: A place for social psychology.* Paper presented at the Society for Experimental Social Psychology annual meeting, St. Louis, MO.

Siegel, J., Dubrovsky, V., Kiesler, S., & McGuire, T. (1986). Group processes in computer-mediated communication. *Organizational Behaviour and Human Decision Processes, 37,* 157–187.

Spears, R., & Lea, M. (1994). Panacea or panopticon? The hidden power in computer-mediated com-
    munication. *Communication Research, 21*, 427–459.
Spears, R., Lea, M., & Lee, S. (1990). De-individuation and group polarization in computer-mediated
    communication. *British Journal of Social Psychology, 29*, 121–134.
Spears, R., Lea, M., & Postmes, T. (2001). Social psychological theories of computer-mediated com-
    munication. In P. Robinson & H. Giles (Eds.), *The handbook of language and social psychology*
    (2nd ed., pp. 601–623). Chichester, England: Wiley.
Spears, R., Postmes, T., Lea, M., & Watt, S. E. (2001). A SIDE view of social influence. In J. Forgas &
    K. Williams (Eds.), *Social influence: Direct and indirect processes.* (pp. 331–350). Philadelphia:
    Psychology.
Spears, R., Postmes, T., Wolbert, A., Lea, M., & Rogers, P. (2000). *The social psychological influ-
    ence of ICTs on society and their policy implications* (Report for "Infodrome"). The Hague,
    Netherlands: Dutch Ministry of Education, Culture and Science.
Straus, S. G. (1997). Technology, group process, and group outcomes: Testing the connections in
    computer-mediated and face-to-face groups. *Human-Computer Interaction, 12*, 227–266.
Suler, J. (2000). The psychology of cyberspace [On-line]. Available: www.rider.edu/users/suler/
    psycyber/psycyber.html
Tajfel, H., & Turner, J. C. (1986). The social identity theory of intergroup behaviour. In S. Worchel &
    W. G. Austin (Eds.), *Psychology of intergroup relations* (pp. 7–24). Chicago: Nelson-Hall.
Thomas, G., & Wyatt, S. (in press). Access is not the only problem: Using and controlling the Internet.
    In S. Wyatt, F. Henwood, N. Miller, & P. Senker (Eds.), *Technology and in/equality: Questioning
    the information society.* London: Routledge.
Thomson, R. & Murachver, T. (2001). Predicting gender from electronic discourse. *British Journal of
    Social Psychology, 40*, 193–208.
Turkle, S. (1995). *Life on the screen: Identity in the age of the Internet.* New York: Simon and Schuster.
Turner, J. C. (1985). Social categorization and the self-concept: A social cognitive theory of group
    behavior. In E. J. Lawler (Ed.), *Advances in group processes: Theory and research* (Vol. 2,
    pp. 77–122). Greenwich, CT: JAI.
Van Gelder, L. (1985, October). The strange case of the electronic lover. *Ms.,* pp. 94, 99, 101–104,
    117, 123–124.
Walther, J. B. (1995). Relational aspects of computer mediated communication: Experimental obser-
    vations over time. *Organization Science, 6*, 186–203.
Walther, J. B. (1996). Computer-mediated communication: Impersonal, interpersonal and hyperper-
    sonal interaction. *Communication Research, 23*, 1–43.
Walther, J. B. (1997). Group and interpersonal effects in international computer-mediated collaboration.
    Human Communication Research, 24, 186–203.
Walther, J. B., Anderson, J. F., & Park, D. W. (1994). Interpersonal effects in computer-mediated
    interaction: A meta-analysis of social and antisocial communication. *Communication Research,
    21*, 460–487.
Watt, S. E., Lea, M., & Spears, R. (in press). How social is Internet communication? Anonymity
    effects in computer-mediated groups. In S. Woolgar (Ed.), *Virtual society? The social science
    of electronic technologies.* Milton Keynes, UK: Oxford University Press.
Weisband, S. P., Schneider, S. K., & Connolly, T. (1995). Computer-mediated communication and
    social information—Status salience and status differences. *Academy of Management Journal,
    38*, 1124–1151.
Wellman, B., & Gulia, M. (1999). Virtual communities as communities; Net surfers don't ride alone.
    In P. Kollock & A. Smith (Eds.), *Communities in cyberspace.* London: Routledge.
Wetherell, M. S. (1987). Social identity and group polarization. In J. C. Turner (Ed.), *Rediscovering
    the social group: A self-categorization theory* (pp. 142–170). Oxford: Blackwell.
Wolbert, A. (2000). *Gender in CMC: Anonymity, power and dissimulation.* Unpublished master's
    thesis, University of Amsterdam.
Zimbardo, P. G. (1969). The human choice: Individuation, reason, and order vs. deindividuation,
    impulse and chaos. In W. J. Arnold & D. Levine (Eds.), *Nebraska Symposium on Motivation*
    (Vol. 17, pp. 237–307). Lincoln, NE: University of Nebraska Press.
Zuboff, S. (1988). *In the age of the smart machine.* New York: Basic.

RUSSELL SPEARS received his PhD from Exeter University in 1985 and worked as a postdoctoral fellow at Manchester University. He moved to the University of Amsterdam in 1989 and has been Professor of Experimental Social Psychology there since 1995. His interests are in intergroup relations, social identity, and social influence as applied to computer-mediated communication. He has published on these topics in a range of social psychology and communications journals. He is currently an Associate Editor of *Self and Identity*.

TOM POSTMES received his PhD from the University of Amsterdam in 1997 and became Assistant Professor and then Associate Professor in Communications Studies at the same university. He recently took a position as Senior Lecturer in Psychology at Exeter University. Besides his research on the social psychological aspects of computer-mediated communication and the Internet, he has broad research interests in group processes, social influence, and prejudice and has published his work in both social psychology and communication journals.

MARTIN LEA received his PhD from Lancaster University in 1983 and has been a tenured Research Fellow in the Department of Psychology of Manchester University since 1995. His research interests focus on the social psychological aspects of computer-mediated communication and the Internet and the role of social identity processes. He has published widely in both social psychology and communications journals on these topics and edited a book on the social contexts of computer-mediated communication (1992).

ANKA WOLBERT completed her master's in social psychology at the University of Amsterdam in 2000 and also has a qualification in multimedia studies. She has worked as a research associate in the Social Psychology Program at that university. Her research interests focus on gender and the Internet, and she combines this work with freelance multimedia consulting.

Journal of Social Issues, Vol. 58, No. 1, 2002, pp. 109–124

Negotiating via Information Technology: Theory and Application

Leigh Thompson*

Northwestern University

Janice Nadler

Northwestern University and American Bar Foundation

In this review article, we examine how people negotiate via e-mail and in particular, how the process and outcomes of e-negotiations differ from those of traditional face-to-face bargaining. We review the key tasks of negotiation and then undertake a review of the research literature that has examined e-negotiations. We outline four theories of interaction that provide insights about social behavior in e-media: rapport building, social contagion, coordination, and information exchange. Our research program has focused on the interpersonal factors and social identity factors that can enhance the quality of e-negotiations. E-negotiators often succumb to the temporal synchrony bias, the burned bridge bias, the squeaky wheel bias, and the sinister attribution bias. We discuss social psychological factors that can reduce these biases and the future of research on e-negotiations.

There is a mix of evidence on how information technology affects social behavior (Kiesler & Sproull, 1992; Postmes, Spears, Sakhel, & de Groot, 2001). In this article, we review research and theory on how e-mail, as a particularly important type of information technology, affects negotiation behavior. First, we introduce negotiation theory, which conceptualizes negotiation as a mixed-motive enterprise, involving both cooperation and competition. Next, we review theories of how information technology affects social behavior. We then review our program of research and identify four social interaction biases that are produced when information technology meets negotiation. In particular, we examine

---

*Correspondence concerning this article should be addressed to Leigh Thompson, Management & Organizations, Kellogg School of Management, Northwestern University, 2001 Sheridan Road, Evanston, IL 60208 [e-mail: leighthompson@kellogg.northwestern.edu].

factors that lead to what we term (1) the temporal synchrony bias, (2) the burned bridge bias, (3) the squeaky wheel bias, and (4) the sinister attribution bias. Finally, we examine practical and theoretical implications of this research program.

Negotiation is an interpersonal decision-making process by which two or more people make mutual decisions concerning the allocation of scarce resources (Pruitt & Carnevale, 1993). Negotiation is a mixed-motive endeavor, such that negotiators are motivated to cooperate with one another to reach agreement, but compete with one another to claim resources (Lax & Sebenius, 1986; Walton & McKersie, 1965). For example, an employee and employer may both recognize the value of reaching mutual agreement, yet each is motivated to maximize his or her own gain. Thus, the key tasks of negotiation are expanding the pie of resources (the cooperative aspect) and claiming resources (the competitive aspect). In negotiation theory, these tasks are known as integrative negotiation and distributive negotiation.

Integrative negotiation is the process of how negotiators reach mutually beneficial agreements. Moreover, when people have different preferences, beliefs, and interests, it is possible to craft outcomes that are better for both parties than simple "split it down the middle" solutions. Unfortunately, most people have a fixed-pie perception of negotiation—that is, they believe that the other party's interests are directly and completely opposed to their own interests (Bazerman & Neale, 1983; Thompson & Hastie, 1990; Thompson & Hrebec, 1996), and consequently, often fail to capitalize on their mutual interests.

It is particularly ironic, then, that most negotiation situations contain potential for mutually beneficial agreements. In most negotiation situations, parties' interests are imperfectly correlated with one another, so that the gains of one party do not represent equal sacrifices by the other (Lax & Sebenius, 1986). However, the fixed-pie perception is a powerful and pervasive heuristic. A meta-analysis of several laboratory and some field investigations of negotiations revealed that people fail to realize compatible interests about 50% of the time (Thompson & Hrebec, 1996).

The task of claiming resources in negotiation is known as distributive bargaining (Deutsch, 1985; Walton & McKersie, 1965). For distributive bargaining to result in an agreement, a positive bargaining zone must exist, meaning that there must be a range of possible agreements that both parties would be willing to accept. For example, if the buyer of a car is willing to pay a maximum of $8,000, and the seller is willing to accept a minimum of $6,500, there is a positive bargaining zone (i.e., any price between $6,500 and $8,000), and the parties must simply decide how the pie will be divided.

Negotiating via Information Technology

Given the pervasiveness of negotiation as a form of social interaction, coupled with the rising prominence of information technologies as a communication mechanism, the question of how negotiation is conducted via e-mail is of great theoretical and practical importance (Turban, Lee, King, & Chung, 2000). We review four theoretical principles: interpersonal rapport, coordination, social contagion, and information; we then consider their implications for negotiation behavior.

Interpersonal Rapport

Most definitions of rapport include in their descriptions the feeling of being "in sync" with the other person in the interaction. Tickle-Degnen and Rosenthal (1990) note that there are three components to rapport: (1) mutual attentiveness (i.e., my attention is focused on you and your attention is focused on me), (2) positivity (i.e., we are friendly to each other), and (3) coordination (i.e., we are in sync, so that we each react spontaneously to the other).

Empirical investigations reveal that rapport enhances the quality of social interaction. Morris and his colleagues (Drolet & Morris, 1995, 2000; Moore, Kurtzberg, Thompson, & Morris, 1999) have examined how rapport mediates negotiated outcomes. More face-to-face contact produces more rapport, which in turn leads to more favorable outcomes for both parties. In another investigation (Drolet & Morris, 1995), rapport was a powerful determinant of whether people developed the trust necessary to reach integrative agreements. Nonverbal cues, such as body orientation, gestures, eye contact, head nodding, and paraverbal speech, such as fluency, use of fillers, such as "uh-huhs," were key to building rapport.

Coordination

Coordination in a negotiation context is the ability of negotiators to agree, implicitly or explicitly, on a course of action that results in a particular outcome. For example, in one bargaining game, called the "double auction" (Myerson & Satterthwaite, 1983), each party simultaneously submits an offer; if there is no overlap, no transaction takes place; if there is a positive overlap (e.g., the buyer demands $30, and the seller is willing to pay $40), the final price is the outcome midway between the two offers (i.e., $35). Although rational choice theory predicts that the communication medium should be inconsequential, empirical investigations have revealed that communication medium makes a large and dramatic difference, such that negotiators who communicate face to face or via telephone are more likely to converge on a single offer prior to submitting their bids, compared to those who communicate only via written offer (Valley, Moag, & Bazerman, 1998; Valley, Thompson, Gibbons, & Bazerman, in press). Valley, Thompson, Gibbons, and Bazerman refer to this strategy, which emerges only in an information-enhanced medium (i.e., face-to-face or telephone interaction), as coordination.

Information

Physical proximity presents certain advantages for social exchange in general and for the exchange of information in negotiation. People who are located in physical proximity have opportunities to interact more frequently. The casual conversations that negotiators have in the restroom, by the water cooler, or walking back from lunch are often where many difficult negotiation problems are solved. Conflicts are expressed, recognized, and addressed more quickly if negotiators are in physical proximity. Problems can be recognized and resolved more quickly when people interact in the same physical space. Thus, it is often the case that more information is exchanged between people in physical proximity simply because they interact more often.

A second reason why information is exchanged more readily face to face than over e-mail arises from fundamental differences between verbal and written exchange. People talk faster than they write or type. In addition, face-to-face verbal interaction occurs all in one session: People sit down and interact for 10 min, and then get up and leave. By contrast, the exchange of the same amount of information over e-mail might be accomplished over the course of hours or even days. However, several investigations of face-to-face versus more restricted forms of communication reveal that people engage in more non-task-relevant discussions in face-to-face discussions, resulting in less efficient discussions (Paulus et al., 1998). In one of our investigations, we asked participants to negotiate a buyer-seller task. Half the negotiation dyads used face-to-face verbal communication exclusively, and the other half used e-mail exclusively (Morris, Nadler, Kurtzberg, & Thompson, 2000). We found that the face-to-face negotiators exchanged more than three times the amount of information, on average, than the e-negotiators. Thus, interactions that are removed physically and are lacking in temporal contiguity (such as in e-negotiations) can result in less overall information exchange and less than optimal social outcomes.

Social Contagion

Social contagion is defined as "the spread of affect, attitude, or behavior from Person A (the 'initiator') to Person B (the 'recipient') where the recipient does not perceive an intentional influence attempt on the part of the initiator" (Levy & Nail, 1993, p. 266). According to Levy and Nail (1993), there are three subtypes of contagion, the most relevant one for the study of e-negotiation being "echo contagion," which occurs when a social actor imitates or reflects spontaneously the affect or behavior of an initiator. The term *echo* refers to a tendency toward automatic imitation of another (cf. Polansky, Lippitt, & Redl, 1950). There are several behavioral measures of echo contagion, such as when people cough, sneeze, or yawn when others do (Pennebaker, 1980); modify their overall activity level to accommodate a partner's activity level (Jaffe & Feldstein, 1970); synchronize temporal aspects of the conversational activities with those of an interviewer (Matarazzo, Saslow, & Guze, 1956); regulate gaze patterns (Exline, 1971); and amplify their voices (Natale, 1975). Emotional contagion (Gump & Kulik, 1997; Hatfield, Cacioppo, & Rapson, 1994; Schachter, 1959) is a particular type of social contagion wherein people mimic the facial expressions and behaviors or others and in turn feel the same emotions of others. The "chameleon effect" refers to nonconscious mimicry of the postures, mannerisms, facial expressions, and behaviors of others (Chartrand & Bargh, 1999). Chartrand and Bargh suggest that the mere perception of another's behavior automatically increases the likelihood of engaging in that behavior oneself.

Whereas the great bulk of research on social contagion processes has been carried out in face-to-face settings, we suggest that social contagion can also occur in e-interaction. An excellent early empirical investigation is Starch's (1911) study of unconscious imitation in handwriting. Although participants never interacted directly, they imitated the handwriting (slant and size) of another participant. We suggest that e-actors nonconsciously imitate not only the linguistic structure of each other's messages (e.g., message length, informational content, grammar) but also the social-emotional connotations of the other's message (e.g., tone, directness) and perhaps even the rate at which the message is attended to (in terms of e-reply lag time). Indeed, McGrath and Kelly's (1986) entrainment model suggests that interacting dyads and groups will match one another in terms of the rate and quality of their task performance. On the other hand, failure to match these cues, such as delaying a long time in responding to an e-mail message during a critical phase of relationship development, can impart powerful meaning about the status of the relationship (Lea & Spears, 1995).

In addition to basic social contagion factors, communication media such as e-mail have been associated with counternormative social behavior (Kiesler & Sproull, 1992). Kiesler and Sproull (1992; see also Sproull, Subramani, Kiesler, Walker, & Waters, 1996) argue that to the extent that situations fail to provide cues relevant for normative behavior, there are fewer constraints on counternormative behavior. In short, e-interactors show feelings that otherwise might be masked in socially appropriate ways. Our own work examining negotiation behavior has revealed that e-negotiators feel less restrained about expressing normatively inappropriate behavior and as a result make more threats and issue more ultimatums than do face-to-face negotiators (Morris et al., 2000).

In addition to counternormative behavior, the absence of social cues in electronic communication can cause people to become disengaged. Sproull et al. (1996) argue that people's responses to e-communication differ as a function of the "humanness" of the interface. For example, in an investigation of a career counseling system, when interacting with a "talking-face" interface, people were more aroused, attributed personality traits to the other party, and presented themselves in a more favorable light as compared to when they interacted with a "text-display" interface (Sproull et al., 1996).

On the other hand, Spears and Lea (1992) argue that group computer-mediated communication can actually promote normatively positive behavior among group members. Salient group norms can be enhanced in e-communication because the group image is uncontaminated by the physical presence of individuals who might deviate from the group (Spears, Lea, & Lee, 1990). Furthermore, in e-communication, visual anonymity and physical isolation encourage self-disclosure (McKenna, Green, & Gleason, this issue), and as a result, group members engaged in e-communication feel greater identification with the group and have more positive impressions of one another than they would in face-to-face communication (Spears & Lea, 1992).

Our Research Program

During the past 5 years, we have conducted a program of research that examines the dynamics of negotiation behavior conducted via electronic mail. In this section, we briefly review our methodological paradigm and highlight our findings. Our basic paradigm involves Master's in Business Administration students at Kellogg Management School negotiating via e-mail with students at Stanford University. Occasionally, departure from this paradigm was required. For example, because of distance constraints, participants in face-to-face negotiations were from the same school. Thus, our e-mail comparison group also contained students from the same school as the face-to-face group.

All students completed the "e-mail negotiation" as part of a 10-week-long course on negotiations. Specifically, students at each university were randomly assigned to either a buyer or a seller role in a classic buyer-seller negotiation involving the purchase of company cars. The eight-issue negotiation task contained integrative potential, but this had to be discovered by the students. Students were given printed instructions containing the e-mail address of their counterpart and strict guidelines to complete the negotiation within 7–10 days. Following the completion of the negotiation, students forwarded all of their e-correspondence for data analysis. The e-correspondence was coded and analyzed according to a coding scheme developed and published in our first empirical article (Moore et al., 1999). Then the participants completed the postnegotiation measures.

In all studies, we were careful to counterbalance and/or randomize all factors, such as role, gender, and university. Whereas there are equal proportions of men and women across universities, there are substantially fewer women in relation to men overall. Thus, in several of our investigations, we are not able to include female-female dyads. Another unexplored issue concerns race and ethnicity, as our participant population does not contain sufficient diversity on this variable.

Using analysis of variance techniques, we tested several different treatments for effects on negotiation performance and process. For example, we compared e-negotiations following a brief telephone conversation (the treatment group) with e-negotiations that took place without any telephone contact (the control group). Our key research questions have centered on three major issues:

1. What are the major behavioral and performance differences of e-mail versus face-to-face negotiation (Morris et al., 2000)?
2. What are the key social factors that can affect the nature and quality of negotiating via e-mail (Moore et al., 1999)?
3. What steps can be taken by people who must negotiate via e-mail, so that they can enhance the social as well as economic outcomes of negotiation (Moore et al., 1999; Morris et al., 2000; Thompson, Morris, & Nadler, 2000)?

Our paradigm allows investigation of interpersonal factors (such as the nature of the relationship between the two parties in the interaction) and social identity factors (such as ingroup vs. outgroup interactions) as well.

Key Research Findings

The major research findings from our program of research are summarized in Table 1, which identifies both social and economic outcomes. Compared to face-to-face negotiations, what appears to be starkly absent from e-mail negotiation is communication with others that is non-task-related and is more relationship-focused, which we call "schmoozing" (Moore et al., 1999; Morris et al., 2000). We hypothesized that schmoozing plays an important role in building rapport in the negotiating relationship and that the rapport developed between negotiators in turn sets the stage for the kind of cooperation and trust that facilitates agreements that are beneficial to both parties. We tested the "schmoozing" hypothesis in several ways (Moore et al., 1999; Morris et al., 2000). The results were dramatic: Negotiators who schmoozed (on the phone) developed more realistic goals, resulting in a larger range of possible outcomes, and were less likely to impasse compared to nonschmoozers. The key mediating factor was rapport. In short, even though both schmoozers and nonschmoozers conducted all of the business aspects of the deal via e-mail, there were dramatic differences in the negotiators' strategies and in the result of the negotiation.

Moreover, negotiators who schmoozed on the phone prior to conducting the e-mail negotiation expressed greater optimism about a future working relationship with the other party, compared to negotiators who did not schmooze (Morris et al., 2000). Negotiators who attempt to build rapport engender more positive emotion and trust than do those who attempt to dominate (Tiedens, Thompson, Morris, & Nadler, 1999). Further, negotiators' feelings and memories about a business

Table 1. Negotiating via E-mail: Effects of Rapport and Social Identity on Negotiation Outcomes

	Key findings: Social outcomes	Key findings: Economic outcomes
Interpersonal (dyadic) factors	As compared to face-to-face negotiation, e-mail reduces rapport building (Morris, Nadler, Kurtzberg, & Thompson, 2000)	As compared to face-to-face negotiation, e-mail increases multi-issue offers (Tiedens, Thompson, Morris, & Nadler, 1999)
	Brief telephone call prior to e-mail results in greater cooperation and better working relationship (Morris, Nadler, Kurtzberg, & Thompson, 2000)	Brief telephone call prior to e-mail improves outcomes (Morris, Nadler, Kurtzberg, & Thompson, 2000)
	Negotiators who attempt to build rapport engender more positive emotion and trust than do those who attempt to dominate (Morris, Nadler, Kurtzberg, & Thompson, 2000)	Brief personal disclosure over e-mail reduces likelihood of impasse (Moore, Kurtzberg, Thompson, & Morris, 1999)
Group and social identity factors	Outgroup e-negotiators express more negative affect and develop less rapport compared to ingroup negotiators (Moore, Kurtzberg, Thompson, & Morris, 1999)	Negotiators concerned about their group's reputation use more aggressive strategies, leading to lower outcomes than negotiators concerned about their personal reputation (Thomas-Hunt, Nadler, & Thompson, 2000)
	Males e-negotiating with other males develop less cooperative working relationships compared to males e-negotiating with females (Morris, Nadler, Kurtzberg, & Thompson, 2000)	Outgroup e-negotiations result in more impasses than do ingroup e-negotiations (Moore, Kurtzberg, Thompson, & Morris, 1999; Thomas-Hunt, Nadler, & Thompson, 2000)

encounter are highly driven by their perception of the relationship, not the economic outcome (cf. Galinsky, Mussweiler, & Medvec, 1999; Thompson, 1995). In sum, rapport building between negotiators leads to trust and optimism about the future that motivates people to form long-lasting relationships and to maintain contact in the future.

In addition to explicit rapport-building rituals, another route to successful negotiation outcomes exploits existing features of relationships involving social identification with the other party. Comparing e-negotiations between parties at the same university to e-negotiations between parties at different universities reveals that membership in the same social group (e.g., the same university) can reduce the likelihood of impasse in e-negotiations (Moore et al., 1999; Thomas-Hunt, Nadler, & Thompson, 2000; Tiedens et al., 1999).

It is worth noting that in our experiments, the control group (negotiators who did not share social ties with their counterparts) consistently underperformed on the relevant measures of negotiation performance, in comparison to our treatment groups (negotiators who did share social ties with their counterparts). The implication is that left to their own devices, e-negotiators are not as successful as they might be in terms of establishing rapport with the other party, reaching agreement when a positive bargaining zone exists, and reaching integrative outcomes. Our research has revealed a set of biases or assumptions that characterize the cognitions of e-negotiators that we review below.

Biases That Affect E-Negotiations

Just as research on face-to-face negotiations has identified a set of cognitive-motivational biases that threaten the quality of negotiated outcomes, our research program has identified a set of biases that can threaten the quality of negotiated interactions. We identify four of these biases below.

Temporal synchrony bias. The temporal synchrony bias is the tendency for negotiators to behave as if they are in a synchronous situation when in fact, they are not. E-negotiators are aware on some level of the asynchronous aspect of e-negotiation but discount it and ignore some of its implications. E-negotiators often behave as if they believe that they can control the rate of message exchange that occurs within the interaction. Such control is often possible in face-to-face interactions, because people tend to converge in the length of their utterances and rate of speech. This process of convergence is an example of social contagion. This difference in how senders and receivers parse the interaction in terms of time can lead to frustration and very commonly, negative dispositional attributions (see "Sinister Attribution Bias," below).

One of the widely cited advantages of e-mail is that any one can send a message whenever he or she wants. The problem is that there may not be anyone there to listen. In e-negotiations, this can be especially problematic, given that most negotiators have a "tennis game" mental model of negotiations; that is, they expect the other party to "volley back" offers much faster than is actually possible using asynchronous media. Indeed, in our research, we found less turn-taking behavior in negotiations conducted via e-mail than in face-to-face negotiations (Morris et al., 2000). And turn taking is positively correlated with schmoozing behavior (e.g., discussion of background issues) that leads to trust and rapport (Morris et al., 2000).

Conversational turn taking does not just make interaction seem smoother, it also serves an important informational function, with interactants engaging in a process of mutual corrections. In face-to-face interactions, receivers and senders typically engage in a process of rapid correction of information. In e-negotiations, by contrast, negotiators must attempt to interpret what the other party has said without the opportunity for brief requests for clarification as the other party is talking. Thus, e-negotiators make assumptions. For example, in our investigation of e-mail versus face-to-face negotiation, e-negotiators asked fewer clarifying questions than did face-to-face negotiators (Morris et al., 2000). These assumptions, however, are often egocentrically tainted, which leads to anger.

Burned bridge bias. The burned bridge bias is the tendency for e-negotiators to engage in risky interpersonal behaviors in an impoverished medium that they would not engage in when interacting face to face. For example, negotiators may create "tests" for the other party that lead to a high probability of failure (e.g., negotiators may say, "If I don't hear from you in 1 hr, then I am going to assume that you don't want to reach an agreement and I will refuse to send any more offers.") In face-to-face interactions, there are a variety of behaviors that negotiators engage in—many of them on a micro level—that enhance relationships (Sproull et al., 1996). For example, politeness rituals, such as smiling, nodding, making direct eye contact, and verbalizations that endorse what the other is saying (e.g., "uh-huh," "OK"), serve to strengthen the relationship between negotiators. Negotiators who build positive rapport are less likely to burn bridges or create situations that imperil the relationships (Morris et al., 2000). A lack of rapport encourages feelings of anonymity and social distance, leading people to reason that the relationship is more temporary and fleeting.

One of the reasons why e-negotiators may burn bridges is that there is less accountability for the relationship. In this sense, e-negotiation often occurs in a vacuum, meaning that short of people explicitly inviting others, such as colleagues or third parties, to witness the interaction, the nature of the interaction is oblivious to others. In contrast, face-to-face negotiations often take place in a richly grounded social network, and in this sense there is greater accountability for one's behaviors (cf. Wicklund & Gollwitzer, 1982). Indeed, observers of face-to-face interactions are able to immediately assess the felt rapport among interactants. Furthermore, observers appear to pay attention to the right cues: The greater the synchrony of nonverbal displays, the more likely an outside observer will judge that a high level of rapport is present in the interaction (Bernieri, 1991; Bernieri, Davis, Rosenthal, & Knee, 1994). An important question for further investigation is whether introducing an accountability mechanism into e-negotiation (such as copying each message to a designated third party who has social ties to both parties) would reduce the risky interpersonal behaviors that occur via e-mail.

Squeaky wheel bias. The squeaky wheel bias is the tendency for negotiators to adopt an aversive emotional style when interacting via an impoverished media, such as e-mail, to achieve their goals, whereas the same negotiator might use a positive emotional style in a face-to-face interaction. Thompson, Medvec, Seiden, and Kopelman (2001) identified three common emotional styles that negotiators can adopt: positive, rational, or negative. The positive negotiation style is the "win more flies with honey" approach. In contrast, the rational emotional approach is devoid of emotion. The inherent belief is that emotion is weakness and that it is best to be rational. Finally, the negative emotional style is a manifestation of the belief that it is more effective to behave in a slightly irrational fashion and use negative emotion to achieve one's goals. One such negative style is the squeaky wheel approach, which captures the idea that a negotiator who throws a temper tantrum is most likely to achieve her goals. Negotiators are likely to use a squeaky wheel approach when they believe intimidation will be effective (cf. Rothbart & Hallmark, 1988). Our argument is that the squeaky wheel approach is most likely to emerge in an e-mail context.

As we discussed earlier in the context of social contagion, communication media such as e-mail have been associated with counternormative social behavior (Kiesler & Sproull, 1992). Indeed, as compared to face-to-face negotiations, strangers negotiating over e-mail are more likely to negatively confront one another. Rude, impulsive behavior, such as flaming, increases when strangers interact on e-mail, in part because people pay more attention to content and less attention to etiquette over e-mail and in part because people perceive the squeaky wheel strategy as most effective. In fact, one study suggests that people are eight times more likely to flame in e-discussion than in face-to-face discussion (Dubrovsky, Kiesler, & Sethna, 1991). On the other hand, when e-discussion members are part of a cohesive group, the anonymity and lack of physical contact of electronic communication makes group norms more salient and can increase conformity to communication norms over time (Postmes, Spears, & Lea, 2000; Postmes et al., 2001; Spears et al., 1990). Nonetheless, e-mail negotiators for whom group norms are not salient (e.g., strangers who have not had the opportunity to schmooze before negotiating) find that conflict escalates more often and more quickly, and this process of conflict escalation frequently serves as a roadblock to the process of information exchange often required for integrative outcomes.

Sinister attribution bias. People often misattribute behavior of others to personal dispositions and overlook the influence of temporary, situational factors (Ross, 1977). The sinister attribution bias is a type of mutation of the fundamental attribution error, wherein attributions of the other person's behavior are not only dispositional, but also diabolical. People do in fact behave in less appropriate ways when communicating via e-mail (and other impoverished media); we argue that the likelihood of making dispositional attributions increases disproportionately to the rate of counternormative e-behavior.

Social identity theory suggests that more similar we perceive others to be, the more cooperative and trusting we are; conversely, if someone is perceived as an outgroup member, particularly from a threatening group, the less likely people are to show trust and cooperation (Tajfel & Turner, 1986). The more we perceive the other party as a member of an outgroup, the more we attribute his actions to malevolent motives, a phenomenon Kramer (1995) refers to as the "sinister attribution error." Attributing sinister motives to outgroup members is especially prevalent in e-mail communication, where the absence of social cues leads to feelings of social distance. Indeed, Fortune and Brodt (2000) found that negotiators interacting via e-mail were more likely to mistrust and suspect the other party of lying or otherwise deceiving them, relative to negotiators interacting face to face. Yet e-negotiators were in fact no more likely than face-to-face negotiators to deceive the other party. Thus, the increased suspicion of the other party on the part of e-negotiators had no factual basis.

Perceived ingroup status of the e-negotiation opponent can reverse the sinister attribution effect and can have a dramatic effect on e-negotiation outcomes and processes. In one study, the likelihood of impasse was reduced to nearly zero when e-negotiators perceived that their counterpart was a member of their ingroup (Moore et al., 1999). E-negotiators who did not perceive the other party as an ingroup member were economically the worst off: They left more money on the table than other e-negotiators, because their suspicion and distrust of the other party hindered the kind of information exchange necessary to engage in mutually profitable trade-offs. Moreover, Spears and his colleagues (Postmes et al., 2001; Spears et al., 1990) have demonstrated that, under conditions of salient social identity and ingroup status, the very anonymity of electronic communication causes e-group members increase their group allegiance and normative behavior.

Implications for Theory and Practice

The investigation of e-mail naturally raises questions that are central in the study of social psychology: How do people make first impressions, build rapport, recover from a breach of trust (Fiske & Neuberg, 1990; Wieselquist, Rusbult, Foster, & Agnew, 1999)? Social psychological theory has much to offer in explaining how people build relationships and exchange information (Berscheid & Reis, 1998; Rusbult & Van Lange, 1996). An important question, we believe, concerns impression development (Fiske & Neuberg, 1990). In face-to-face interaction, people have a panoply of cues to help them form impressions of others (Brewer, 1988). Further, social psychological research has revealed that the most important cues, perhaps to the chagrin of most people, are physical attractiveness, gender, and race (Brewer, 1988; Eagly, Ashmore, Makhijani, & Longo, 1991; Fiske & Neuberg, 1990; Mazur, 1985). Generally speaking, e-mail communication may cultivate relationships between people that would have otherwise never formed (McKenna & Bargh, 2000). Indeed, the availability of e-mail as a medium for initial negotiations might help to create opportunities for job candidates, sales representatives, consultants, and agents, to name just a few. The "gating features" (McKenna et al., this issue) present in face-to-face interaction that impede relationship formation for people who are physically unattractive or socially anxious are largely absent in e-mail. Thus, other information presumably forms the basis of e-impressions, including expressions of self-disclosure (Bargh, McKenna, & Fitzsimons, this issue). This suggests that rapport-building opportunities we discussed earlier are specific to computer-mediated communication but not unique to negotiation. McKenna et al. (this issue) reported that gating features are the most salient features of face-to-face meetings, preventing people from forming bonds based on the quality of the interaction, whereas over the Internet substantive features of an encounter, such as the degree to which the participants got to know one another and the quality of the conversation, drive initial liking.

Practice and Policy Recommendations

Rapport and perceived ingroup status emerge as powerful factors that influence the quality of negotiated outcomes. Negotiators who have a positive relationship, either through perceived shared membership in an ingroup or through the process of engaging in a personal, getting-to-know-you exchange prior to the negotiation, are more likely to express positive affect during the negotiation process. This expression of positive affect, in turn, leads to lower impasse rates and increased integrative agreement.

A second factor influencing the quality of negotiated outcomes is trust. Negotiators who establish rapport prior to commencing negotiations via e-mail report significantly higher levels of trust in their counterpart compared to negotiators who fail to establish rapport prior to commencing negotiations (see Wieselquist et al., 1999, for a review of emotion and trust). Conversely, negotiators who don't feel a connection with their counterpart or perceive their counterpart as a member of an outgroup are more likely to engage in a negotiating style motivated by negative affect, resulting in flaming and escalation of conflict, which makes mutually beneficial information exchange less likely to occur and less trustworthy and thus makes the likelihood of agreement lower. Thus, the positive influence of trust and rapport on negotiated outcomes suggests that there are prescriptive techniques that can be employed to minimize losses that can occur in communication-impoverished negotiations. Organizations whose members rely on e-mail for negotiating with others outside of their own work groups might adopt policies for e-mail use that reflect the influence of rapport-building techniques on affect, trust, and ultimately, negotiated outcomes.

However, we fully expect that there are different classes of skills, currently not under standard social psychological investigation, that may prove to be important for helping people to be competent in an e-business world. Thus the challenge for the investigation of e-negotiation, and e-interactions in general, will be to develop concepts and theories that are unique to the medium, rather than merely borrowing from established disciplines. In this sense, it may be useful to combine experimental investigations, in which manipulations and treatments are introduced and their effect on preestablished indices are measured, with more passive observation in natural settings.

References

Bazerman, M. H., & Neale, M. A. (1983). Heuristics in negotiation: Limitations to effective dispute resolution. In M. Bazerman and R. Lewicki (Eds.), *Negotiating in organizations* (pp. 51–67). Beverly Hills, CA: Sage.

Bernieri, F. J. (1991). Interpersonal sensitivity in teaching interactions. *Personality and Social Psychology Bulletin, 17,* 98–103.

Bernieri, F. J., Davis, J. M., Rosenthal, R., & Knee, C. R. (1994). Interactional synchrony and rapport: Measuring synchrony in displays devoid of sound and facial affect. *Personality and Social Psychology Bulletin, 20*(3), 303–311.

Berscheid, E., & Reis, H. T. (1998). Attraction and close relationships. In D. Gilbert, S. Fiske, & G. Lindzey (Eds.), *Handbook of social psychology* (4th ed., pp. 193–281). New York: Oxford University Press.

Brewer, M. B. (1988). A dual process model of impression formation. In T. K. Srull & R. S. Wyer (Eds.), *Advances in social cognition* (Vol. 1, pp. 1–36). Hillsdale, NJ: Erlbaum.

Chartrand, T. L., & Bargh, J. A. (1999). The chameleon effect: The perception-behavior link and social interaction. *Journal of Personality & Social Psychology, 76,* 893–910.

Deutsch, M. (1985). *Distributive justice: A social-psychological perspective.* New Haven, CT: Yale University Press.

Drolet, A. L., & Morris, M. W. (1995). *Communication media and interpersonal trust in conflicts: The role of rapport and synchrony on nonverbal behavior.* Unpublished manuscript, Stanford University, Stanford, CA.

Drolet, A. L., & Morris, M. W. (2000). Rapport in conflict resolution: Accounting for how nonverbal exchange fosters cooperation on mutual beneficial settlements to mixed-motive conflicts. *Journal of Experimental Social Psychology, 36,* 26–50.

Dubrovsky, V. J., Kiesler, S., & Sethna, B. N. (1991). The equalization phenomenon: Status effects in computer-mediated and face-to-face decision-making groups. *Human-Computer Interaction, 6,* 119–146.

Eagly, A. H., Ashmore, R. D., Makhijani, M. G., & Longo, L. C. (1991). What is beautiful is good, but . . .: A meta-analytic review of research on the physical attractiveness stereotype. *Psychological Bulletin, 110,* 109–128.

Exline, R. V. (1971). Visual interaction: The glances of power and preference. In J. K. Cole (Ed.), *Nebraska Symposium on Motivation* (Vol. 19, pp. 163–206). Lincoln, NE: University of Nebraska Press.

Fiske, S. T., & Neuberg, S. L. (1990). A continuum of impression formation, from category-based to individuating processes: Influences of information and motivation on attention and interpretation. *Advances in Experimental Social Psychology, 23,* 1–74.

Fortune, A., & Brodt, S. (2000). *Face to face or virtually, for the second time around: The influence of task, past experience, and media on trust and deception in negotiation* (Working paper). Durham, NC: Duke University.

Galinsky, A. D., Mussweiler, T., & Medvec, V. H. (1999). *Disconnecting subjective and objective utility: The role of negotiator focus* (Working paper). Evanston, IL: Northwestern University.

Gump, B. B., & Kulik, J. A. (1997). Stress, affiliation, and emotional contagion. *Journal of Personality and Social Psychology, 72,* 305–319.

Hatfield, E., Cacioppo, J. T., & Rapson, R. (1994). *Emotional contagion.* New York: Cambridge University Press.

Jaffe, J., & Feldstein, S. (1970). *Rhythms of dialogue.* New York: Academic.

Kiesler, S., & Sproull, L. (1992). Group decision making and communication technology. *Organizational Behavior and Human Decision Processes, 52,* 96–123.

Kramer, R. M. (1995). Power, paranoia and distrust in organizations: The distorted view from the top. In R. J. Bies, R. J. Lewicki, & B. H. Sheppard (Eds.), *Research on negotiation in organizations* (Vol. 5, pp. 119–154). Greenwich, CT: JAI.

Lax, D. A., & Sebenius, J. K. (1986). *The manager as negotiator.* New York: Free.

Lea, M., & Spears, R. (1995). Love at first byte? Building personal relationships over computer networks. In J. T. Wood & S. Duck (Eds.), *Under-studied relationships: Off the beaten track* (pp. 197–233). Thousand Oaks, CA: Sage.

Levy, D. A., & Nail, P. R. (1993). Contagion: A theoretical and empirical review and reconceptualization. *Genetic, Social and General Psychology Monographs, 119,* 235–285.

Matarazzo, J. D., Saslow, G., & Guze, S. B. (1956). Stability of interaction patterns during interviews: A replication. *Journal of Consulting Psychology, 20,* 267–274.

Mazur, A. (1985). A biosocial model of status in face-to-face groups. *Social Forces, 64*, 377–402.

McGrath, J. E., & Kelly, J. R. (1986). *Time and human interaction: Toward a social psychology of time*. New York: Guilford.

McKenna, K. Y. A., & Bargh, J. A. (2000). Plan 9 from cyberspace: The implications of the Internet for personality and social psychology. *Personality and Social Psychology Review, 4*, 57–75.

Moore, D., Kurtzberg, T., Thompson, L., & Morris, M. W. (1999). Long and short routes to success in electronically-mediated negotiations: Group affiliations and good vibrations. *Organization Behavior and Human Decision Processes, 77*, 22–43.

Morris, M. W., Nadler, J., Kurtzberg, T., & Thompson, L. (2000). *Schmooze or lose: Social friction and lubrication in e-mail negotiations* (Working paper). Evanston, IL: Northwestern University.

Myerson, R. B., & Satterthwaite, M. (1983). Efficient mechanisms for bilateral trading. *Journal of Economic Theory, 48*, 179–220.

Natale, M. (1975). Convergence of mean vocal intensity in dyadic communication as a function of social desirability. *Journal of Personality and Social Psychology, 32*(5), 790–804.

Paulus, P. B., Larey, T. S., Brown, V., Dzindolet, M. T., Roland, E. J., Leggett, K. L., Putman, V. L., & Coskun, H. (1998, June). *Group and electronic brainstorming: Understanding production losses and gains in idea generating groups*. Paper presented at Learning in Organizations Conference, Carnegie-Mellon University, Pittsburgh, PA.

Pennebaker, J. W. (1980). Perceptual and environmental determinants of coughing. *Basic and Applied Social Psychology, 1*, 83–91.

Polansky, N., Lippitt, R., & Redl, F. (1950). An investigation of behavioral contagion in groups. *Human Relations, 3*, 319–348.

Postmes, T., Spears, R., & Lea, M. (2000). The formation of group norms in computer-mediated communication. *Human Communication Research, 26*, 341–371.

Postmes, T., Spears, R., Sakhel, K., & de Groot, D. (2001). *Social influence in computer-mediated communication: The effects of anonymity on group behavior*. Manuscript submitted for publication.

Pruitt, D. G., & Carnevale, P. J. (1993). Negotiation in social conflict. Pacific Grove, CA: Brooks-Cole.

Ross, L. (1977). The intuitive psychologist and his shortcomings: Distortions in the attribution process. In L. Berkowitz (Ed.), *Advances in experimental social psychology* (Vol. 10, pp. 173–220). Orlando, FL: Academic.

Rothbart, M., & Hallmark, W. (1988). In-group and out-group differences in the perceived efficacy of coercion and conciliation in resolving social conflict. *Journal of Personality and Social Psychology, 55*, 248–257.

Rusbult, C. E., & Van Lange, P. A. M. (1996). Interdependence processes. In E. T. Higgins & A. W. Kruglanski (Eds.), *Social psychology: Handbook of basic principles* (pp. 564–596). New York: Guilford.

Schachter, S. (1959). *The psychology of affiliation: Experimental studies of the sources of gregariousness*. Stanford, CA: Stanford University Press.

Spears, R., & Lea, M. (1992). Social influence and the influence of the "social" in computer-mediated communication. In M. Lea (Ed.), *Contexts of computer-mediated communication* (pp. 30–65). London: Harvester-Wheatsheaf.

Spears, R., Lea, M., & Lee, S. (1990). De-individuation and group polarization in computer-mediated communication. *British Journal of Social Psychology, 29*, 121–134.

Sproull, L., Subramani, M.., Kiesler, S., Walker, J., & Waters, K. (1996). When the interface is a face. *Human-Computer Interaction, 11*, 97–124.

Starch, D. (1911). Unconscious imitation in handwriting. *Psychological Review, 18*, 223–228.

Tajfel, H., & Turner, J. C. (1986). The social identity theory of intergroup behavior. In S. Worchel & W. G. Austin (Eds.), *Psychology of intergroup relations* (pp. 7–24). Chicago: Nelson-Hall.

Thomas-Hunt, M., Nadler, J. & Thompson, L. (2000). *Social identity and group reputation in e-mail negotiations*. Manuscript in preparation.

Thompson, L. (1995). The impact of minimum goals and aspirations on judgments of success in negotiations. *Group Decision Making and Negotiation, 4*, 513–524.

Thompson, L., & Hastie, R. (1990). Social perception in negotiation. *Organizational Behavior and Human Decision Processes, 47*, 98–123.

Thompson, L., & Hrebec, D. (1996). Lose-lose agreements in interdependent decision making. *Psychological Bulletin, 120,* 396–409.

Thompson, L., Medvec, V. H., Seiden, V., & Kopelman, S. (2001). Poker face, smiley face, and rant 'n' rave: Myths and realities about emotion in negotiation. In M. Hogg & S. Tindale (Eds.), *Blackwell handbook in social psychology: Vol. 3. Group processes* (pp. 139–163). Oxford, UK: Blackwell.

Thompson, L., Morris, M. W., & Nadler, J. (2000, September). *Information technology and negotiation behavior.* Paper presented at Auctions and Negotiations.com Conference on Electronic Exchange, Northwestern University, Evanston, IL.

Tickle-Degnen, L., & Rosenthal, R. (1990). The nature of rapport and its nonverbal correlates. *Psychological Bulletin, 1*(4), 285–293.

Tiedens, L., Thompson, L., Morris, M. W., & Nadler, J. (1999). *Rapport, dominance, and social identity in e-mail negotiations.* Manuscript in preparation.

Turban, E., Lee, J., King, D., & Chung, H. M. (2000). *Electronic commerce: A managerial perspective.* Upper Saddle River, NJ: Prentice Hall.

Valley, K., Moag, J., & Bazerman, M. H. (1998). A matter of trust: Effects of communication on the efficiency and distribution of outcomes. *Journal of Economic Behavior in Organizations, 34,* 211–238.

Valley, K., Thompson, L., Gibbons, R. & Bazerman, M. (in press). How communication improves efficiency in bargaining games. *Games and Economic Behavior.*

Walton, R. E., & McKersie, R. B. (1965). *A behavioral theory of labor relations.* New York: McGraw-Hill.

Wicklund, R. A., & Gollwitzer, P. M. (1982). *Symbolic self-completion.* Hillsdale, NJ: Erlbaum.

Wieselquist, J., Rusbult, C. E., Foster, C. A, & Agnew, C. R. (1999). Commitment, pro-relationship behavior, and trust in close relationships. *Journal of Personality and Social Psychology, 77,* 942–966.

LEIGH THOMPSON is the J. Jay Gerber Distinguished Professor of Dispute Resolution and Organizations in the Kellogg School of Management at Northwestern University. She is the director of the AT&T Behavioral Research Laboratory at Kellogg and an executive member of the Dispute Resolution Research Center, and she also directs the Negotiation Strategies and Leading High Impact Teams Executive Programs at Kellogg. She received an MA in Education from the University of California at Santa Barbara and a PhD in Psychology from Northwestern University. Thompson is a recipient of the National Science Foundation's Presidential Young Investigator Award, a fellowship at the Center for Advanced Study in the Behavioral Sciences at Stanford, and a grant from the Citigroup Behavioral Sciences Research Council of Citibank. Her research areas focus on negotiation, group decision making, learning and creativity, and team performance. She is the author of three books and over 60 articles in leading management journals and books.

JANICE NADLER is an Assistant Professor of Law at Northwestern University and a Research Fellow at the American Bar Foundation. She received a PhD in social psychology from the University of Illinois at Urbana-Champaign and a JD from the University of California at Berkeley. Her research interests focus on distributive justice, deference to legal authority, negotiation, and conflict resolution.

Journal of Social Issues, Vol. 58, No. 1, 2002, pp. 125–141

Civic Culture Meets the Digital Divide: The Role of Community Electronic Networks

Eugene Borgida,* John L. Sullivan, Alina Oxendine, Melinda S. Jackson, and Eric Riedel
University of Minnesota

Amy Gangl
University of Colorado at Boulder

The concept of social capital *reflects the norms and social relations embedded in the social structure of societies that enable people to coordinate community action to achieve desired goals. Our research focuses on the role that norms of cooperation and civic and political culture play in addressing the "digital divide" in computer use and Internet access. We review evidence from mail surveys of randomly selected respondents in two rural Minnesota communities as well as qualitative focus group and archival evidence suggesting that the communities have adopted different approaches to technology diffusion. Whether information technology is viewed as a public or private good depends in part on the civic culture of a community.*

Community Context and Technological Change

The effects of social and political context on the diffusion of information technology have emerged as a recent theme in the social scientific study of

*Correspondence concerning this article should be addressed either to Eugene Borgida, Department of Psychology, University of Minnesota, Minneapolis, MN 55455 [e-mail: borgi001@tc.umn.edu], or to John L. Sullivan, Department of Political Science, University of Minnesota, Minneapolis, MN 55455 [e-mail: jsull@polisci.umn.edu]. This research was supported by National Science Foundation Grant No. SBR9619147 to Eugene Borgida and John L. Sullivan. Melinda Jackson is also supported in part by a National Science Foundation graduate fellowship. We thank Ashleigh Smith and Jill Doerfler for research assistance on the preliminary historical analysis of the two communities and Mark Snyder for his comments on an earlier version of this article.

technological change (Tsagarousianou, Tambini, & Bryan, 1998). For example, Guthrie and Dutton (1992) conducted a case study of four California communities, three of which implemented a version of a community electronic network. They found that existing uses of technology and the local political climate, rather than the financial resources of the communities, played the most important roles in determining the structure of the networks, including public access, availability of electronic mail, and restrictions on content. Virnoche (1998) also concluded that the social context surrounding the development of several electronic community networks in Colorado significantly affected the shape of the networks. She contrasted nonprofit and market-based networks, the choice of which depended on considerations such as access for underserved populations, the status of local businesses as part of the community, and civic idealism. Other studies, focusing on the implementation of computer networks in organizations, suggest that patterns of technology use rest on the social networks and organizational culture already in place (Ashburner, 1990; Kanungo, 1997; Pickering & King, 1995; Rubinyi, 1989; Sankar, 1988).

In exploring the role that social context plays in the implementation of information technology, we draw upon the concept of social capital. *Social capital* is defined as the norms and social relations embedded in the social structure of societies that enable people to coordinate action to achieve desired goals (World Bank, 2000). It is described as a feature that communities possess to varying degrees, with the key elements being social trust and civic engagement (Coleman, 1988, 1990; Putnam, 1993, 2000). The presence of these elements supports norms of cooperation and reciprocity, creating a "civic community" that is able to address public issues collectively, as a community of citizens rather than a collection of private individuals. Putnam (1993), in his study of differences between northern and southern regions of Italy, observed that regions of the country with differing levels of social capital showed marked differences in political culture. Regions with high levels of social capital were marked by a respect for political equality and an expectation that civic participation would be organized on the basis of co-operation among citizens for the common good, rather than competition between citizens of unequal status and resources.

The role of social capital and its attendant norms of cooperation in fostering collective action has been illustrated in several contexts including local economic development (Fukuyama, 1995; Putnam, 1993, 2000), education (Coleman, 1988; Schneider, Teske, Marshall, Mintrom, & Roch, 1997), political participation (Knack & Kropf, 1998; La Due Lake & Huckfeldt, 1998), and public health (Kawachi, Kennedy, Lochner, & Prothrow-Stith, 1997; Wilkinson, 1996, 2000). The concept of social capital has also been applied to the study of technological change, with research focused on whether new information technologies have the potential to create new forms of social capital and reverse the current trend of declining social capital in American society (Calabrese & Borchert, 1996; Kling,

1996; Wellman et al., 1996). In our program of research, we take a somewhat different approach by viewing access to information technology in a community as a potential collective action problem. In this article, we focus on the role that norms of cooperation and civic and political culture play in addressing disparities in access to information technology. We maintain that whether information technology is viewed as public good, with an accompanying collective obligation to provide access, or as a private good, best provided by the free market, is in part determined by the civic culture of a community. Drawing on our longitudinal study of two rural Minnesota communities, we present evidence based on survey results, focus groups, and historical contextual analysis to suggest that the two communities have adopted different approaches to technology diffusion. We conclude that these different avenues to providing access to information technology in turn have different consequences for equality of access.

The Narrowing but Persistent Digital Divide

Along with the rapid spread of computer technology among households in the United States over the past decade, disparities based on income, race, and urban versus rural settings have also emerged. The National Telecommunications and Information Administration (NTIA) has been tracking this digital divide since 1994 and most recently reported that gaps between groups based on income levels, education levels, and geographic locations began to shrink dramatically at the end of the last decade (NTIA, 2000). The NTIA reported that by August 2000, 51% of American households owned computers, compared to 42% in 1998, and 41.5% had access to the Internet at home, compared to 26.2% in 1998. Despite these recent gains, however, the NTIA finds a persistent divide in computer use and Internet access that separates the information haves and have-nots. The NTIA 2000 survey found that 85% of households with incomes of $75,000 and higher have a computer at home, compared to just 19% of households in the $15,000-and-under income bracket. Similarly, 78% of households at the highest income levels have Internet access, compared to only 13% of low-income households. In addition, there is a significant racial digital divide, with Blacks and Hispanics continuing to experience the lowest household Internet penetration rates, at 23.5% and 23.6%, respectively, compared to 46.1% among Whites.

Of particular interest to our study, the NTIA survey reports that Americans living in rural areas also continue to lag behind their urban and suburban counterparts, despite recent gains. The gap between rural households and the nation as a whole with regard to Internet access narrowed from 4.0 percentage points in 1998 to 2.6 percentage points in 2000. This represents an impressive 75% increase in Internet access among rural households, from 22.2% in December 1998 to 38.9% in August 2000. However, low-income rural households continue to have the lowest rate of Internet access, 11.3%, compared to low-income households in other geographic areas. Furthermore, rural cities and towns are lagging behind urban areas in access to high-speed broadband services, the most recent information technology development (NTIA, 2000). This disparity in high-speed Internet access limits opportunities for rural businesses with regard to electronic commerce and puts rural communities at a disadvantage in trying to attract new high-tech companies to their areas.

Rural communities have thus begun searching for collective solutions to reduce this digital divide between their citizens and the rest of the nation. One approach they have increasingly turned to is the community electronic network. Such a network may provide a number of services, including electronic access to government employees and information, community-oriented discussions, electronic mail, electronic bulletin boards, information about community organizations, and access to the Internet. Ideally, community electronic networks also seek to fulfill a number of civic goals, including access to technology, education and training, enhancing community cohesion, and bolstering informed citizenship and public participation (Anderson, Bikson, Law, & Mitchell, 1995; Schuler, 1994). In order to maintain a healthy economy and a vibrant workforce, electronic networks are one way some rural communities are attempting to catch up to urban areas and reduce the information gaps that exist among their own citizens.

Introducing ItascaNet

One of the first rural communities in Minnesota to initiate an electronic network was the town of Grand Rapids, located in the north-central area of the state, with a population of 8,400. In Minnesota, there are significant differences between the Twin Cities metropolitan area and rural cities and towns such as Grand Rapids. As in many small Minnesota towns, the average Grand Rapids resident is getting older, and the tax base is shrinking. Trying to convince the city's youth to stay in the area to ensure the community's future has become a common concern. Trailing metro Minnesota on measures of economic strength, education levels, population growth, standard of living, and percentages of citizens living in poverty, the citizens of Grand Rapids have a firm desire not to be left behind as technology advances explode across the country.

Against this backdrop, planning for a community electronic network was initiated in 1995 when the local superintendent of schools gathered leaders from various community agencies to discuss the state of their computer technology. After exploring their options, a partnership was formed and the group decided to create GrandNet, a community electronic network, to meet their collective technology needs. In late 1995, grant funding was sought and secured locally from the nonprofit Blandin Foundation and through the Telecommunications and Information Infrastructure Assistance Program (TIIAP) of the U.S. Department of Commerce. GrandNet's goals included several of TIIAP's aims: increasing the community's access to and use of the national information infrastructure, reducing disparities in access levels among community residents, increasing information available to community members, and facilitating the sharing of data and information among the partner organizations.

In late 1997, with five partner agencies in place and routinely cooperating to achieve common goals, the group purchased a server and laid cable for connections, and the partners linked into GrandNet. In keeping with the network's community goals, Internet-linked computers were made available to students in the public schools and citizens in the public library, and free computer training classes were offered to the community. Over the last several years, the GrandNet project has expanded. Efforts to provide computer access and training to residents in all of Itasca County, where Grand Rapids is located, are underway. To reflect this goal of providing access to a broader rural community, the project has been renamed ItascaNet.

To facilitate the long-term study of the effects of the ItascaNet community network on the community of Grand Rapids, we identified a similar Minnesota community on the basis of a cluster analysis of demographic and social factors across Minnesota (see Sullivan et al., in press, for details). The city of Detroit Lakes proved to be a close statistical match to Grand Rapids and was therefore selected to serve as a nonequivalent control group. The city of Detroit Lakes initiated its own electronic network, called LakesNet, through its municipal utility in 1997. This city-managed network supplies low-cost Internet access to the local schools and public library and offers Internet service to citizens for a monthly fee. There is also a small private communications company based in Detroit Lakes that has recently begun offering Internet access to local residents at competitive rates. By contrast with the city of Grand Rapids, the approach to networking in Detroit Lakes has thus been driven by an entrepreneurial spirit in which various networking enterprises in the community in effect compete with each other to establish a dominant market share in town. The kind of cooperative social networking that gave rise to a multigroup partnership in Grand Rapids was not present in the Detroit Lakes community. As such, Detroit Lakes represents an ideal comparison to Grand Rapids in assessing the roles of community resources and civic culture in the approach taken to technological change.

Survey Assessment of the Two Communities

In 1997, we conducted a baseline mail survey of 2,000 randomly selected households in Grand Rapids and Detroit Lakes, with a response rate slightly above 40% for each community. The survey covered attitudes toward computer use, technology ownership, attitudes toward the community, political engagement (interest, knowledge, efficacy, and participation), membership in civic organizations, social attitudes (alienation and interpersonal trust), and sociability (frequency of social interactions), as well as various demographic indicators. In late 1999, we administered a second round of surveys in the two communities, expanding the sample to include residents in the counties surrounding Grand Rapids (Itasca County) and Detroit Lakes (Becker County). This second survey also included the revised UCLA Loneliness Scale (Russell, Peplau, & Catrona, 1980) and the social support subscale assessing "belonging" used in the original HomeNet survey (Kraut et al., 1998). Surveys were sent to a total of 2,791 households in the second round, with an overall response rate of 64%.

Using our two rounds of surveys from 1997 and 1999, we investigated whether the ItascaNet network in Grand Rapids was making a difference in terms of access to computer technology (Gangl et al., 2000). Linear regression models were estimated for each community with computer use (having ever used a computer) as the dependent variable. While controlling for demographic characteristics commonly associated with the digital divide (income, education, social class, gender, age, and political knowledge) we examined the interaction effects of each characteristic with city (or county). In the 1997 survey data, we found that income predicted computer use in both communities, but to a significantly lesser extent in Grand Rapids. With the 1999 data, income ceased to predict differences in computer use in Grand Rapids, but the income-based divide remained in Detroit Lakes. This evidence suggests that the cooperative community-based approach to electronic networking in Grand Rapids has had a positive impact on improving equality of access in that community, whereas the competitive, market-based approach in Detroit Lakes has so far failed to reduce existing disparities in access.

Historical Perspectives on Community Differences

In our efforts to understand why these two very similar rural Minnesota communities have taken such different approaches to technology diffusion, we have begun to examine the historical and cultural aspects of civic life in each community from the time of their founding in the 19th century. A systematic historical analysis of civic organizations and public participation in these two communities over time is currently underway. However, our preliminary investigation suggests that the differences in civic culture that we have observed in our surveys may have their roots in historical trends. A key facet of Putnam's (1993) theory of social capital is the extent to which social capital is strongly tied to historical patterns. In his extensive case study of Italy, for example, Putnam (1993) located the roots of differences between the northern and southern regions in social patterns originating centuries ago. Likewise, the different approaches these two Minnesota towns have adopted to bring information technology to their citizens may reflect historical differences in cooperation between the public and private sectors and community support for projects providing public goods.

Grand Rapids began as a settlement when Itasca County was formed in 1849. Like other towns in northern Minnesota, including Detroit Lakes, it primarily provided services for farmers and lumberjacks. In contrast to Detroit Lakes, civic organizations and projects have proliferated throughout Grand Rapids' history. At the turn of the century, women's church organizations often sponsored well-attended events, and secret societies and fraternal organizations were popular among the town's residents, with a dozen different clubs to choose from (Boese, 1984). An analysis of youth services in Grand Rapids conducted in the early 1950s documented 39 civic organizations that met regularly in the town, with 14 of these devoted specifically to helping young people (State of Minnesota Youth Conservation Commission, 1952). Grand Rapids also has a long history of successfully supporting local projects to assist the poor. In 1916, for example, local voters approved a $50,000 levy to establish the first county hospital in Minnesota, and in 1917 Itasca County became one of the first in the state to establish its own welfare program (Boese & Cain, 1991).

Although the timber industry played an important role in the origins of many northern Minnesota towns, it took a particularly central role in the Grand Rapids community that it retains to the present day. The Blandin paper mill, which began operation in 1902, has long been a major employer in the city, accounting for about one fifth of the local labor force. The original owner of the mill, C. K. Blandin, professed a strong commitment to promoting the advancement of Grand Rapids and northern Minnesota and to that end established the nonprofit Blandin Foundation in 1941. The foundation has supported a variety of civic groups, public buildings, scholarships, and economic development projects in the region, disbursing $35 million between 1941 and 1991 in Grand Rapids and Itasca County alone (Boese & Cain, 1991). Although the role of the Blandin Foundation in promoting civic life in Grand Rapids has been significant, it cannot single-handedly account for the community's active civic culture. Local organizations and projects that may benefit from the foundation's support also require the ongoing commitment and participation of community members to remain vital. Many projects that received initial funding from the Blandin Foundation have successfully gone on to become self-sustaining through the active support and involvement of community members.

Detroit Lakes was founded in 1868, aided by the Federal Homestead Act, which granted Civil War soldiers 160 acres of land. It quickly grew, becoming a township by 1871, with its economy based mainly on agricultural services. By 1873, it became the home of the "first grain elevator built on the Northern Pacific Railroad west of Duluth" (Wilcox, 1907, p. 344). Although many northern Minnesota communities have turned to tourism in recent decades to revitalize declining local economies, Detroit Lakes did so quite early in the century and has remained oriented toward attracting tourists ever since. As early as 1912, pamphlets were published with the aim of drawing convention visitors to the city.

By the 1920s, a number of associations took an active part in promoting tourism, and events were added to the city's winter carnival with this purpose in mind (Becker County Record, 1971).

Despite the mutual interest of promoting tourism by civic associations and businesses, the history of Detroit Lakes reveals a rather mixed record on public projects oriented toward the local residents. For example, in 1902 the *Detroit Lakes Record* suggested that a lack of civic concern resulted in the failure, due to poor community attendance, of several meetings called to investigate the feasibility of building a municipal electrical plant. "Of one thing there is no doubt and that is that it would be folly to invest in a municipal plant or to make our village government any more cumbersome than it is at present, until our most responsible businessmen are willing to give public affairs that careful attention which alone will insure economical management and success. We are far from that at present" ("Public Meeting," 1902).

Other projects, aimed more directly at those lacking economic resources, also tended to receive little public support throughout Detroit Lakes' history. A county-sponsored food stamp program closed in 1943 after serving only 200 cases. Proposals to issue bonds to build new schools were defeated in 1895, 1969, and 1970, with a 1930 addition to the high school approved only by a narrow margin of 30 votes (Detroit Lakes Centennial Committee, 1971). Exclusively private endeavors, such as the founding of the Detroit Lakes Boys Club in 1958, the first one chartered in the state of Minnesota, were more typical of the civic successes enjoyed by Detroit Lakes.

Focus Group Insights

In addition to our survey research in these two communities, we have periodically conducted focus groups, first in Grand Rapids and later in Detroit Lakes, to assess community members' attitudes on a host of issues related to our study. Such issues have included general opinions about the community and its strengths and weaknesses, the extent of residents' experiences with computers and the Internet and their perceptions of those technologies, and attitudes toward their community's involvement in fostering the availability of information technology. This last component specifically tapped into perceptions and attitudes toward ItascaNet in Grand Rapids and LakesNet in Detroit Lakes. Focus group participants were selected from among respondents who completed the 1997 or 1999 mail surveys. Respondents were initially asked to indicate on a postcard whether they would be willing to participate in a focus group. Survey data were then used to select a sample of willing participants who were diverse in terms of age, gender, and socioeconomic resources.

In summer and winter 2000, two sets of focus groups were conducted in Detroit Lakes and Grand Rapids, with the second set retaining several members of the previous group, in a quasi-panel design. Content analysis of the transcripts of the December focus groups in each community was carried out in which moderators' and participants' comments were coded as reflecting individualistic, interpersonal, or community-oriented issues and concerns. Comments coded as *individualistic* included, for example, references to personal computer use, individual initiative, responsibility, choice, and individual privacy concerns. Comments reflecting *interpersonal* themes included references to computer-mediated interpersonal communication and concerns over decreasing face-to-face communication and increasing social isolation. Comments were coded as *community-oriented* if they made reference to the local community or economy, public institutions, civic organizations, or community concerns such as public access to technology or education. Two members of the research team coded the focus group transcripts for each community using a standard coding scheme. Intercoder rates of agreement were 88.5% for moderator statements and 84.5% for participant statements.

The types of questions and comments made by the *moderators* were consistent across both focus groups, with the majority of comments reflecting community-oriented themes (79% in Grand Rapids; 88% in Detroit Lakes) and the remainder classified as individualistic (21% in Grand Rapids; 12% in Detroit Lakes). Difference of proportions tests show that there are no statistically significant differences between the two communities for moderators' comments. *Participants'* comments did reveal significant differences across the two communities, however. Grand Rapids focus group participants made significantly more community-oriented statements (62%) than their Detroit Lakes counterparts (48%, $p < .05$). Detroit Lakes participants made twice as many comments reflecting interpersonal concerns (14%) as Grand Rapids participants (7%, $p < .05$), reflecting greater concern about social isolation and decreasing face-to-face interaction. The percentage of individualistic comments was not statistically different across the two communities (31% in Grand Rapids, 37% in Detroit Lakes). This quantitative summary of the content analysis thus reflects qualitative differences in the types of issues and concerns raised by residents of these two communities with regard to the social impact of technology diffusion. Excerpts from the focus group discussions also provide insight into the substantive significance of these differences.

In the Detroit Lakes focus group, for example, the issue of providing access to information technology for those who cannot afford it was raised several times by the moderators. Detroit Lakes participants generally liked the free computer access provided by the local public library, although this access is currently limited to two machines with a 15-min time limit. Several participants also suggested that a new community center that is currently under construction should provide similar public computer resources. However, they also expressed the view that technology access was not an obligation of the community and that to the extent that it was provided, the private sector should be relied upon for grants and donations. The following excerpt from the December Detroit Lakes focus group illustrates this viewpoint:

> Moderator: Is there a sense among the people who may not be able to afford to have computers at home or Internet access, that the community has a responsibility to provide those services? To provide free access? Or are you not hearing that kind of thing? It sounds like with the suggestion to make computers available at the community center, that some people think that would be a good idea. But is there, a sort of movement, or a lot of talk about that, or not?
>
> Detroit Lakes (DL) Participant: No, I just thought through a grant they could get it . . . .
>
> DL Participant: This is something private business and service organizations and clubs in town can take over as a project.
>
> Moderator: Sounds like there's some general feeling that it's not a community responsibility—it may be goodwill, but it's not a community responsibility. But I'm kind of curious, why is it not a community responsibility, or for those who might disagree and haven't said much so far, why is it a community responsibility?
>
> DL Participant: No, I don't think so.
>
> Moderator: Why not?
>
> DL Participant: I would think that would be picked up eventually by those various companies. They're interested in putting this out. And we have enough welfare fringes and benefits. I think that for the most part, I think this is something we're capable of doing on our own, or some corporation.

By contrast with the Detroit Lakes focus group, when Grand Rapids participants were asked about opportunities to use computers and the Internet, they readily described a number of community programs, several of which involved ItascaNet. These included computer training classes provided by Itasca Community College and the public school district as well as public access provided by the local library, access that had recently expanded to 30 machines with a new, larger library building. In further contrast to their Detroit Lakes counterparts, Grand Rapids focus group participants readily supported the goal of reducing disparity in information technology access, as the following excerpt demonstrates:

> Moderator: Do you think there are people in this community that are being left behind? Who can't afford computers at home and may not know about the resources that are available?
>
> Grand Rapids (GR) Participant: Absolutely.
>
> (General assent from the rest of the group)
>
> GR Participant: That's the problem with me, I was left behind in school. It took me all my life to get where I am now.
>
> GR Participant: But they weren't doing computers then, you know . . .
>
> GR Participant: No, but I was doing stuff that we were into. You know, it's the same difference whether it's computers or reading or writing, it's the same difference. And, you get the slower ones and somebody's got to take care of them, whether it's computers or what it is, they need help.
>
> Moderator: Who do you think needs to take care of them? Is that the responsibility of the community or the government? Whose responsibility do you think it is to make sure there's not this divide, or that people are not left behind?

GR Participant: The community. Every individual has their own problem, so you have to set up a governmental unit that will do the best they can. You know there's bureaucrats and that, but you know it's not a perfect world. But you have to start someplace and you have to help the ones that need the help. Actually, they will learn, and they'll be interested. It'll take time.

When the possibility of greater community involvement in computer technology was mentioned favorably in the Detroit Lakes focus group, it was by a relative "outsider" to the community, a woman who had recently moved to Detroit Lakes from a larger city in the region and worked in a senior citizens' residential facility. She suggested that there was need for public leadership on this particular issue:

Moderator: You mentioned that you deal with computers every day, kind of all the time. What's your sense about Detroit Lakes? Is there all the opportunity that people want? Is there too much opportunity to use information technology? What do you hear?

DL Participant: Well, I guess in my experience I think, you know I lived in Fargo [North Dakota] before. It used to be the thing. It probably is a little slower here. But that's just from a small town. And I grew up in a small town and it's the same way there. But I think it is catching on. I think what we probably need in Detroit Lakes is some energetic leaders to kind of bring to the limelight of the community what kind of opportunities exist that we can do with the Internet. You know, I would love with my work to set up programs between the schools and the students and my residence, and hooking up on e-mail, on a weekly or monthly basis, where they can communicate and do those intergenerational programming types of things.

This participant also went on to talk about opportunities and her plans to participate in college courses on-line. For the Detroit Lakes focus group, this quickly led to a discussion between the participants over how the Internet may affect social relationships and concerns that on-line relationships might become a substitute for the initiation and maintenance of off-line relationships (McKenna, Green, & Gleason, this issue). This focus on the effects of the Internet on interpersonal communication and patterns of social interaction became a recurring theme in the Detroit Lakes group, as the following exchange illustrates.

DL Participant: The disadvantage is the fact that, people relations, you're losing that. We're becoming so technological that we're forgetting the whole purpose of people.

Moderator: Do you think that's happening even here in Detroit Lakes?

DL Participant: I think that's funny . . . . I taught for 23 years and I think back in the '80s when I got out of teaching, the seventh graders were coming up and getting passes from study hall to go down and work in the computer room. What really fascinated me was how they were absorbed in this thing. And just observing young people today and people in general, I get the feeling almost that people are losing the ability to articulate. I think they spend almost too much time in front of this thing. That they're absorbed and don't have the opportunity to communicate with other human beings. Well, it's not quite that bad. But it's not like a group situation where you sit around and shoot the breeze.

DL Participant: I get all these e-mails. I get all these e-mails with stories over and over from one person, about four of them right in a row. It's like, don't you have a life? Get outside or something!

Several times near the end of the discussion, Detroit Lakes participants were asked about the danger of negative effects from information technology, particularly that of social isolation, and what could be undertaken to alleviate those effects. Their answers were generally individualistic in tone, even when they pushed for more community-centered action. Most respondents ultimately emphasized personal self-control and family responsibility. It is not that Detroit Lakes participants thought of the community as lacking cohesion and civic involvement. As a group they were unanimous in the opinion that Detroit Lakes fared better than many other towns and regions of the country in this regard. Social and community involvement was in fact touted as the appropriate alternative to spending time on-line.

Only one of the Detroit Lakes participants expressed an awareness of the social science–based debate about technology and social isolation (e.g., Kraut et al., 1998; Markoff, 2000). But concerns about the social effects of computers did arise in different ways in each community. In both focus groups, the potential for technology to either isolate people or foster relationships was not asked about directly by the moderator until it was raised first by a participant. In the Detroit Lakes group, such concerns arose rather early in the discussion after the moderators asked about the general effects and availability of information technology. In Grand Rapids, on the other hand, the potential effects of computers and the Internet did not focus on social relationships. Rather, other issues were more central to the discussion, including concern over the availability of pornography over the Internet, privacy concerns, and the use of computers for education and for developing the local economy. It was only at the very end of the Grand Rapids focus group that one of the participants asked other group members about the effects of information technology on social relationships:

GR Participant: I've got a question to pose to the group, just something to think about. How do you feel sitting in front of the computer, maybe back in your computer room, spending a few hours there, compared with picking up the newspaper, sitting in your living room, and your wife is knitting next to you and you're talking about different things that are going on in the paper, the relationship in your family. Are we getting off by ourselves more with computers?

Moderator: What do you guys think?

GR Participant: That hasn't happened in our house.

GR Participant: It hasn't happened in ours either. Everytime I get on the computer I've got the whole family talking . . . .

GR Participant: I think that there are different things, I mean, I wouldn't want to spend the whole day with my husband. *(Laughter)* I'd rather spend the whole day with him than anybody else, but I don't want to spend the whole day with him, because I have my life and he has his life. But there may be some of that, that some people just focus on the computer, but I don't know if anybody here does that.

GR Participant: That's what I've heard, I have friends that they'll be on there til 2 in the morning . . . .

GR Participant: There are people addicted, addicted to the Internet. I mean, it is a problem.

GR Participant: But I think at our house at least, there's a lot of times like when we're planning a vacation or something where we'll go on the Internet, and we'll sit there together and kinda go through it, and look at all the options.

GR Participant: In my family it's improved communications, I'll say hey, come here and look at this.

GR Participant: But it does sound like that sometimes in the newspaper, that you read about people that are just focused on it, and some senior citizens. Actually, it's broadened their lives tremendously, so they don't feel so alone, when actually they are alone in their apartments, but they can communicate. They can't even get out, but they communicate over the Internet. So I don't, I don't know, I think it's like anything else, you know you've got a lot of men that'll just sit and watch football all the time!

The responses by focus group participants in Detroit Lakes and Grand Rapids thus reflect rather different views of information technology and the Internet and help to provide qualitative insights into the potential effects of technology in these two communities. In Detroit Lakes opportunities and choices about how to use such technology tended to be seen in individualistic terms. Access is mainly left up to the free market and possibly private organizations. Detroit Lakes residents were not ignorant of the potential community-based uses for such technology but still viewed technology use primarily in terms of individual choice and responsibility. Social isolation resulting from the use of computer technology was also a concern raised frequently in the Detroit Lakes focus groups. Grand Rapids participants, by contrast, made reference to computer technology in relation to the community more often. They tended to discuss technology use in both individual and community terms, with participants readily agreeing that there is an obligation to provide access to this technology. Fears of social isolation and concerns about the negative impact of this technology on social life were also much more subdued in the Grand Rapids focus groups.

Conclusions

As the evidence reviewed in this article suggests, the two communities we have been tracking over time have been responding in very different ways to the question of how to create and maintain access to information technology. Our survey data to date suggest that the competitive, market-based approach in the community of Detroit Lakes has not been successful in reducing existing disparities in access, whereas in the community of Grand Rapids, income no longer predicts differences in computer use and Internet access. Our preliminary historical analysis of the civic cultures of these two towns also suggests, though not in a systematic sense, that Grand Rapids and Detroit Lakes have in the past adopted different approaches to cooperation between the public and private sectors with regard to a range of other civic issues.

Finally, our focus group analyses in both communities provide additional and more in-depth insights into the nature of the concerns that citizens have about technology diffusion. Importantly, these findings are in line with the insights drawn from our survey database and from our historical analysis. Participants from Grand Rapids were generally more supportive of the goal of reducing the digital divide as it exists in their community. They indeed recognize that such a divide exists and recognize the importance of public leadership in moving the community toward effective solutions. In Detroit Lakes, by contrast, technology access was not seen as a community responsibility, but rather as a matter that the private sector should address more directly. Interesting, from our perspective, were the findings from our focus groups suggesting that participants in Detroit Lakes had more interpersonal concerns about technology diffusion than their Grand Rapids counterparts. There was more concern in Detroit Lakes about social isolation and decreasing face-to-face interaction than there was in Grand Rapids, where participants were much more focused on other community-oriented issues and concerns.

Although our data, as presented in this article, generally address the question of whether Internet access is improving participation and the store of social capital in community life, the data do not directly address the extent to which technology diffusion and Internet access are improving *or* harming patterns of social interaction and social relationships (see McKenna & Bargh, 2000). The data presented here also cannot address the long-term question of whether civic life is enhanced or hindered by the different patterns of technology access and use, though we are currently examining these issues in our ongoing longitudinal project. What our focus groups *do* suggest, however, is the intriguing possibility that extant community structure and levels of social capital may play an important mediating role in understanding the impact of Internet access on social relationships and psychological well-being. Similarly, extant community structure and levels of social capital also may mediate the impact of Internet access on the forms of individual and collective action in a community. Research on the personal and social motivations that dispose people to volunteer and to sustain their volunteerism (e.g., Snyder & Omoto, 2000), for example, suggests that communities with strong social ties and connectivity may be more promotive of volunteerism and other forms of citizen participation than communities characterized by lower levels of social capital (Snyder & Omoto, 2001). Certainly a more complete understanding of these issues should take into consideration the social and political context of Internet access and technology diffusion. Our program of research, especially the next waves of our survey panel study, will, we hope, enable us to examine these latter questions more directly.

References

Anderson, R. H., Bikson, T., Law, S. A., & Mitchell, B. M. (1995). *Universal access to e-mail: Feasibility and societal implications* (RAND Report MR-650-MF). Santa Monica, CA: RAND Corporation.

Ashburner, L. (1990). Impact of technological and organizational change. *Personnel Review, 19*, 16–20.

Becker County Record. (1971). *Centennial papers.* Becker County, MN: Author.

Boese, D. L. (1984). *Papermakers.* Grand Rapids, MN: Blandin Foundation.

Boese, D. L., & Cain, R. R. (1991). *Grand Rapids companion.* Grand Rapids, MN: Grand Rapids Centennial Committee.

Calabrese, A., & Borchert, M. (1996). Prospects for electronic democracy in the United States: Rethinking communications and social policy. *Media, Culture, and Society, 18*, 249–268.

Coleman, J. S. (1988). Social capital in the creation of human capital. *American Journal of Sociology, 94*, 95–120.

Coleman, J. S. (1990). *Foundations of social theory.* Cambridge, MA: Harvard University Press.

Detroit Lakes Centennial Committee. (1971). *100 years of progress: Sod to shoreline.* Detroit Lakes, MN: Author.

Fukuyama, F. (1995). *Trust: The social virtues and the creation of prosperity.* New York: Free.

Gangl, A., Oxendine, A. R., Jackson, M. S., Riedel, E., Sullivan, J. L., & Borgida, E. (2000, July). *The role of community electronic networks in bridging the digital divide.* Paper presented at the 23rd annual scientific meeting of the International Society of Political Psychology, Seattle, Washington.

Guthrie, K. K., & Dutton, W. H. (1992). The politics of citizen access technology: The development of public information utilities in four cities. *Policy Studies Journal, 20*, 574–597.

Kanungo, S. (1997). An empirical study of organizational culture and network-based computer use. *Computers in Human Behavior, 14*, 79–91.

Kawachi, I., Kennedy, B. P., Lochner, K., & Prothrow-Stith, D. (1997). Social capital, income inequality, and mortality. *American Journal of Public Health, 87*, 1491–1498.

Kling, R. (1996). Synergies and competition between life in cyberspace and face-to-face communities. *Social Science Computer Review, 14*, 50–54.

Knack, S., & Kropf, M. E. (1998). For shame! The effect of community cooperative context on the probability of voting. *Political Psychology, 19*, 585–600.

Kraut, R., Patterson, M., Lundmark, V., Kiesler, S., Mukopadhyay, T., & Scherlis, W. (1998). Internet paradox: A social technology that reduces social involvement and psychological well-being? *American Psychologist, 53*, 1017–1031.

La Due Lake, R., & Huckfeldt, R. (1998). Social capital, social networks, and political participation. *Political Psychology, 19*, 567–584.

Markoff, J. (2000, February 16). Portrait of a newer, lonier crowd is captured in an Internet survey [On-line]. *New York Times.* Available: www.nytimes.com/library/tech/00/02/biztech/articles/16online.html

McKenna, K. Y. A., & Bargh, J. A. (2000). Plan 9 from cyberspace: The implications of the Internet for personality and social psychology. *Personality and Social Psychology Review, 4*, 57–75.

National Telecommunications and Information Administration (NTIA). (2000, October). *Falling through the net: Toward digital inclusion: A report on Americans' access technology tools* [On-line]. Available: http://www.ntia.doc.gov

Pickering, J. M., & King, J. L. (1995). Hardwiring weak ties: Interorganizational computer mediated communication, occupational communities, and organizational change. *Organization Science, 6*, 479–486.

Public meeting goes by Detroit. (1902, May 9). *Detroit Lakes Record.*

Putnam, R. D. (1993). *Making democracy work: Civic traditions in modern Italy.* Princeton, NJ: Princeton University Press.

Putnam, R. D. (2000). *Bowling alone: The collapse and revival of American community.* New York: Simon & Schuster.

Rubinyi, R. M. (1989). Computers and community: The organizational impact. *Journal of Communication, 39*, 110–123.

Russell, D., Peplau, L. A., & Cutrona, C. (1980). The revised UCLA Loneliness Scale: Concurrent and discriminant validity. *Journal of Personality and Social Psychology, 39*, 472–480.

Sankar, Y. (1988). Organizational culture and new technologies. *Journal of Systems Management, 39*, 10–17.

Schneider, M., Teske, P., Marshall, M., Mintrom, M., & Roch, C. (1997). Institutional arrangements and the creation of social capital: The effects of public school choice. *American Political Science Review, 91*, 82–93.

Schuler, D. (1994). Community networks: Building a new participatory medium. *Communications of the ACM, 37*, 39–51.

Snyder, M., & Omoto, A. M. (2000). Doing good for self and society: Volunteerism and the pychology of citizen participation. In M. Van Vugt, M. Snyder, T. Tyler, & A. Biel (Eds.), *Collective helping in modern society: Dilemmas and solutions* (pp. 127–141). London: Routledge.

Snyder, M., & Omoto, A. M. (2001). Basic research and practical problems: Volunteerism and the psychology of individual and collective action. In W. Wosinska, R. B. Cialdini, D. W. Barrett, & J. Reykowski (Eds.), *The practice of social influence in multiple cultures* (pp. 287–307). Mahwah, NJ: Erlbaum.

State of Minnesota Youth Conservation Commission. (1952). *Grand Rapids Survey of Youth Services.*

Sullivan, J. L., Borgida, E., Jackson, M. S., Riedel, E., Oxendine, A., & Gangl, A. (in press). Social capital and community electronic networks: For-profit vs. for-community approaches. *American Behavioral Scientist.*

Tsagarousianou, R., Tambini, D., & Bryan, C. (1998). *Cyberdemocracy: Technology, cities, and civic networks.* London: Routledge.

Virnoche, M. E. (1998). The seamless web and communications equity: The shaping of a community network. *Science, Technology, and Human Values, 23*, 199–220.

Wellman, B., Salaff, J., Dimitrova, D., Garton, L., Gulia, M., & Haythornthwaite, C. (1996). Computer networks as social networks: Collaborative work, telework, and virtual community. *Annual Review of Sociology, 22*, 213–238.

Wilcox, A. H. (1907). *A pioneer history of Becker County, Minnesota.* St. Paul, MN: Pioneer.

Wilkinson, R. G. (1996). *Unhealthy societies: The affliction of inequality.* New York: Routledge.

Wilkinson, R. G. (2000). Social relations, hierarchy, and health. In A. R. Tarlov and R. F. St. Peter (Eds.), *The society and population health reader: A state and community perspective* (pp. 211–235). New York: New.

World Bank. (2000). PovertyNet: Social capital for development website. Available: http://www.worldbank.org/poverty/scapital

EUGENE BORGIDA is Professor of Psychology and Law and a Morse-Alumni Distinguished Teaching Professor of Psychology at the University of Minnesota. He is also an Adjunct Professor of Political Science and Co-Director of the Center for the Study of Political Psychology and coeditor of the journal *Political Psychology*. His research and publications are in the areas of social cognition, attitudes and persuasion, political psychology, and psychology and law.

JOHN L. SULLIVAN is Regents' Professor of Political Science and holds the Arleen Carlson Chair in American Government and Politics at the University of Minnesota. He also codirects the Center for the Study of Political Psychology. He has published six books and 70 articles on political tolerance, research methodology, political psychology, and public opinion.

ALINA OXENDINE is a doctoral student in the political science program at the University of Minnesota. She received her BA and MA from Emory University in Atlanta, Georgia. Her research interests include American and comparative politics, political psychology, political culture, and social capital. She serves as editorial assistant for the journal *Political Psychology*.

MELINDA S. JACKSON is a PhD candidate in the Political Science Department at the University of Minnesota. Her research interests include political psychology, public opinion, social identity, and civic participation. She is a National Science Foundation graduate fellow.

ERIC RIEDEL received his doctorate in political science from the University of Minnesota, where he currently serves as a postdoctoral fellow at the Center for the Study of Political Psychology. His research interests include political socialization, civic education, political psychology, and mass political behavior.

AMY GANGL is an Assistant Professor in the Department of Political Science at the University of Colorado at Boulder. She received her doctoral degree in political science from the University of Minnesota. Her research interests include political psychology, public opinion, and political communication.

Journal of Social Issues, Vol. 58, No. 1, 2002, pp. 143–159

Dark Guests and Great Firewalls: The Internet and Chinese Security Policy

Ronald J. Deibert*

University of Toronto

Some believe that the Internet is immune to regulation and is contributing to the demise of the state. Others see the same technology as facilitating surveillance on behalf of states and corporations. To help explore this debate further, this article examines the case of the Internet in China. China—a nondemocratic, authoritarian state—is a "hard case" for those who argue that the Internet cannot be controlled. Even while pushing for the expansion of new information technologies, mostly for economic reasons, China has attempted to maintain strict controls over the Internet. After summarizing the debate outlined above, a review of China's Internet security policies is conducted, and the ways in which prodemocracy activists have attempted to circumvent these policies is examined.

Like previous changes in modes of communication, the expansion of the Internet around the world is bound to affect the "nature" of governance. But in what ways? Some believe that these technologies are, by their very nature, immune to regulation and are fast contributing to the demise of the state. This predominate view, most often associated with so-called cyber-libertarians, argues that the Internet is a fundamentally new technology that will inevitably stifle government restrictions, destroy hierarchical forms of authority, and free up the exchange of information and ideas worldwide (see Barney, 2000; Pye, 1990; Toffler, 1980; Wriston, 1992).

This *unfettered* view of Internet communications has two dimensions. The first emphasizes the contradiction between the global spread of the Internet and the territorial organization of political-jursidictional spaces. Although states may

*Correspondence concerning this article should be addressed to Ronald J. Deibert, Department of Political Science, University of Toronto, Toronto, Ontario, Canada M5S 3G3 [e-mail: r.deibert@utoronto.ca]. Thanks to Ces Ruggiero, Mike Downie, John Bucyk, and Adam Samarillo for research assistance and to the Program on International Studies in Asia for facilitating field research in China.

desire or even enact regulations against certain types of Internet communications, their authority extends only to their territorial borders, making enforcement problematic. A prime example of this dynamic was the German government's attempts in 1996 to prohibit German citizens from accessing neo-Nazi Web sites found on the Compuserve computer network. Although the Germans were successful in pressuring Compuserve to remove the sites in question, people from around the world "mirrored" them dozens of times over, not in support of the site's content, but rather to demonstrate the futility of the German regulations (Froomkin, 1997).

The second dimension emphasizes the unique properties of the Internet qua technology. It is now well known that the Internet was intentionally designed as a *distributed network* with no central node or hierarchy in order to facilitate communications in the event of a nuclear war (Baran, 1964). Indeed, the unique properties of the Internet as a distinct mode of communication center on its dispersed, packet-switching architecture, which breaks up information, sending it along numerous trajectories to be reassembled at its destination. Such a distributed architecture, by its very design, is difficult to control, since there is no central node or gateway through which all information passes. The many peer-to-peer file sharing systems that have been established on the Internet offer a prime example of this particular dimension. Through these systems, computer users can store and share information without having the information contained in a single node or on a single server. What makes these technologies such an apt illustration of the second critical dimension of the Internet regulation argument is that, short of the state entering into individual homes, offices, and business and seizing computers attached to the Internet that are capable of engaging in peer-to-peer communications, there is apparently no way to control such distributed communication networks or prevent them from operating effectively (Kuptz, 2000). Together, these Internet characteristics seem to point in the direction of a coming "borderless" world where state control is increasingly obsolete.

The unfettered perspective on the Internet does not go unchallenged, however. Others see the very same technology facilitating greater surveillance and control on behalf of both states and corporations (Gandy, 1993; Whitaker, 2000). Although they recognize that the Internet has spread far and penetrated societies deeply, these more pessimistic observers stress the manner in which tools of surveillance embedded in Internet communications allow for a much greater invasion of personal privacy. Noting the way in which the use of electronic communications leaves traces that can be compiled and compared as a record of people's activities, some go so far as to argue that we are living in an "electronic panopticon" (Lyon, 1993). Stemming from a long theoretical tradition that sees technology as a force for, rather than against, centralized control and authoritarianism (Ellul, 1964; Huxley, 1932; Mumford, 1970), this perspective portrays the Internet and other new media as forces helping to solidify and extend, rather than undermine, state control.

To help push this debate further, abstract generalizations must give way to careful empirical analyses of individual cases. To this end, this article examines the case of the Internet in China. Along with only a handful of other states, China has the requisite mix of communication, commerce, and security policies to speak directly to this debate. Like many authoritarian regimes, China maintains strict controls on free speech and political competition and has vigorously applied regulations on Internet communications to such ends. It has imposed draconian restrictions on Internet access for much of China's citizens and has handed down severe penalties for those caught breaching them. Unlike many other authoritarian regimes, however, China has also energetically expanded its communications infrastructure and promoted the Internet primarily for economic reasons. To put it simply, China wants to be able to reap the benefits of new information technology while at the same time minimizing and even eliminating its negative political effects—something the "unfettered" perspective suggests cannot happen. The potential sustainability of China's policies is the subject of this article.

The article first outlines China's promotion of information technology over the last decade, demonstrating China's vigorous adoption of new information technologies primarily for economic reasons. It then examines China's security policies designed to control Internet communications and sustain centralized, authoritarian control. Finally, a discussion of some of the ways in which we might determine whether China's Internet security policies will succeed or fail is offered. Given the available evidence to date, this article concludes that although Chinese Internet security policies may work in the short run to slow down or impede dissident movements, in the long run they will likely fail. Although such a conclusion falls short of fully supporting the "unfettered perspective," it does suggest that the material properties of the Internet, as well as broader economic and political structures, place considerable constraints on China's security policies.

A Networked Empire

Beginning in 1979 with the accession to leadership of Deng Xiaoping, the Chinese state has pursued a concerted strategy of increasing industrial and technological modernization. Although this strategy has not gone so far as to fundamentally affect the basic one-party nature of the regime, it has moved China dramatically away from the isolation and economic autarky characteristic of the Mao leadership period. One of the centerpieces of Deng's reforms was an "opening to the outside world" to encourage expanded trade, foreign direct investment, and cultural exchanges (Joseph, 1993). This strategy of openness, along with a tentative and periodically reversed decentralization of economic decision making, has had an enormous impact on the Chinese economy. In 1978, 80% of the Chinese population had incomes of less than US$1 per day; by 1998 that number had been reduced to just 12% (World Bank Country Data, 2001). China's gross domestic product has quadrupled since 1978, making it the second largest economy in the world after the United States (CIA World Factbook, 2000).

Widely recognized as critical to this modernization strategy has been the development of telecommunications, computers, and communication networks. China has invested heavily in its information infrastructure at the same time as it has encouraged foreign investment in key information-related sectors, a strategy promoted by China's communist rulers ("Special: Wired China," 2000). Starting from the ground up, China has quickly built a vast information infrastructure. Since 1993, 16 high-capacity fiber-optic lines have been laid in a grid across China, connecting its major urban centers. Because of this development, over 80% of China's communications backbone and 40% of its urban networks now use fiber-optic cables (Wong, 1999). Telephone lines have accordingly been laid by the state telecommunications monopoly, China Telecom, at an astonishing rate. In 1990, there were fewer than 10 million telephone lines in China; today, there are over 125 million, with 2 million more being laid every month ("Special: Wired China," 2000). Although small in comparison to the overall population, there are 110 million telephone users in the country, second in absolute terms only to the United States (Wong, 1999). Mobile phone use has skyrocketed as well, from 5 million users in 1995 to over 65 million today ("Qualcomm," 2000; "Special: Wired China," 2000). Other media, such as satellite and cable television and radio, have seen an analogous explosion.

The Internet has been one of the cornerstones of the information technology explosion in China ("Chinese Minister," 2000; Lawrence, 1999). China first established a connection to the Internet in April 1994 through the China Science and Technology Network (China Internet Network Information Center, 2001), making it the 71st state to establish a connection to the Internet. It is estimated that there were around 23,000 Chinese who had restricted Internet access at the time connection was established, all government officials and select academics (Court, 1998). Since then, the number of Chinese who have regular connections has grown exponentially, to the point where today it more than doubles on average every 6 months. Official government statistics on Internet usage have been supplied by the China Internet Network Information Center since November 1997 (China Internet Network Information Center, 2001). Recent reports indicate that by the end of July 2000 there were 16.9 million Internet users in China, up from 8.9 million at the end of 1999, 4 million in July 1999, and 2.1 million at the end of 1998.

China has also increasingly seen the type of cross-media convergence common in Western countries whereby mobile and wireless communications devices are made Internet accessible, increasing the penetration and depth of the Internet ("Chinese Try Internet," 2000). Foreign investment in Internet startups and Web portals in China has been vigorous in anticipation of China's entry into the World Trade Organization (WTO), in spite of the present unclear investment regulations ("Asian Trade," 2000; "China-Interview," 2000). Indicative of the ferment, more than 540,000 applications to register Internet domain names were received by the CNNIC in the first two days that it began accepting them. Sixty thousand applications were received in the first hour alone ("Rush for Chinese," 2000). With all of this investment and growth, some forecasts anticipate that China will have the largest numbers of Internet users in the world by 2005, surpassing the United States (Lu, 2000).

Empire of Regulations

Although it is clear that China has aggressively adopted information and communication technologies as a cornerstone of its economic development, it has not done so without attempting at the same time to minimize their undesired consequences. Such seemingly contradictory swings between liberalization and control have long characterized China's relationship with the outside world, with encouragement of trade and investment periodically giving way to strong official sentiments of "antiforeignism" (Chan, 1994, p. 70). China's attitude toward the Internet is but the latest episode in this long-running saga, seemingly combining both sentiments simultaneously in a single phase. These regulations and actions have become, on the surface at least, increasingly strident.

Controlled Access: The Great Firewall

One of the main ways in which China is attempting to control the Internet is by, in effect, *territorializing* China's computer networks into a large national *intranet* whose connections to the global Internet are then restricted and funneled through only a few major nodes. By contrast, most countries' access to the Internet is distributed through multiple national nodes and a combination of private and public providers. In China, however, all of the numerous Internet service and content providers that compete with each other must, in connecting to the global Internet, make their connections through one of four state-controlled corporations (Higgins and Azhar, 1996). Such funneled access provides the most important outer layer of control and the basis for "firewall" technologies to be implemented that ostensibly block controversial or politically undesirable Web sites.

As far back as 1995, China began to employ such filtering technologies and tunneling strategies to block what it called "spiritual pollution" (Smith, 1995, p. B3; "China Tells Internet," 1996). Although the sites that are blocked tend to vary, they typically include foreign news sites, such as those of the *Economist*, the Cable News Network, and the *New York Times*; human rights sites, such as those for Amnesty International and Human Rights Watch; and dissident or prodemocracy Web sites, such as VIP Reference or those maintained by the religious group Falun Gong.[1]

---

[1] I tried to access all of these sites from an Internet café in Shanghai but found that they were blocked by the firewall.

In an ironic twist to the forces of globalization, major Western corporations, such as Sun Microsystems, Cisco Systems, and Bay Networks, have all contracted with the Chinese state to develop such firewall technologies (Barme and Ye, 1997).

These macro-level controls are then complemented by more micro forms of controlled access. Although anonymous e-mail accounts are technically available (as will be discussed below), the conventional way to get an Internet account involves the completion of lengthy and intrusive application forms that go to both the local and regional Public Security Bureaus. There is also an Internet Access Responsibility Agreement that must be completed, in which the user pledges not to use the Internet to threaten state security, reveal state secrets, or communicate information that "endangers the state, obstructs public safety, or is obscene or pornographic" (Barme and Ye, 1997). Internet service and content providers, including Internet cafés, must register with the Public Security Bureau as well.

Restrictions on Content and Internet Activity

Complementing the constraints on access are regulations that define the type of content that can be posted on the Internet by providers and users. China has adopted a very broad set of rules that outline appropriate Internet content. Beyond the type of prohibited content discussed above, it is also illegal to "spread rumours," "hurt China's reputation," "harm ethnic unity," or "advocate cults and feudal superstitions" (Rennie, 2000). Such lack of specification provides the state with wide latitude to react to any type of Internet activity that it finds threatening or contrary to the regime's political interest. Not surprisingly, a number of arrests have been made under these rules, resulting in sharp sentences for the accused.

In January 1999, 30-year-old Lin Hai was sentenced by a Chinese court to 2 years in jail for charges of "inciting the overthrow of the state." Lin was accused of sending 30,000 e-mail addresses to the underground electronic newsletter *Dacankao* (translated as VIP Reference) based in Washington, D.C. ("China Jails," 1999; Faison, 1999). In addition to the 2-year sentence, Lin was stripped of his "political rights" for a year. Other arrests include that of Qi Yanchen, a dissident who was arrested while preparing to redistribute copies of VIP Reference ("China Engineer," 2000). Qi was sentenced to 4 years in prison ("Unappealing Case," 2000). Huang Qi was arrested in June 2000 for creating a human rights Web site commemorating the Tiananmen Square protests ("China Arrests," 2000). In August 2000, a high school computer teacher, Jiang Shihua, was arrested for posting information critical of the Chinese Communist Party on the Internet from the Web café that he owns ("Chinese Internet Café," 2000). Five hundred twenty-five of Shanghai's 1,000 Internet cafés were shut down in September 2000 for allowing youth to play "morally corrupting" computer games ("China Cracks Down," 2000; "China to Shut Down," 2000). In May 2000, the China Finance Information Network Web site was temporarily shut down and fined for publishing information "that damaged the government's image" ("China Shuts Down," 2000). To facilitate the content controls, Internet service providers are required to maintain for 60 days records of all of the information that has been posted on the Web sites and all of the users who have connected with their servers (Smith, 2000a).

More recently, content controls were strengthened further by placing restrictions on what type of foreign content Chinese sites could post. Commercial Web sites are banned from hiring their own reporters or from publishing "original" content. The only news that can be posted on the Internet by these sites is that which is provided by the official government information organs, such as the *People's Daily* or the Xinhua state news agency ("Special: Wired China," 2000). One example of this type of content control is the Web site ChinaByte. ChinaByte technology and financing is provided by Rupert Murdoch's News Corp—a Western corporation— but the actual content for the site is provided by China's *People's Daily* (Leonard, 1997). Such content controls are meant to further winnow the type of information that China's citizens can access.

Aggressive Policing and Countermeasures

Beyond restrictions aimed at controlling Internet activities, China has also taken several aggressive steps of its own as an active participant in the Internet. Like many Western industrialized states, China has attempted to minimize the flood of global content by actively subsidizing and in some cases producing its own content. One site contains anti–Falun Gong propaganda and is entitled "Expose the Fallacies of Falun Gong; Safeguard the Well-Being of the People" (Williams, 1999). China's Propaganda Department has recently ordered "ideological education" to be spread on Internet chatrooms and Web sites by cadres and officials ("China: Net Laws," 2000).

More dramatically, China's intelligence, police, and armed forces have all adopted tactics that involve an active presence of the state in the Internet—in some cases, violating communication networks in other state jurisdictions. Such tactics were demonstrated in late 1999 when Internet service providers that hosted Falun Gong's Web sites were crippled by a series of distributed denial-of-service attacks. Attacks on providers in Missouri, the United Kingdom, and Canada were then traced back to accounts belonging to the Internet Monitoring Bureau of the Public Security Ministry, the Beijing Application Institute for Information Technology, and the Information Center of Xin An Beijing (Williams, 1999). The attacks suggest that recommendations that China develop a "cyberwar" capability, as expressed in the *Liberation Army Daily*, may actually have been carried out (Lombardo, 1999).

Closer to home, it was reported in 1999 that the Ministry of State Security had connected monitoring devices to the computers of major Internet service providers based in Beijing in order to monitor e-mail traffic (Laris, 1999). As with the filtering technologies described above, major Western technology corporations were said to be actively involved in helping China to develop an Internet surveillance capacity along these lines (Fackler, 2000). These technologies have apparently been instrumental in the identification and detention of "more than 15,000 suspected criminals . . . wanted for murder, smuggling, counterfeiting, and theft" (Laris, 1999). To help manage the surveillance, at least 20 provinces and cities have set up special Internet police forces to "administrate and maintain order" on the Internet ("China Says Provinces," 2000).

Encryption Regulations

Lastly, like many other states, China has made attempts to control the use of encryption technologies. Sophisticated encryption products are widely distributed on the Internet, with some of the best being virtually uncrackable by even the most advanced system of supercomputers in the employ of state intelligence organizations. Encryption technologies thus undermine the ability of states to monitor communications, and in particular to intercept e-mail traffic. In 1999, regulations were issued by the State Encryption Management Commission banning Chinese companies or individuals from using foreign encryption software.[2] Although some exceptions were later made under pressure from foreign corporations, as will be explained below, individual Chinese still must use Chinese-approved encryption products and must also register with the commission to use them.

Together, these four major areas of security policy form the bulwark of China's attempt to exploit, while controlling, Internet technology. The trajectory of these policies has been in the direction of greater control, with more vigorous policing measures and aggressive offensive actions. These two seemingly contradictory interests suggest that China is indeed a "hard case" for the unfettered view of Internet communications outlined above.

Networked Constraints

In spite of the exaggerated claims often made on behalf of its democratizing power, it is clear that the Chinese state is not going to collapse under the weight of the Internet any time soon. The formidable measures taken above ensure that at the very least a climate of caution and even self-censorship pervade Internet culture in China. Moreover, the lack of a well-developed civil society and tolerance for open opposition means that social movements with interests opposed to the regime tend to be segregated and often work through clandestine channels. These conditions

---

[2] By State Council Order No. 273, "Commercial Use Password Management Regulations," October 15, 1999. See Crypto Law Survey, at http://cwis.kub.nl/~frw/people/koops/lawsurvy.htm

complement China's restrictive policies. But can such policies be sustained indefinitely? Political, economic, and technological constraints suggest that they will at the very least face numerous impediments as the Internet deepens and expands.

One major constraint concerns the long-term incompatibility of China's restrictive Internet policies and its strong interest in promoting information and communication technologies through trade, foreign direct investment, and industrial policy. Since 1979, China has introduced liberalizing measures meant to move its economy in a capitalist direction, and as outlined above, these policies have begun to transform the Chinese economy. Promotion of e-commerce has become a central feature of this transformation. In Shanghai, for example, the streets are festooned with billboard upon billboard of commercial advertisements for cellphones, pagers, software, Web portals, and computers. In many shopping districts, computer hard drives, monitors, peripherals, and software quite literally spill out onto the street.

As this sector continues to expand as the central processor of China's new economy, regulations that have either the intended or unintended consequence of disadvantaging their competitiveness will be unpopular. A good example concerns China's encryption policies. As discussed above, in January 2000, China enacted stiff encryption laws that prohibited foreign corporations from using anything but the encryption products sanctioned by the state. Multinational corporations depend on the ability to communicate information across distributed networks securely and so have developed sophisticated firewall, virus protection, and encryption technologies. Yet China's laws would have had them substitute state-sanctioned versions for their own technologies—something that would put corporations in a position of uncertainty with respect to local competitors and the privacy of their business communications ("Controlling the Net," 2000). The regulations were assailed, with U.S trade officials and corporations in particular engaging in aggressive lobbying efforts. Microsoft Corporation was among the chief concerned as it was forced to delay the launch of its Windows 2000 operating system in China because of the new restrictions. Faced with this pressure and the peril of fleeing foreign investment, China eventually relented. The government issued a revised statement that allowed foreign corporations to include encryption in their technologies and products (Oleson, 2000).

A similar set of pressures will likely manifest themselves in the area of China's most recent regulations concerning foreign content and direct investment in Internet industries. The new regulations prohibit Internet content providers from posting foreign news on their Web sites as well as sharply restrict foreign ownership and investment in Internet-related industries and services in China. Almost immediately after the restrictions were announced, the values of Chinese Internet companies listed on American stock exchanges sharply plummeted. Many companies were quickly facing bankruptcy as foreign venture capitalist pulled their investments out in the face of the uncertainty. The content provisions are particularly troublesome for many of China's most popular Web portals, like Sina and Sohu, which rely on news to attract surfers ("New Internet Regulations," 2000). One Web portal operator remarked that there has been a dramatic change in foreign investors' enthusiasm for China's Internet startup market: Before, "if you said you were a Chinese dot.com they would lead you by the hand through the door. Now if you say you are a Chinese dot.com, generally they say 'Oh we don't do that anymore'" (Wingfield-Hayes, 2000). One Western executive said that his company would "pull out of our joint venture and move equipment, the brand name and foreign staff overseas" ("China Bans," 1999).

These business pressures will be coupled with those coming from states and international organizations once China enters the WTO. As part of the trade-off necessary to be considered for membership in the WTO, China agreed to cut tariffs on imports, let foreign companies sell goods directly to Chinese in the banking and telecommunications services sectors, and allow foreign ownership stakes in Internet companies up to 49% the first year, to be followed by increases in following years (Kurtenbach, 2000). Once embedded in the WTO, China's ability to discriminate between foreign and domestic investment—one key element of its Internet control strategy—will be severely hampered. Moreover, such pressures will likely have a kind of "ratchet effect" on China's regulatory climate: As liberalization encourages increased foreign direct investment in a variety of economic sectors, the pressures to liberalize further the country's rules concerning Internet control will increase, which in turn will encourage yet more liberalization and investment (see Cerny, 1995).

Another major constraint on China's Internet security policy is a less indirect one that concerns both the skills of China's Internet users and the distributed nature of the Internet itself. Although the number of China's Internet users is still small relative to the entire population, there is nonetheless a very formidable pool of technological expertise. Some of this expertise derives from the formal training that has naturally accompanied the rapid growth of the information and communication technology sectors in China over the last 20 years. But some of it derives from a less formal source: what might be called the Chinese tradition of hacking. Media piracy has a long history in China, reaching back at the least to a thriving black market for pirated television programs and movies in the 1970s and 1980s (see Chan, 1994; Ho, 1995). With the introduction of the Internet, such skills have been applied to pirated software, CD-ROMs, and DVDs, all of which are widely—even openly—available in public markets throughout China.[3] One remarkable illustration of this phenomenon was the government-sponsored

---

[3] During my visit to Shanghai, not only did I see dozens of pirated CDs containing movies and software for sale in public booths, but I also witnessed a full Internet café with scores of students watching movies (presumably pirated copies) that were still in their first run in theaters in Canada and the United States.

anticorruption movie, *Life and Death Choice, pirated copies* of which were being shown in state-run cinemas around China (Smith, 2000b). In spite of the relatively small number of Internet users overall, in other words, this is not a neophyte culture of technology.

Although such well-honed technology skills are most often employed for business and entertainment, they have been eagerly applied to dissident movements as well. The Internet has supplied the infrastructure for a variety of social movements operating either on the fringes or the outside of the law in China. For example, the outlawed Falun Gong religious group uses e-mail campaigns to communicate with its members as well as to organize them for protests and demonstrations. The group stunned China's government when on April 25, 1999, 10,000 of its members showed up in silent protest at Zhongnanhai, the seat of power of the Communist Party ("Falungong Founder's," 1999). When the exiled leader was asked how, in spite of a lack of formal organizational structure in China, such a coordinated protest could take place, he replied that "[t]hey learned it from the Internet" ("Falun Dafa," 1999). Another dissident set up an infamous Web site critical of the Communist regime called New Culture Forum. When the state shut down the site, the operators of the site moved it offshore and continued to maintain it through false e-mail accounts registered at numerous Internet cafés.[4] To this day, the operators continue to remain anonymous and harangue the government through postings on the Web site.

As that last example suggests, what makes the Internet such a potent tool of organization is that the activities of these social movements are coordinated not just within China but beyond as well. Many dissident organizations' main Web nodes are actually located abroad, out of effective reach of the Chinese authorities. The appendix to this article provides a list of some of the most important of these Web sites, including some of their main features. As described, many of them contain regularly updated news, information, and discussion forums in which dissidents within China can communicate with each other and with Chinese abroad. Although China's firewall technology routinely blocks direct access to these types of nodes, Chinese citizens can still receive information and communicate with them in several different ways.

First, firewalls can be easily sidestepped by the use of proxy servers, which reconnect users to sites that are officially blocked by the state. A good example is the proxy servers that are maintained by a news site, *China News Digest,* which each day provides a list of thousands of different proxy servers that are available to Internet users in mainland China as well as detailed instructions on how to sidestep China's firewall technology (China News Digest, 2001). As the list varies daily and includes many university servers from countries around the world, the Chinese authorities simply cannot block all or even many of them without in effect cutting themselves off from outside academic and scientific contacts.

---

[4] The site is mirrored here: http://www.hrichina.org/Xinwenming/index.htm

Second, many dissident organizations based outside of China send their publications and newsletters en masse to thousands of e-mail addresses in China. Such a "spamming" strategy allows dissidents that receive the e-mail a plausible denial.[5]

Significantly, then, although the Internet does play an important part in organizing the activities of dissident groups based within China, the links that have been established between dissident organizations in countries outside of China are equally, if not more, important. As these organizations operate outside of the restrictions of the Chinese state, they are able to provide Chinese citizens with unfettered access to news and information that otherwise would be blocked. And although firewalls are formally employed to block access to them, in practice such firewalls are easily sidestepped by net-savvy Chinese users. In the long run, the establishment of these transnational social networks among political and religious dissidents may be the most important way in which the Internet directly facilitates and enlarges prodemocracy activism within China.

Conclusion

The picture presented in this article, then, is of a rather mixed character. On the one hand, China has aggressively adopted severe restrictions on the type of communications that can take place over the Internet. These range from control over access to the Internet, to content controls, to aggressive offensive measures designed to propagate information conducive to the regime while undercutting dissident activities. Such policies will undoubtedly curb democratic change in China, engendering a climate of apprehension and self-censorship. They may also actually facilitate surveillance on behalf of the state, as computer networks are applied to the law enforcement, military, and intelligence areas. In light of these measures, simplistic assertions about the inherently democratizing potential associated with the unfettered perspective of the Internet need to be seriously qualified.

Yet at the same time, these more strident policies have come alongside equally assertive policies designed to facilitate the penetration and extension of new information and communication technologies into all sectors of Chinese society, primarily for economic reasons. As these technologies permeate China, it will be increasingly difficult for the state to effectively regulate the more strident control policies outlined above. Economic pressures from global market forces, particularly those both within and beyond China who have a stake in encouraging foreign direct investment, will likely tend to push China further in the direction of greater liberalization, as evidenced by the change in China's encryption regulations. Further changes are likewise expected in rules governing foreign ownership in Internet industries once China enters the WTO.

---

[5] The VIP Reference newsletter operates in this manner. See http://come.to/dck/

At the same time as economic pressures are pushing China's networks in a more liberal direction, transnational social networks are actively developing links that move in and around China's firewalls. Although these networks face enormous coercive pressures within China, their links established abroad are formidable and show no signs of dissipating. Moreover, China's technologically sophisticated Internet population is able to use the Internet to access these offshore nodes in spite of China's firewall restrictions.

Taken together, these two forces present a considerable set of environmental constraints against the long-term viability of China's Internet control strategy (cf. Kalathil & Boas, 2001). Even though the bulk of China's Internet elite today wants simply to make money, rather than overthrow the regime, doors are being opened, and path dependencies created, that cannot easily be reversed. Transnational social, political, and economic networks are beginning to permeate Chinese society, burrowing deeper and wider into more sectors of life. As each day goes by, the economic and practical costs of reversing these changes will be increasingly high, and the incentives to move in a more liberal direction will be great. In the end, however, forestalling rather than prohibiting democratic political change may be all that the regime realistically desires.

The significance of these conclusions for the theoretical debates outlined above is also mixed. Clearly, material factors within the media and Internet impose limits on the types of policies that governments can implement. But it seems equally clear that inventive and determined government officials are capable of utilizing technology in such a way as to minimize politically negative effects, at least in the short run. Such a mixed picture suggests that a more nuanced theoretical approach to the relationship between the Internet and state control is required, one that gives due attention not only to the properties of specific technologies qua technologies, but also to the political, economic, and geographic context in which they are deployed (see Deibert, 1997).

This conclusion has implications for how far the Chinese case be generalized to other countries and potential "hard" cases, such as Singapore and Malaysia. Singapore, being a small island state governed by an undemocratic regime with a strong interest in information technology and global commerce, displays an interesting mix of variables. Like China, it has tried to walk a fine line between promoting new information and communication technology and controlling free speech and dissent. Yet unlike China, its population is much more tightly confined within a small geographic space, creating circumstances much more favorable to state control and surveillance. It may, therefore, have more success than China in minimizing the undesirable impacts of the Internet. Malaysia, with a slightly less undemocratic regime, larger geographic area, and five times the population of Singapore, may experience more difficulty. How far we can safely generalize the case of China to other potential "hard" cases depends, then, not just on the technology, but on the circumstances of each particular state.

Appendix: Prodemocracy Web Sites with Links to Dissident Movements in Mainland China

Beijing Spring	http://www.bjs.org/	Prodemocracy online journal; links to other journals; history of Chinese Alliance for Democracy
China Democracy Party (Overseas)	http://www.freechina.net/cdp/	Global membership with links to mainland dissidents; links, news, discussion forum
China Democracy Party (China)	http://members.tripod. com/~chinadp/	Chinese version of the overseas site; links to dissident publications and forums
Chinese Democracy and Justice Party	http://come.to/dcjp/	Exiled dissident democracy party; links, forums
China Spring	http://www.chinaspring.com/	On-line journal and newsletter written by Chinese dissidents and distributed via e-mail
Chinese Community Information Center	http://www.ifcss.org/ccic/	Forum for the Independent Federation of Chinese Students and Scholars; chat rooms, proxy servers, links
City University of Hong Kong Student Union	http://www.cityu.edu.hk	
Hong Kong Alliance in Support of Patriotic Democratic Movement in China	http://www.alliance.org.hk/	
Hong Kong Journalists Association	http://www.hkja.org.hk/	
Hong Kong University Students Association	http://www.hku.h,/hkusu/	
Hong Kong Voice of Democracy	http://www.democracy.org.hk	
Inner Mongolian Peoples Party	http://www.innermongolai.org/	Political party constituted by exiled dissidents; press releases, FAQ, links
Global Petition Campaign for the 10th Anniversary of June 4th	http://www.june4.org/	Coalition of exiled dissidents and prodemocracy groups; links, news, chat rooms
Global Petition Campaign (Chinese version)	http://www.june4.net/	
Laogai Research Foundation	http://www.laogai.org/	China labor watch and human rights group, headed by Harry Wu of the Free China Movement
Alliance of Hong Kong Chinese in the US	http://www.ahkcus.org/	
China News Digest	http://www.cnd.org/	Popular news site on China
Democratic China Magazine	http://www.chinama.org/	Prodemocracy e-journal
Democracy for China Fund	http://www.6-4.org/	
Free China Movement	http://www.freechina.net	Coalition of Chinese dissidents based in the mainland and around the world; links, discussion forum

Human Rights and Democracy in China Information Centre	http://Speednet.net/~frankwet	Gateway in Hong Kong for Chinese Internet users to access blocked prodemocracy sites
Human Rights in China	http://www.hrchina.org	New York based organization run by Chinese human rights activists; links, resources; forums
Tunnel	http://www.freechina.net/tunnel	Mainland China's underground e-journal; publishes dissident works and distributes via e-mail to the mainland; news, links, newsletterrs
VIP Reference Dacankao	http://come.to/dck	E-magazine circulating among Chinese students, scholars, and activists

References

Asian trade: How do you say Yahoo in China? (2000, May 29). *Barrons*.

Baran, P. (1964). On distributed communications networks. *IEEE Transactions on Communications, CS-12*, 1.

Barme, G., & Ye, S. (1997, May 6). The great firewall of China [On-line]. *Wired*. Available: http:/www.wired.com/wired/5.06/China_pr.html

Barney, D. (2000). *Prometheus sired: The hope for democracy in the age of network technology*. Toronto: UBC.

Cerny, P. (1995). Globalization and the changing logic of collective action. *International Organization, 49*(4), 595–625.

Chan, J. (1994). Media internationalization in China: Processes and tensions. *Journal of Communications, 44*(3), 70–88.

China arrests Internet editor [On-line]. (2000, June 7). *BBC News Online*. Available: http://news.bbc.co.uk/hi/english/world/asia-pacific/newsid_780000/780787.stm

China bans Internet investment [On-line]. (1999, September 15). *BBC Monitoring*. Available: http://news.bbc.co.uk/hi/english/business/the_economy/newsid_448000/448305.stm

China cracks down on Internet cafés [On-line]. (2000, February 2). *BBC News Online*. Available: http://news.bbc.co.uk/hi/english/world/asia-pacific/newsid_628000/628432.stm

China engineer who helped dissident newsletter is freed [On-line]. (2000, March 6). *Digital Freedom Network*. Available: http://dfn.org/focus/china/linhai.htm

China Internet Network Information Center [On-line]. (2001). Available: http://www.cnnic.net.cn/

China-interview: German firm guiding $2 billion into China telecoms [On-line]. (2000, May 27). *Reuters*. Available: http://news.muzi.com/ll/english/1085771.shtml

China jails engineer in first Internet dissent case [On-line]. (1999, January 20). *Reuters*. Available: http://209.75.88.206/eforum/messages/325.html

China: Net laws set to combat "Web crime." (2000, October 26). *South China Morning Post*.

China News Digest [On-line]. Available: http://www.cnd.org/

China says provinces setting up Internet police [On-line]. (2000, August 5). *Reuters*. Available: http:www.tibet.ca/wtnarchive/2000/8/8_7.html

China shuts down financial Web site [On-line]. (2000, May 15). *Digital Freedom Network*. Available: http://drn.org/focus/china/cfinet.htm

China tells Internet users to register with police. (1996, February 15). *Wall Street Journal*, p. A11.

China to shut down half of Shanghai's Internet cafés. (2000, September 28). *China News Digest*.

Chinese Internet café owner arrested. (2000, August 24). *Digital Freedom Network*.

Chinese minister says e-commerce part of globalization strategy [On-line]. (2000, June 11). *BBC Monitoring*. Available: http://news.bbc.co.uk

Chinese try Internet phone services. (2000, June 2). *Los Angeles Times.*
CIA World Factbook [On-line]. (2000). Available: http://www.odci.gov/cia/publications/factbook/index. html
Controlling the Net [On-line]. (2000, January 31). *Digital Freedom Network.* Available: http://dfn.org/ focus/china/netregulations.htm
Court, R. (1998, March 11). Excite follows Yahoo in China [On-line]. *Wired: News.* Available: http:// www.wired.com/news/business/0,1367,12665,00.html
Deibert, R. J. (1997). *Parchment, printing, and hypermedia: Communication in world order transformation.* New York: Columbia University Press.
Ellul, J. (1964). *The technological society.* New York: Vintage.
Fackler, M. (2000, November 7). The great fire wall of China? [On-line]. ABC News.com. Available: http://www.abcnews.go.com/sections/tech/DailyNews/chinanet001108.html
Faison, S. (1999, January 21). China sentences Internet entrepreneur to 2 years in jail. *New York Times,* p. C7.
Falun Dafa and the Internet: A marriage made in Web heaven [On-line]. (1999, July 30). *The China Matrix Perspective.* Available: http://www.virtualchina.com/matrix/perspective/index.htm#next
Falungong founder's arrest sought as China keeps up anti-sect blitz [On-line]. (1999, July 29). *Agence France Presse.* Available: http://asia.yahoo.com/headlines/290799/news/933262500-9072915301.newsasia.html
Froomkin, M. (1997). The Internet as a source of regulatory arbitrage. In B. Kahin and C. Nesson (Eds.), *Information policy and global information infrastructure* (pp. 129–163). Cambridge, MA: MIT Press.
Gandy, O. H., Jr. (1993). *The panoptic sort: A political economy of personal information.* San Francisco: Westview.
Higgins, A., & Azhar, A. (1996, February 5). *The Guardian,* p. 9.
Ho, K. (1995). *A study into the problem of software piracy in China* [On-line]. Master's thesis, London School of Economics. Available: http://www.info.gov.hk/ipd/piracy.html
Huxley, A. (1932). *Brave new world.* London: Granada.
Joseph, W. (1993). China. In J. Krieger (Ed.), *The Oxford companion to the politics of the world* (p. 131). New York: Oxford University Press.
Kalathil, S., & Boas, T. (2001). *The Internet and state control in authoritarian regimes* (Working paper no. 21). Carnegie Endowment.
Kuptz, J. (2000, August 10). The peer-to-peer network explosion [On-line]. *Wired.* Available: http:// www.wired.com/wired/archive/8.10/p2p_intro.html
Kurtenbach, E. (2000, October 16). Investors eye China's Internet market. *Columbian.*
Laris, M. (1999, August 4). Beijing turns the Internet on its enemies. *Washington Post,* p. A1.
Lawrence, S. (1999, March 4). China surf's up. *Far Eastern Economic Review.*
Leonard, A. (1997, February 27). Chairman Rupert's little red bucks [On-line]. *Salon.* Available: http:// www.salon.com/feb97/21st/murdoch970220.html
Lombardo, H. (1999, August 3). Chinese military seek to train cyberwarriors [On-line]. *AsiaInternet News.* Available: http://asia.internet.com/asia-news/article/0,,161_650911,00.html
Lu, P. (2000). Internet development in China [On-line]. *Virtual China.* Available: http://www. virtualchina.com/infotech/analysis/chinanet-cnnic-7.html
Lyon, D. (1993). An electronic panopticon? A sociological critique of surveillance theory. *Sociological Review, 41*(4), 653–678.
Mumford, L. (1970). *The pentagon of power.* New York: Harcourt Brace Jovanovich.
New Internet regulations to control Internet news service. (2000, November 9). *China News Digest.*
Oleson, A. (2000, March 14). China reverses encryption regulations [On-line]. *Virtual China.* Available: http://www.virtualchina.com/archive/news/mar00/031400-cryptoreg-alo-jst.html
Pye, L. (1990). Political science and the crisis of authoritarianism. *American Political Science Review, 84*(1), 3–19.
Qualcomm still on China's radar [On-line]. (2000, October 9). *Wired: News.* Available: http://www. wired.com/news/business/0,1367,39343,00.html
Rennie, D. (2000, October 4). New clamp on Internet by China [On-line]. *Daily Telegraphy (London).* Available: http://news.telegraph.co.uk/news/main.jhtml?xml=/news/2000/10/04/wchina04.xml
Rush for Chinese Net names [On-line]. (2000, November 10). *China.com.* Available: http://english. china.com/cdc/en/home/news/0,1073,18187-100000,00.html

Smith, C. (1995, July 5). China's state firms to get some access to global Internet. *Wall Street Journal*, p. B3.

Smith, C. (2000a, October 5). Piracy a concern as China trade opens up. *New York Times*, p. A1.

Smith, C. (2000b, October 4). Tough new rules don't faze Chinese Internet start-ups. *New York Times*, p. C2.

Special: Wired China. (2000, July 22). *Economist*, pp. 24–28.

Toffler, A. (1980). *The third wave*. Toronto: Bantam.

Unappealing case [On-line]. (2000, October 2). *Digital Freedom Network*. Available: http://dfn.org/focus/china/qiyanchen-appeal.htm

Whitaker, R. (2000). *The end of privacy*. New Press.

Williams, M. (1999, August 2). Falun Gong war explodes online [On-line]. *CNET News*. Available: http://hongkong1.cnet.com/briefs/news/asia/19990802ao.html

Wingfield-Hayes, R. (2000, October 4). Tough times for China's dot.coms [On-line]. *BBC News*. Available: http://news.bbc.co.uk/hi/english/world/asia-pacific/newsid_956000/956404.stm

Wong, B. (1999). *Improving Internet access in China* [On-line]. Digital Freedom Network. Paper presented at the Computers, Freedom and Privacy 1999 Conference. Available: http://www.dfn.org/Voices/Asia/china/chinanet.htm

World Bank Country Data [On-line]. (2001). Available: http://www.worldbank.org/html/extdr/regions.htm

Wriston, W. (1992). *The twilight of sovereignty: How the information revolution is transforming our world*. Toronto: MacMillan Canada.

RONALD J. DEIBERT is Associate Professor of Political Science at the University of Toronto, specializing in media, technology, and world order. He is the author of *Parchment, Printing, and Hypermedia: Communication in World Order Transformation* (New York: Columbia University Press, 1997) as well as articles in *International Organization, European Journal of International Relations, International Studies Perspectives*, and *Review of International Studies* on topics ranging from space technology to civic activism on the Web. He is currently completing a manuscript for a book, *Network Security and World Order*, on the politics of Internet security.

Journal of Social Issues, Vol. 58, No. 1, 2002, pp. 161–176

E-Research: Ethics, Security, Design, and Control in Psychological Research on the Internet

Brian A. Nosek* and Mahzarin R. Banaji
Harvard University

Anthony G. Greenwald
University of Washington

Differences between traditional laboratory research and Internet-based research require a review of basic issues of research methodology. These differences have implications for research ethics (e.g., absence of researcher, potential exposure of confidential data and/or identity to a third party, guaranteed debriefing) and security (e.g., confidentiality and anonymity, security of data transmission, security of data storage, and tracking participants over time). We also review basic design issues a researcher should consider before implementing an Internet study, including the problem of participant self-selection and loss of experimental control on the Internet laboratory. An additional challenge for Internet-based research is the increased opportunity for participant misbehavior, intentional or otherwise. We discuss methods to detect and minimize these threats to the validity of Internet-based research.

The potential of the information highway to advance understanding of psychological science is immense, and it is likely that the Internet will decisively shape the nature of psychological research. Yet as any researcher who has attempted to use the Internet to obtain data will have discovered, a host of methodological issues

Correspondence concerning this article should be addressed to Brian Nosek, Department of Psychology, Harvard University, William James Hall, 33 Kirkland Street, Cambridge, MA 02138 [e-mail: bnosek@wjh.harvard.edu]. We thank Katelyn McKenna for sharing ideas that were directly incorporated in this article and Susan Bouregy for discussions about Internet-based experiments. This research was supported by National Science Foundation grants SBR-9422241, SBR-9422242, SBR-9709924, and SBR-9710172, and National Institute of Mental Health grants MH-41328, MH-01533, and MH-57672 to M. R. Banaji and/or A. G. Greenwald.

161

require consideration because of differences between standard laboratory research and Internet-based research concerning research methodology. They concern the treatment of participants, the security of the data that are transmitted and obtained, and the internal and external validity of the data. In this article, we identify and review selected issues concerning (1) conducting ethical research on the Internet, (2) personal and data security, (3) experimental design, and (4) experimental control. We raise these issues only insofar as they concern Internet research with an emphasis on on-line experimental and quasi-experimental design. For each methodological issue raised, some potential solutions or strategies are offered.

Ethics

The absence of an experimenter engaged in face-to-face interaction with the participant removes the most obvious source of coercion that has been a source of concern in psychological experimentation. The removal of this concern is a nontrivial benefit of Internet-based research and should play an important role in the cost versus benefit analysis of a research program. Here, we focus on the threats to ethical treatment of participants that can potentially affect Internet-based research. Three differences between Internet and standard laboratory research have implications for ethics: absence of a researcher, uncertainty regarding adequate informed consent and debriefing, and potential loss of participant anonymity or confidentiality. These aspects of Internet research will have a direct influence on the practices of informed consent, debriefing, research with (and without) children, and the protection of privacy on the Internet.

In any study, Internet-based or otherwise, participants ought to be given enough information to judge whether they wish to participate. In Internet laboratories, the manner in which informed consent is obtained is especially important because of the inability of an experimenter to respond to adverse reactions while the experiment is underway. Consent forms should be especially clear and accompanied by FAQs (frequently asked questions) that anticipate potential questions and concerns.

Debriefing

Internet participants could involuntarily end participation in the event of a computer or server crash, a broken Internet connection, a program error, or even a power outage. Participants might also voluntarily end participation because of boredom, frustration, confusion, being late for class, not wanting to miss a favorite television show, or hearing the footsteps of an approaching supervisor. Whatever the cause, early withdrawal from a study is a threat to ensuring adequate debriefing.

There are several options available to an Internet-researcher to enable debriefing even if participants leave the experiment early:

1. Participants could be required to enter an e-mail address at the beginning of a study. Debriefing statements could later be e-mailed to the participant. (This option is not available in studies that assure full anonymity.)

2. A "leave the study" button, made available on every study page, would allow participants to leave the study early and still direct them to a debriefing page.

3. The program driving the experiment could automatically present a debriefing page if the participant prematurely closes the browser window.

In face-to-face debriefings, researchers can make idiosyncratic adjustments for participants who have found the experience unsettling. A number of strategies are available to the Internet researcher to accommodate debriefing requirements that may vary across participants:

1. A list of FAQs that address participant concerns immediately and provide feedback that those concerns are normative, even expected.

2. Debriefing and FAQs should be engaging, making it more likely that the participant will appreciate the purpose of the study and the importance of psychological research.

3. Researchers can offer participants an e-mail address to which to send their questions and concerns about the study.

4. The researcher can be available in a chat room following participation to interactively address concerns or answer questions. In this type of design, the study might be made available only when the researcher is on-line.

Protection of Children

Internet research designed to use children as participants should proceed with care similar to that in standard laboratory settings. A more difficult issue for Internet research is controlling participation in research *not* designed for children. Whereas the participation of an 8-year-old (even a 16-year-old) is not likely to pass unnoticed in a standard laboratory, "catching" such participants on the Internet can be difficult. Asking participants to report their age may be sufficient to remove minors from data analysis, but it is not sufficient to prevent them from completing the study itself. There are, however, strategies available to minimize the opportunity and/or likelihood that children will participate:

1. Design decisions for an experimental Web site should maximize its appeal to adults while simultaneously minimizing its appeal to children. This might be

as simple as avoiding cartoons or popular-culture images that attract children or as involved as gearing the site description and text toward adults.

2. Participant recruiting could target adults by advertising only in adult-dominated list-servs, chat rooms, Web sites, and other places.

3. A password for participation could be required that is available only through adult-targeted advertisements or direct invitation.

4. Experimenters could implement an "adult check" system. Such systems require individuals to register with a centralized database by providing some evidence that they are 18 or older.

U.S. regulations have been developed to protect the privacy of children under the age of 13. Internet researchers should review these instructions before implementing their own projects, particularly the Children's Online Privacy Protection Act. Resources are available at http://www.ftc.gov/bcp/conline/pubs/online/kidsprivacy.htm; http://www.ftc.gov/bcp/conline/edcams/kidzprivacy/resources.htm; http://www.ftc.gov/ogc/coppa1.htm; and http://www.ftc.gov/bcp/conline/pubs/buspubs/coppa.htm

Protecting Participants

The preceding discussion suggests that researchers must pay attention to a different set of issues in Internet research compared to those in standard laboratory paradigms. That does not, however, mean that protecting participants is more difficult in Internet research. In fact, there may be better guarantees for participant protection in Internet research. For instance, the physical absence of a researcher decreases situational demands to remain in an experimental situation that is uncomfortable or unrewarding. Although explicitly coercive tactics are not likely to pass review by ethics committees, implicit situational pressures in most research designs (such as politeness norms) may well discourage participants from prematurely discontinuing participation. The physical absence of a researcher in Internet study designs eliminates these social demands to continue participation, thereby allowing participants greater freedom to withdraw. This fact should not lead investigators to place greater responsibility on the participant to self-regulate participation, but rather to make good use of this added advantage in ensuring the ethical treatment of participants (for additional discussion on Internet research ethics, see Frankel & Siang, 1999).

Security: Protecting Participant Privacy

Many experimental designs do not require identifying information from the participants. In this case, a number of factors indicate that Internet research can guarantee anonymity even more effectively than standard laboratory research.

First, the data can be encrypted, rendering them meaningless to any third party that might intercept them in transit between the participant's machine and the server. Additionally, if no identifying information is collected, the only piece of information that could possibly be used to identify a participant is the Internet Protocol (IP) address. This information typically accompanies data transmitted from the participant's machine to the server, but a researcher can choose not to record this datum. Even IP addresses do not identify information for many Internet surfers. For one, IP addresses identify machines, not individuals. Also, most Internet service providers use floating IP addresses, which identify a particular machine only for the course of a single session. For users who connect to the Internet through such providers, the IP address will change each time they log on. Even so, a small proportion of users have a single machine with a fixed IP address by means of which they can reliably be identified as the "owner" of that machine. Because of this, the IP address must be considered identifying information. Even if IP addresses do not identify a single machine, they can often be used to identify the school, company, or location from which the connection occurred.

There are many types of research designs, however, that do require identifying information. The Internet does afford a perception of anonymity, but in some circumstances that perception may be false. Three elements of Internet research require consideration for protection of confidentiality: data transmission, data storage, and poststudy interaction with participants.

Data Transmission

In an Internet study, there is a small but real possibility that the data will be intercepted by a third party. The standard approach for dealing with this possibility when conducting a Web page–based study is to implement secure server line (SSL) technology. SSL is an encryption technology that encodes information from the client machine to make it meaningless if it is intercepted in transit. If this technology is out of reach (because of cost or sophistication), simpler methods of encryption may effectively protect participant confidentiality. For example, responses to survey questions could be transformed by an algorithm, leaving the researcher to reverse the transformation during analysis. Also, questionnaire items could be given identifying labels that, even if intercepted in transmission, are meaningless to anyone but the researcher. Finally, separating transmissions of identifying information from transmissions of experimental data can increase the assurance of confidentiality. For example, demographic data could be collected with one questionnaire and all experimental data collected with a second questionnaire, with only a randomly assigned identification number to associate them. In survey research conducted through e-mail, it is a simple matter to save responses separately from the e-mail addresses and other identifying information provided in the headers that contain identifying information.

Data Storage

Although only the most intrepid of data burglars may be able to gain access to a laboratory's locked filing cabinet, data stored in files on an Internet-connected server are significantly more vulnerable. The procedures for securing data vary extensively across server designs, so techniques for maintaining strong security of stored data will not be reviewed here. Even so, Internet researchers should be sure to investigate the procedures necessary for securing data on their servers.

Internet Sampling

Internet Samples: Greater Diversity

The Internet has a clear sampling advantage for populations that are difficult to access because (1) the sample is difficult to bring to a laboratory, (2) the population is small, or (3) group members are difficult to find. In addition, although participant recruitment is often constrained to a local community, without leaving the office, Internet researchers from the South can collect samples from the North, psychologists from Japan can sample Nisei and Issei in the United States, and Asians and Asian Americans can be simultaneously sampled via a Web site set up in England.

To date, efforts comparing Internet and laboratory samples find them to show comparable results for a variety of experimental effects (Birnbaum, 1999, 2000; McGraw, Tew, & Williams, 2000). Even so, potential sampling biases should be taken seriously if the researcher intends to claim generalizability from the sample to the population.

Recruiting Particpants for Internet Research

Whatever the needed sample, the method of recruiting will have a strong impact on who chooses to participate. Who participants are will depend on two features of participant recruitment: the accessibility of the study and the type of advertising.

Accessibility. Internet researchers have three options for the availability of a study for participation: open, specific, and invited accessibility. Open access refers to studies open to whoever is able to find the Web site. *Open accessibility* studies have the advantage of sampling from the broadest pool possible but are disadvantageous to the extent that it is difficult to control the type of sample that ultimately chooses to participate, not to mention the nonrandom nature of the sample.

Specific accessibility studies constrain participation to individuals who meet specific selection criteria assessed before beginning the study. For example, researchers interested in age bias among elderly people might have participants who visit their Web site complete a preselection questionnaire with age as one of the preselection questions. Participants meeting selection criteria would be assigned to the age study, whereas others would be assigned to an alternative study or dropped. The specific design also enables a reduction in self-selection biases. A Web site administering multiple studies can advertise itself at a general level (e.g., psychology studies) rather than specifically recruiting for a specific topic (e.g., age attitudes). If random assignment to a study does not occur until after the participant agrees to participate, then selection bias is reduced. However, like any study, attention should be paid to disclosing enough information so that participants can make an informed choice about whether they wish to participate.

A final accessibility option is a more private or *invited accessibility* design. To control participation, researchers can contact a randomly selected sample of participants (for example, from among those who take part in on-line forums for the elderly) and provide each individual with a unique access code and a link directing him or her to the Web site. Only those with viable access codes would then be admitted to the experimental area of the Web site, so those who simply surf onto the site would not be eligible for participation. This procedure also allows the researcher to verify that each participant is engaged in the study on only one occasion. Additional assurance can come from the use of small files called "cookies" that can be stored on user machines. These can be an effective means of tracking visits to a Web site from individual machines. However, users have the option of setting their browsers to reject cookies, rendering them ineffective.

Recruiting. Researchers interested in attracting as many people to their research Web site as possible will often use a *widespread* recruitment method. Widespread recruitment can be as easy as registering the site with some popular search engines (e.g., Excite). A more intensive (and costly) recruitment effort might involve advertising with ad banners at popular Web sites with general appeal (e.g., www.cbs.com). Despite the fact that these methods are the most popular ways to promote a Web site, they are not necessarily the most effective at netting traffic. Simply posting a Web site may not be sufficient to generate adequate samples quickly. Researchers interested in widespread recruitment of participants for an e-mail-based survey might simply post the survey in hundreds of newsgroups and list-servs.

Becoming "viral" is often considered the most effective means for generating traffic to a Web site. Becoming viral depends on having a Web site that is interesting enough that visitors are likely to forward the address to friends. This behavior results in exponential growth in Web site traffic. For example, in November 2000 an artist at www.pixelspill.com produced humorous "proposed Florida ballots" poking fun at the 2000 presidential election debacle in Florida. Showing significant viral spreading, daily traffic at his Web site went from 1,700 to 35,000 to 263,000 in 3 days. Similarly, individuals may forward an e-mail survey to friends who might also be interested in participating.

Although widespread recruiting offers the best opportunity for recruiting a large and diverse sample, it does come with a significant risk: loss of control in the content of advertising for the site. When a research Web site is widely advertised, and especially when it becomes viral, links to the Web site set up by others may present misleading information that biases the sample choosing to visit through that link. For example, the authors of this article maintain a Web site on which participants can measure their implicit attitudes and implicit knowledge of social groups, individuals (political candidates), and themselves (Nosek, Banaji, & Greenwald, in press). Significant press coverage of the site opening and a viral response to the site content led to substantial traffic such that, 3 years after opening, the site averages over 700 hits per day. However, a subset of links to the Web site suggests that the implicit measures reveal "true" preferences (i.e., the task is a lie detector), a claim not endorsed by the researchers or espoused at the Web site. Even though the researchers did not write or control these advertisements, they still operate as recruiting tools. If widespread, these types of advertisements could affect both the types of individuals who decide to participate and the invalid expectations of those participants upon arrival.

Targeted advertising is another recruitment method that can help to increase the researcher's control over who hears about the study and how the study is described. In targeted advertising, particular groups of interest are contacted directly. For example, messages to newsgroups or chat rooms about auto repair are likely to generate samples interested in auto repair. Targeted advertising, if accompanied by password access or other screening, guarantees that a Web site will be visited only by people contacted directly.

Conclusions for Internet sampling and recruiting. Internet samples are likely to underrepresent populations that have low levels of access to the Internet (e.g., minorities, the poor). The challenges to generalizability posed by Internet samples place some limits on Internet research. Nonetheless, in this regard, the challenges for Internet research are similar to the challenges of all experimental research paradigms. The Internet can be a boon to theory testing in psychology: Large samples can increase the power of tests and allow more confident interpretation of null results, special populations are more accessible, and experimenter bias is minimized.

Web-Based Experimental Design

Creating an Effective Lab Setting

Aronson, Ellsworth, Carlsmith, and Gonzales (1990) described four essential components for the creation of an effective laboratory setting: (1) *coherence*: each event should appear to be an integral element of the study, (2) *simplicity*: avoid unnecessary complication, (3) *involvement*: participants should never lose interest in the study tasks (also known as "impact"), and (4) *consistency*: the design should contribute to the *creation of the same basic state* in all participants (e.g., similar mood, distractions in the environment, and cognitive load). These elements are as important for Internet research as they are for any other type of design.

The absence of an experimenter introduces some challenges for the coherence and simplicity of Internet-based designs. Although such absence significantly minimizes researcher bias, it increases the likelihood of misunderstanding. Any confusion will lead the participant either to discontinue participation or to incorrectly complete the experimental materials. Also, without a researcher present, it is more difficult to communicate the cover story. Live researchers are able to adapt a script in order to maintain study integrity, but the Internet typically does not allow flexibility in this regard. Finally, live researchers can catch problems in the design quickly, especially if the problems lie in the cover story or instructions. In Internet research, feedback about a manipulation or instruction that "just isn't working" is not readily available. As a consequence, greater effort will be needed in Internet research to ensure that the instructions are coherent, simple, and similarly interpreted by all participants.

Maximizing experimental impact. In standard laboratory research participants typically appear at a laboratory at a designated time, are greeted by an experimenter, given verbal instructions, and shown into a room expressly designed for the experiments. These features of the experimental setting assist in creating the appropriate signals for setting up the research environment. Unfortunately, none of these signals is available in Internet research. Effective Internet studies have to utilize other means to maximize experimental impact. In short, participants should be made aware of what they will gain, as well as give, by participating. There is no definitive prescription on how to increase the impact of an experimental design in Internet research. The procedural variations that will maximize experimental impact will vary significantly with the nature of the study.

Standardizing the experience for participants. The traditional laboratory environment is usually designed to minimize distracting information and to create the same basic state in all participants. Most laboratory walls are bare, chairs are generally plain and lacking cushy comfort, and colors are neutral and bland. Unfortunately, psychologists do not have keys to Internet participants' homes and offices to reproduce that venerable, if sterile, ambiance. The variation in environments during Internet research participation is likely to lead to much greater variability in states of the participants compared to standard laboratory settings. Internet participants might participate in any variety of environments—at home, in the office during a coffee break, or in an Internet café at 3 A.M. Also, these participants might complete the study alone, with a group of friends, while holding a baby, while talking on the phone, while listening to music, or while smoking marijuana (only a very small minority will likely be doing all five at once). The variation in environments is a challenge to researchers trying to create the same basic state in participants.

Some strategies for creating the same basic state (or at least control for variation in state) on the Internet include (1) presenting a list of "requirements" for completing the research, including items such as "be in a quiet place," "reserve 15 min to complete the task," and "close other programs"; (2) having all participants complete a warm-up task designed to get participants involved and focused on the study (and, perhaps, standardize participant states); and (3) having a list of questions at the end of the study asking participants to report various distractions (e.g., "were there other people in the room while you completed this study?"). Extra effort to create a similar state among participants will pay off by increasing the power of the experimental design.

Maintaining Experimental Protocols

Components of studies that are relatively straightforward to control in a traditional laboratory become remarkably difficult to control in a Web-based laboratory. For example, the following are events that are unlikely to occur during a standard laboratory study but could easily occur during an Internet study: (1) immediately following a priming induction, the participant could be distracted with a phone call and stop participating for 15 min before returning to finish the study; (2) in a study with a surprise memory task, a participant could return to the original list by hitting the back button on the browser; or (3) after finishing a study, a participant might decide to participate in the same study again. A selection of strategies for dealing with these types of threats to the procedural integrity of Internet studies is reviewed below.

Timing

Many studies depend on completion of the measures in a fixed order and within a specified period of time. Without any safeguards, Internet participants could discontinue participation in the middle of a study only to finish it minutes, hours, or even days later. Controlling the amount of time available for each section of a study is straightforward if an applet (a small program designed to run over the Internet) is used, because deadlines and time limits can be programmed directly into administration of the materials. However, the easiest and most commonly used approach for presenting and collecting information is HTML (Hypertext Markup Language) forms. These forms are easy to produce and have the advantage of being familiar to Internet users. However, some additional design considerations are needed to maximize experimental control when using HTML. Timing details might be handled with some of the following strategies:

1. Include a specific instruction at the beginning of the study stating the minimum and maximum amount of time needed to complete the study.
2. Include a time stamp in the data collected with HTML forms. Participants can be included or excluded based on the time difference between the submission of the various forms the study.
3. Code the HTML page to automatically forward to a different page after a specified period of time. If that time expires before the participant submits his or her data, the participant can be removed from the study.

Direction and flow. Another issue for Internet studies is the back and reload buttons on Internet browsers. These buttons allow the participant to self-navigate through a study, which is generally undesirable for experimental design. The use of an applet (or similar technology) can eliminate problems of self-navigation because the opportunity to back up can be excluded. However, for users of HTML, a couple of other options exist:

1. A study can be run in a window that does not contain a back or reload button, so that participants do not have an easy means of self-navigating through the study.
2. With use of some programming to help manage presentation of HTML pages such as CGI (common gateway interface) scripts or JSPs (Java server pages), a "tilt" mechanism can be established that ejects participants from the study who attempt to go back or reload.

Multiple data points for single individuals. Experimental design requires that data assumed to be from different participants are clearly identified as such. This requirement disallows participation of a given individual more than once in a single study. Complete prevention of multiple submissions from single individuals is difficult. Even so, a variety of solutions are available to prevent or disallow multiple submissions from a single individual. Below is a selection of strategies for detection or prevention of multiple submissions:

1. During informed consent, ask participants if they have participated in the study before.
2. HTML forms typically, by default, record the IP address of the source. In data analysis, multiple submissions from the same IP address can be removed. In addition to sacrificing anonymity, this solution is not ideal for two reasons. First, acceptable data will be needlessly removed. There are many instances in which data from the same IP address is not coming from a single individual:

a proxy server may service multiple computers from a single IP, a floating IP address may connect to two different computers on two different occasions, and more than one individual may use a single computer. Second, using only one instance from each IP address does not guarantee that all multiple submissions from individuals are removed. Participants could participate in a study from more than one IP address by either using more than one machine, or more likely, using a machine that connects to the Internet with a floating IP address.

3. Require participants to register (have a log-in process). This could be as simple as requiring participants to enter a piece of identifying information (e.g., e-mail address) or as complex as setting up an individual "account" with log-in name and password. With this information, a participant ID tag could be attached to each questionnaire and only the first instance from any participant would be used, or, more impressively, a CGI script could be written to prevent participants from participating in studies that they have already completed.

Deceptive Participants: Intentional or Otherwise

In any method of research, identifying participants who are deliberately or un-intentionally responding inaccurately can be challenging. More attention may need to be paid to this issue for Internet research because of the decreased accountability associated with lack of an experimenter and absence of situational cues increasing the impact of the experimental situation. Most techniques for identifying deceptive participants in the standard laboratory can be applied for use in Internet research. In this section, we discuss deceptive practices that are unique to Internet research and identify some methods for deception detection that may be particularly useful for Internet designs.

Two or more participants appearing as one. In most experimental designs, a participant is defined as a single individual, not the collective thoughts of two or more individuals. The Internet, however, can be a group activity. Families, friends, or colleagues may enter an Internet study and take turns responding to questions or discuss them as a group. This type of behavior may be rare. Even so, there is no way to guarantee that it does not occur. To minimize the likelihood that groups of individuals are counted as a single participant, a researcher can (1) state clearly in the instructions that the study is for an individual and not for a group, (2) use marker questions more than once in a study, such as birth date or height (because these are more likely to change if more than one individual is completing the study), and (3) explicitly ask participants to report how many individuals were involved (or were in the room) when the study was completed.

Detecting intentional deception. The Internet allows individuals to conceal their identity and even to adopt an alternative one (e.g., a 20-year-old might pose as a 70-year-old in a chat room). Also, lack of an experimenter may decrease accountability to such a degree that participants "play" with the study and make up responses that do not accurately reflect their beliefs or identity. Below are some strategies that may help to detect deceptive responding:

1. Repeat questions with definitive answers (e.g., birth date) or that are not likely to change during the course of a study (e.g., occupation). Deceptive responders may be detected by changes in responses to these types of questions.

2. Ask questions in which one of the provided responses is unlikely to be true. Participants who are not taking the study seriously or who are trying to be deliberately deceptive may be more likely to select odd responses. (Excessive use of this strategy may backfire and decrease the impact of the experimental design.)

3. Require that the participant supply identifying information at the beginning of the study. (This approach should be treated with care because of the loss of anonymity and the importance of confidentiality.)

4. Give participants the opportunity to correct their responses by showing them their responses a second time before recording them.

Additional Web-Based Research Methodologies

The Internet is a burgeoning resource, not only for experimental and quasi-experimental research, but also for other research methods, including surveys, natural and archival research, and interviews or participant observations. In this section we briefly discuss some issues of particular relevance to these methods.

Surveys

There are two ways to conduct surveys on the Internet. The first is to set up a Web page containing the survey. Currently, SPSS software is available to create an on-line survey from a data file and automatically encode survey responses into that data file. The methods discussed earlier in this article apply to recruitment, security, and control for this type of survey. Surveys can also be carried out through e-mail, and different techniques are required for reaching specific participant populations. A variety of virtual communities including newsgroups, chat rooms, and MUDs (multiple-user dialogues) offer a space for people with specific interests (e.g., clam baking), traits (e.g., narcoleptics), or qualities (e.g., identical twins) to gather and converse. For psychologists, these groups offer unique opportunities to access survey data from specific participant populations. For instance, one can easily obtain a random sample of active newsgroup participants, as the e-mail address for each user is contained in the header of his or her newsgroup posting, and surveys can then be mailed out to a randomly selected subset of users. However, with this method it is not possible to obtain a random sample of newsgroup readers who do not actively participate in discussion. Some electronic groups (e.g., Yahoo) provide e-mail addresses for all newsgroup members whether they are active participants or not, enabling random selection. In other cases, users are not identified by their e-mail addresses but rather by a chosen nickname and must be contacted individually to participate. (For a more detailed description of newsgroups, chat rooms, and MUDs and surveying techniques within them, see McKenna & Bargh, 2000).

Natural and Archival Research

The Internet presents a unique opportunity to study individuals and groups within a naturalistic setting without the presence of an intrusive researcher. One can, for instance, observe and code the verbal content of newsgroup posts or chat room comments to test hypotheses about individual or group behavior. One can easily collect data on individuals' or groups' reactions to naturally occurring historical events such as wars, elections, or public figures. One useful feature of the Internet is that one need not wait for events to happen, nor wait months while data are being collected, because archives of newsgroup posts are available through several sources. The most popular source is Google Groups at http://groups.google.com/. Messages dating back to 1995 are organized within a searchable database by the newsgroup, date, and time the article was originally posted, as well as by author. Archived posts for the more newly formed Yahoo electronic groups also exist. However, Yahoo does not provide a searchable database for these posts, which appear within digests specific to each group. Thus, the researcher must first identify the groups, and then individually work through the digests and articles within them.

Interviews and Participant Observation

Both in-depth interviews and participant observation can be profitably combined with the other methodologies discussed above, as well as with one another. Glaser, Dixit and Green (this issue) opted for the latter in their study of racist behavior within chat rooms associated with White supremacist groups. Interviews carried out with users in chat rooms and MUDs or conducted through e-mail exchanges can provide valuable insight and rich data about a given phenomenon. The free-response format of interviews provides information that preconfigured surveys and other data collection methods might miss. Insights gleaned through interviews can be empirically tested by including survey questions addressing such issues or through laboratory or Web page–based experimental designs. Participant observation can also yield rich data and is a method that can be particularly beneficial to survey research. Taking part in the groups under study aids in gaining the trust of the members of those groups and can substantially increase response rates. The researcher must take care, however, to attend to principles of research ethics and not to influence or otherwise affect the responses participants make to the survey by his or her presence in the group. Researchers should participate in no more than half of the groups under study, so that the possibility of participant bias can be checked by comparing survey results from groups in which one participated with those from groups in which one did not. Similarly, as in the study by Glaser et al., when one combines interviews with participant observation, it is important that the interviewer(s) be blind to the hypotheses being tested to reduce the chance of eliciting biased responses.

Conclusion

The challenges of the Internet should not deter investigators from taking advantage of this powerful medium for discovery and education. Yet the responsibility for conducting research that meets the highest standards for ethical treatment and advances science is first and foremost the responsibility of scientists themselves. Expenditure of the requisite resources for research design at the onset of a research enterprise will have major benefits for the ultimate quality of experimental designs and scientific discoveries.

References

Aronson, E., Ellsworth, P. C., Carlsmith, J. M., & Gonzalez, M. H. (1990). *Methods of research in social psychology*. New York: McGraw-Hill.

Birnbaum, M. H. (1999). Testing critical properties of decision making on the Internet. *Psychological Science, 10*, 399–407.

Birnbaum, M. H. (2000). *Psychological experiments on the Internet*. San Diego, CA: Academic.

Frankel, M. S., & Siang, S. (1999, June). *Ethical and legal aspects of human subjects research on the Internet*. Workshop report for the American Association for the Advancement of Science, Washington, DC.

McGraw, K. O., Tew, M. D., & Williams, J. E. (2000). The integrity of Web-delivered experiments: Can you trust the data? *Psychological Science, 11*(6), 502–506.

McKenna, K. Y. A., & Bargh, J. A. (2000). Plan 9 from cyberspace: The implications of the Internet for personality and social psychology. *Personality and Social Psychology Review, 4*(1), 57–75.

Nosek, B. A., Banaji, M. R., & Greenwald, A. G. (in press). Harvesting implicit group attitudes and beliefs from a demonstration Website. *Group Dynamics.*

BRIAN NOSEK is a graduate student at Yale University working under the supervision of Mahzarin Banaji and currently an exchange scholar at Harvard University. He earned his BS from California Polytechnic State University, San Luis Obispo, in 1995 with a major in psychology and minors in computer science and women's studies.

MAHZARIN R. BANAJI received her BA from Nizam College in India in 1976 and her PhD from Ohio State University in 1986. From 1986 to 2001, she was a Professor of Psychology at Yale University. She is now the Richard Clarke Cabot Professor of Psychology, at Harvard University. She has served as Associate Editor for the *Journal of Experimental Social Psychology*, *Psychological Review*, and the *Encyclopedia of Psychology*. She has received a Guggenheim Foundation Fellowship, the James McKeen Cattell Fellowship, and the Gordon Allport Prize for Intergroup Relations.

ANTHONY G. GREENWALD received his BA from Yale College in 1959 and his PhD from Harvard University in 1963. Before moving to his present position as Professor of Psychology at University of Washington, he was a faculty member at Ohio State University from 1965 to 1986. He holds a Research Scientist Award from the National Institute of Mental Health, is a fellow of the Society of Experimental Psychologists, and received the Donald T. Campbell Award from the Society for Personality and Social Psychology. He was previously Editor of the *Journal of Personality and Social Psychology* and Chair of the Society of Experimental Social Psychology.

Journal of Social Issues, Vol. 58, No. 1, 2002, pp. 177–193

Studying Hate Crime with the Internet: What Makes Racists Advocate Racial Violence?

Jack Glaser*
University of California, Berkeley

Jay Dixit
New York City

Donald P. Green
Yale University

*We conducted semistructured interviews with 38 participants in White racist In-
ternet chat rooms, examining the extent to which people would, in this unique
environment, advocate interracial violence in response to purported economic
and cultural threats. Capitalizing on the anonymity and candor of chat room interactions, this study provides an unusual perspective on extremist attitudes. We
experimentally manipulated the nature and proximity of the threats. Qualitative
and quantitative analyses indicate that the respondents were most threatened by
interracial marriage and, to a lesser extent, Blacks moving into White neighborhoods. In contrast, job competition posed by Blacks evoked very little advocacy
of violence. The study affords an assessment of the advantages and limitations of
Internet-based research with clandestine populations.*

Under what conditions do people advocate racial violence? In particular, are
people who openly embrace ideologies of racial hierarchy in a constant state of
readiness to respond to racial threats, or are certain types of threats particularly
evocative? Since Myrdal (1944), scholars have observed that threats of miscegenation tend to evoke the strongest emotional reactions from avowed racists, yet at

---

*Correspondence concerning this article should be addressed to Jack Glaser, Goldman School
of Public Policy, 2607 Hearst Ave., University of California, Berkeley, CA 94720-7320 [e-mail:
glaserj@socrates.berkeley.edu]. We wish to thank Jon Drummond, Rob MacCoun, and seven anonymous reviewers for their very helpful comments on earlier drafts.*

the same time, there exists an extensive literature that explains racial animus by reference to economic competition and other "realistic" sources of conflict (e.g., Olzak, 1990; Tolnay & Beck, 1995).

This topic, like so many in the domain of intergroup conflict, presents the researcher with a wide array of measurement problems. In addition to problems of dissembling and self-presentation (Crosby, Bromley, & Saxe, 1980), special ideological populations, such as those belonging to White separatist movements, are often deeply suspicious of authorities and outsiders. Although interviews with avowed racists have been conducted in past research (Ezekiel, 1995), it remains unclear whether the views expressed have been tailored to the interview setting.

In order to observe this population as unobtrusively as possible, we used the Internet, applying a randomized survey procedure to examine the conditions under which individuals who participate in White racist chat rooms would be willing to advocate violence in response to a racial threat. This approach benefits from a combination of features unique to the Internet: the guarantees of anonymity in communication, and the abundance of hate group communication forums there. It should be noted at the outset, however, that our study does not measure actual illegal conduct. Rather, our approach is to study the advocacy of racially motivated crime, under the assumption that the causes of advocacy are related to the causes of illegal conduct itself.

Motifs of Ethnic Violence

It has long been observed that different types of ethnic groups are targets of different types of prejudice, discrimination, and violence (Horowitz, 1985). Research on hate crime, unlawful conduct motivated by prejudice against a social group, emphasizes this theme by demonstrating quantitatively how different groups are victimized. For example, Jews, often stereotyped as affluent and greedy, are more frequently the victims of vandalism than assault. Gays and lesbians, who are perceived to be a moral and sexual threat, are more often the victims of physical assault. Blacks are attacked in a variety of ways, including acts of vandalism and intimidation, apparently in an attempt to confine African Americans to a subordinate status and keep them physically separate from Whites.

The present analysis focuses on hate crime against African Americans and will compare the factors that have most prominently been thought to precipitate such acts: economic competition, turf violation, and interracial dating, marriage, and/or sex. We focus on anti-Black hate crime for several reasons. First, because the nature of hate crime appears to vary as a function of the target group, it is prudent to focus on one group in order to isolate predictor variables. Given that, we chose to focus on anti-Black hate crime in part because Blacks are by far the most frequently victimized group according to federal statistics (e.g., U.S. Department of Justice, 1997). Additionally, our previous research (e.g., Green, Glaser, & Rich, 1998) on causes of hate crime also focused on Blacks, and the present study allows us to clarify and extend that analysis.

Societal factors and motivation. What kinds of threats trigger the most vigorous racist reaction? Historical analyses have attributed Hitler's rise to poor macroeconomic conditions (e.g., Eberhard, 1998; Turner, 1996). Similarly, dominant social science approaches to understanding hate crime assume instrumental antecedents like competition for material resources. This dates back at least to Hovland and Sears's (1940) demonstration that the price of cotton (and other economic indicators) in the post–Civil War Deep South correlated negatively with the number of lynchings of Blacks. Although Hovland and Sears conducted their analyses to find support for the frustration-aggression hypothesis (Dollard, Doob, Miller, Mowrer, & Sears, 1939), their finding quickly became a cornerstone of sociological studies of economic threat and intergroup violence (e.g., Olzak, 1990; Pinderhughes, 1993; Tolnay & Beck, 1995). Theories of realistic group conflict (e.g., Bobo, 1988), wherein competition for material resources underlies intergroup strife, are also bolstered by such findings.

However, recent analyses of historical and contemporary data indicate that economic variables are not reliable predictors of hate crime (Green, Abelson, & Garnett, 1999; Green, Glaser, & Rich, 1998; Green, Strolovitch, & Wong, 1998). Green, Glaser, and Rich (1998) found that when time series data involved in earlier analyses were reanalyzed and extended in time, economic conditions bore a weak and inconsistent relationship to lynching. Furthermore, contemporary data revealed no reliable correlations between unemployment, an important economic factor, and hate crime against Blacks, Asians, Jews, or gays and lesbians (Green, Glaser, & Rich, 1998). Rather than flowing directly from economic downturns, hate crime seems to coincide with hard times when political leaders seize on economic conditions in order to marshal resentment against minority groups.

What little is known about the motives of those who belong to racist groups or engage in racially motivated crime also suggests the importance of noneconomic factors. Green et al. (1999) conducted a telephone survey of known White supremacists and hate crime perpetrators in North Carolina, having identified such people based on media reports. The respondents were not aware of the selection criteria. Green et al. (1999) found that, in comparison to a general-public control sample, supremacists and hate crime perpetrators were not more economically frustrated or pessimistic about future finances. However, they were considerably more opposed to interracial marriage and migration of minorities into traditionally White communities. Supremacists in particular also appeared more concerned with threats to cultural identity (e.g., banning of the Confederate flag).

With respect to anti-Black violence in particular, historical analyses reveal that lynchings often resulted from the perception and accusation that a Black man had committed sexual assault against, had a consensual relationship with, or even simply looked at a White woman (Hodes, 1997; Tolnay & Beck, 1995; Wright, 1990). More contemporary anti-Black hate crimes (e.g., cross burnings) are often precipitated by territorial incursion by Blacks into predominantly White communities (Green, Strolovitch, & Wong, 1998). Interracial dating and marriage is still taboo, at least implicitly, and in some circles explicitly, with Alabama taking until the year 2000 to expunge a law (albeit one rendered moot by federal legislation) prohibiting interracial marriage, and this by only a 60% to 40% popular vote.

Thus, we theorize that hate crime against African Americans typically results not so much from economic concerns or frustrations, or competition for material resources, but more often from the perceived threat to the integrity, separateness, and hegemony of the ingroup. We set out to test this thesis by examining the differential effects of economic, geographic, and genetic threat on White racists' advocacy of hate crime. All three threats are interrelated, but our hypothesis is that the threat of genetic incursion is the most evocative.

This conceptualization is in some ways consistent with Ezekiel's (1995) theory of the racist mind. Ezekiel argues that White racists often fear for their own survival and that belonging to supremacist groups gives them comfort and reassurance. Support for the importance of cultural threat, especially with regard to interracial sex, also comes from Hodes (1997), whose historical analysis suggests that miscegenation in the 19th-century Deep South came to be perceived by Whites as a threat and a justification for lynching primarily *after* emancipation, when subordination of Blacks was no longer facilitated through the institution of slavery.

The purpose of the present research is to employ and test an Internet-based, unobtrusive survey method to determine the social factors that are most likely to incite bias-motivated violence. The question is, what form of threat by minorities, in this case African Americans, is most likely to yield an inclination by racists to commit violence against them? Accordingly, we posed scenarios that might be perceived as threatening, regarding interracial marriage, minority in-migration (i.e., Blacks moving into one's neighborhood), and job competition (i.e., competing with a Black person for a job). These were selected to reflect genetic (cultural), geographic (cultural), and economic threats, respectively, each representing fundamental and prototypical examples of these types of threats in the interracial realm. In addition to investigating the effects of different types of threats, we assess the impact of threat proximity, that is, whether the threat occurs at the personal, local, or national level. This factor is potentially important because White separatist rhetoric often dovetails with nationalistic concerns (i.e., many separatists advocate deporting racial and ethnic minorities to other countries or continents), but for practical reasons it seems likely that action (e.g., violence) will be taken or advocated when threat is immediate or proximal.

Method

The Utility of the Internet

In order to test hypotheses about the likelihood of committing a hate crime, we required an unusual sample, one that would have sufficient variability in this regard (i.e., contain a relatively large portion who would be inclined to condone hate crimes), and one that would be willing to express such dispositions. Similarly, we needed to conduct this study in a milieu that would enable the expression of hate crime advocacy, with sufficient anonymity and confidentiality for our participants and ourselves. The Green et al. (1999) survey of supremacists and hate crime perpetrators made significant inroads in this regard, but the sample size was very limited and the telephone public opinion poll format restricted the survey to relatively formal and tame questions. Fortunately, with the advent of the Internet, we were afforded the opportunity to gain entrée to the world of White racist hate groups, surveying them in an environment that encourages open expression.

Over 100 million Americans used the Internet in 1999 (Cole et al., 2000). White pride Web sites appear to be particularly active on the Internet (Anti-Defamation League, 1999; Whine, 1999). Organized racist presence on the Internet began no later than 1985 (Anti-Defamation League, 1999) and has increased to include hundreds of Web sites, file archives, chat rooms, mailing lists, newsgroups, etc. (Franklin, 2000; Klanwatch, 1998).

Racists on the Internet tend to express their views rather freely, at least when they are interacting with those they perceive to be like-minded. For this reason, and because of their prevalence there, we decided to use the Internet Relay Chat (IRC) "rooms" affiliated with racist organizations as our venue, and the participants therein as our sample. In this manner we can assess attitudes and behavioral inclinations that racists might otherwise be reluctant to reveal.

Our goal was to compare factors that are likely to inspire hate crime, specifically those discussed above: economic threat (i.e., job competition), territorial threat (i.e., minority in-migration to neighborhoods), and genetic threat (interracial marriage). In order to accomplish this, we visited various IRC chat rooms sponsored by White supremacist groups and conducted randomized interviews. Posing as a new visitor to the chat rooms, our interviewer presented scenarios of different kinds of threats and recorded the responses. These responses were then coded for their advocacy of violence so that we could compare the extent to which different types of threat differentially inspire advocacy of hate crime.

Design

We employed a 3 (threat type: interracial marriage, minority in-migration, job competition) by 3 (threat level: personal, local, national) design. One important feature of the design is that it was neither fully within- or between-participants, nor was it a mixed-factorial design in the typical, orthogonal sense. We adopted an unusual, pseudo–Latin square design to maximize the number of respondents in each condition of the experiment. Although there are a large number of racist Web sites, the number of chat rooms is more limited, and our preliminary monitoring of these rooms indicated that many of the participants were the same people, jumping around from room to room. Consequently, there appeared to be a universe of only several hundred at the most. Because we anticipated that only a subset of this population would be willing to converse one-on-one with a chat room neophyte (the interviewer) with whom they were not familiar, we attempted to increase the number of respondents in each condition of the experiment by utilizing a partial within-participants design. It most likely would be awkward and suspicious for the respondents if all nine scenarios were posed to each of them, or if they were posed a series of similar questions with only one parameter changed. It was decided that we could pose three scenarios each, if only one was drawn from each level of each variable. Specifically, one group of respondents got all the scenarios in the diagonal of Table 1 (personal interracial marriage, local in-migration, and national job competition). Similarly, another group heard about personal in-migration, local job competition, and national interracial marriage. Finally, another group was asked about personal job competition, local interracial marriage, and national in-migration. In this manner, all nine conditions were filled with a limited sized sample without raising suspicion.

Ethics

In order for us to gather candid responses without raising suspicion, we could not obtain informed consent. The Yale human participants committee agreed that respondents would have been very unlikely to participate, that those who did would not have been representative, and that responses would have been significantly biased. We believe, and the Yale committee concurred, that the lack of informed consent was acceptable because respondents participated without

Table 1. Scenarios Comprising 3 × 3 Design of the Quasi-Experimental Survey

	Marriage	In-migration	Job competition
Personal	My sister is talking about getting married to this Black man.	I found out this Black couple is moving in next door to me.	I found out I'm competing with a Black man for my promotion at work.
Local	Lots of White women in my neighborhood are getting married to Black men.	Lots of Blacks are moving into my neighborhood.	At my work, White people have to compete with Blacks for promotions.
National	All over the country, Black men are getting married to White women.	All over the country, Blacks are moving into White neighborhoods.	All over the country, Blacks are taking White people's jobs.

coercion, in a public forum, discussing topics that were common subjects of conversation there. Finally, respondents' identities were protected, through the use of their own pseudonyms and our careful separation in the data set of these pseudonyms from the responses they provided.

Procedure

The interviewer entered various chat rooms, posing as a curious neophyte. In an IRC chat room one can engage in real-time conversations with any or all of the visitors there. Chat rooms are ideal for this study because their participants are especially likely to express otherwise socially taboo sentiments and proclivities (McKenna & Bargh, 1998, 2000). In each visit, the interviewer made small talk until he was able to engage an individual in a dialogue. At this point the interviewer randomly selected a sequence of experimental conditions (e.g., personal-marriage, local-in-migration, and then national-job competition). There were 18 possible orderings to ensure that scenario order would be a random variable and that the interviewer would not be able to anticipate the next scenario he was to give. The interviewer posed each scenario after the respondent appeared to have played out his or her response to the previous scenario. The interviewer typically carried out the discussion "in view of" the chat room but did not engage other participants in the same room on the same day.

We employed a semistructured interview approach (Smith, Harre, & Von Langenhove, 1995) wherein the interviewer engages in a relatively free-flowing discussion, making sure to cover certain topics. This approach allowed for a realistic discussion with survey questions embedded naturalistically, thereby increasing the likelihood of candid and representative responses. The danger that the interviewer's own hypotheses might bias his interactions with respondents was mitigated by the random selection of the conditions just prior to posing each scenario.

Thirty-eight people were interviewed in all. They were all voluntary participants in the chat room in which they were surveyed. No demographic data were obtained on the respondents because this might have served to undermine their anonymity and to raise suspicion about the interviewer.

As described above, three of the nine scenarios were posed to each respondent. A few respondents left the chat room after responding to only one or two of the three scenarios, thus reducing the total number of responses from the expected 114 to 107. Responses were recorded by logging the text of the discussions and downloading it for later coding. The responses were coded for the extent to which the respondent advocated violence in some form during the course of his or her response. Blind to the condition of the experiment, the interviewer and another author rated each response on a 6-point scale from 0 (*no advocacy of violence*) to 5 (*advocacy of extreme violence*). It is plausible that the interviewer could have recognized the responses and recalled the condition, but this was impossible for the other author, who had not seen the data prior to coding. Nevertheless, the interrater correlation was reasonably high ($r = .82$). Although the author who had not participated in data collection was not able to recognize the specific responses, he nevertheless was aware of the design of the experiment, may have been able to infer the scenarios to which some of the responses were made, and may have had hypotheses similar to those of the experimenter, which may have served to bias his ratings. To address this concern, we had a third, doubly blind (i.e., unaware of design or conditions, or for that matter the nature of the study in general) person rate the responses on the same scale for their advocacy of violence. The correlation between this rater's ratings and the average ratings of the first two raters (used in the data analyses) was .90, indicating strong correspondence.

Results

Narrative Analysis

Perhaps the greatest power of this study lies in the qualitative analysis of the types of responses the different scenarios evoked. The specific statements made by our respondents were often very strongly worded, revealing clear opinions that differed substantially as a function of threat type. They offer a rich source for analysis of racists' attitudes toward minorities and committing violence against them. It should be noted that the style of communication in chat rooms is very informal and, even more so than with e-mail, typing is often sloppy. We have not corrected errors in the following quotes.

Interracial marriage. The data clearly reveal that responses with regard to interracial marriage, especially at the personal level, were the most volatile. For example, one respondent stated, "better kill her. kill him and her. pull a oj... im not kidding. i would do it if it was my sister. i would gladly go to prison then live a free life knowing some mud babies were calling me uncle whitey." Another respondent advised, in a manner reminiscent of the days of lynchings, "Hang his black ass." One person cautiously suggested the following: "Im not saying how I would stop it, nor am I encouraging you to do this, but, there are many murders in America today, some for the better of our race, and it is fairly easy to get away with one. Not that I am telling you to go out and murder someone though!" It is not certain, but this respondent appears to be advocating violence while being careful not to do so directly. There is certainly an aspect of encouragement (i.e., "it is fairly easy to get away with one") in his comments.

A few people responded to the personal-interracial marriage scenario without advocating violence (e.g., "well I wouldn't have anything to do with her if I were you."), but the clear majority (9 out of 13) expressed some advocacy of violence, mostly extreme violence. Further evidence for the evocative nature of interracial marriage is available in spontaneous responses to other threats. For example, one respondent stated with regard to in-migration, "I don't let it get to me, they stay with their space and I stay in mine. . . . The thing that upsets me most is seeing so many white girls dating black guys."

Responses to interracial marriage at the local level were, in contrast, notably brief and bland. Respondents expressed some concern (e.g., "Thats sad. Yuck that makes me sick," "man that to bad," "then move"), but were generally more passive and helpless (e.g., "sorry man, I don't know what to say"). Only 1 respondent out of 14 in this condition indicated a disposition toward violence, recounting his own assault of a Black man who married his cousin, for which he claimed to have been prosecuted.

At the national level, the responses to interracial marriage were somewhere between the personal and local in terms of advocacy of violence, with most being tepid, but a few exhibiting support for extreme violence (e.g., "They should all be shot.").

Minority in-migration. At least at the personal level, in-migration evoked a range of responses. Many were mild and even restrained, such as, "I don't like it but we can['t] do anything." Others were more extreme: "I would run the niggers and all non-whites oit of my city. . . kill some nigger ass." Others recommended specific action that would qualify as hate crime but was not necessarily violent (e.g., "Spraypaint 'niggers beware' on the door before they even move in. If they catch wind of it, I doubt they will even finalize the buy"). At the local and national levels, in-migration moved only a few respondents to advocate some form of action (e.g., "make his ass move out of there") but for the most part responses were passive and even resigned (e.g., "move," "Yep. . . . It's happening everywhere").

Job competition. The threat of job competition elicited a more consistently mild reaction. Although one respondent did advocate extreme violence ("kill him") with regard to a personal-level scenario, most responses were tepid and reasoned, such as, "all you can do is try your best." In response to the personal-level threat, several inquired about the qualifications of the Black competitor, one suggesting filing suit for reverse discrimination. At the local level, responses were similar, with the exception of one person who advocated framing the Black competitor: "I say set em up for a bust get em fired and away from our women." Notably, in this case, spontaneous reference is again made to interracial dating/marriage, suggesting that it is a chronically salient threat. At the national level as well, responses tended to be political, focusing on issues of affirmative action, rather than violent. One person volunteered, "asian are taking white jobs too!" suggesting that whereas job competition from Blacks may not be much of a threat, competition from other groups may be.

The clear differences in the types of reactions to different scenarios reveals to some extent that the threat to the integrity of the group, be it cultural or genetic, is a relatively potent predictor of violent tendencies toward outgroup members. The genetic aspect of this is evidenced by the specific references to the outcome of interracial marriage: "mud babies." This conclusion is bolstered by data from additional inquiries we made. On one occasion, after completing the relatively structured part of the interview, the experimenter asked, more comparatively, "Of blacks marrying white women, blacks moving into white neighborhoods, and blacks taking white jobs, which of these do you think is the most threatening?" The response was "integration of races, obviously!" When the interviewer pressed further the respondent indicated that he meant integration through intermarriage, restating, "obviously."

Quantitative Analysis

Although the analytic strength of this research appears to lie in the compelling narrative of the responses, the data can also be analyzed quantitatively. Accordingly, Table 2 reports the mean degree of advocacy of violence in each condition of the experiment, based on the 6-point (0–5) scale ratings. These results reinforce our qualitative assessment. The average level of advocated violence was greatest when respondents were presented with the issue of interracial marriage as compared to job competition or in-migration. Averages were also higher when these threats were framed in personal terms. Local threats elicited low levels of advocated violence, with national threats falling in between.

These results can be tested more rigorously using regression analysis, making allowances for the unusual design of this experiment. The quasi–Latin square

Table 2. Advocacy of Violence as a Function of Threat Type and Level

Threat type	Threat level			
	Personal	Local	National	Row mean
Interracial marriage	2.46	0.18	1.43	1.34
	(2.21)	(0.67)	(2.44)	(2.04)
	$n = 14$	$n = 14$	$n = 7$	$n = 35$
In-migration	1.5	0.0	0.0	0.46
	(2.23)	(0.0)	(0.0)	(1.38)
	$n = 11$	$n = 16$	$n = 9$	$n = 36$
Job competition	0.54	0.0	0.29	0.32
	(1.47)	(0.0)	(1.21)	(1.18)
	$n = 12$	$n = 7$	$n = 17$	$n = 36$
Column mean	1.54	0.07	0.46	
	(2.11)	(0.41)	(1.46)	
	$n = 37$	$n = 37$	$n = 33$	

Note. Scores represent mean responses from ratings on a 6-point scale from 0 (*no advocacy of violence*) to 5 (*advocacy of extreme violence*). Standard deviations are in parentheses.

design of the experiment, in which each respondent was presented with multiple scenarios (but not all scenarios), increased the number of participants in each condition, but the observations are not statistically independent. The disturbances associated with one observation are likely to be correlated with others. In order to address this problem, we report robust standard errors derived from bootstrapping. That is, 150 samples of size 107 (the size of the total sample) were drawn (with replacement, necessarily) from the original data set. The empirical sampling distribution of these regression estimates is used to calculate the standard errors.

The second problem also arises from the limited size of each treatment condition. In randomizing the placement of respondents into conditions, and due in large part to false starts (e.g., refusals to engage in discourse), our group sample sizes became lopsided. Before we could fully rectify this, it became evident that we had tapped out much of the available sample and suspicion was beginning to mount about our presence and repeated statements and questions. As a result, we were left with condition cells of varying sizes (ranging from 7 to 17). This imbalance reduces the statistical power of our test but does not lead to biased inference.

The regression includes four predictors of advocated violence. The first two are dummy variables associated with the type of threat: one dummy marks interracial marriage and the other in-migration (with job competition being the omitted category). The second set of dummy variables marks the level of threat: one dummy for personal threat and the other for local (with national threats being the omitted category). The regression reported in Table 3 indicates that interracial marriage significantly increases advocated violence by an average of 1.1 scale points relative to job competition ($t = 2.7$, $p < .01$, two-sided test). Similarly, personal threats significantly increase advocated violence ($t = 2.22$, $p < .05$, two-sided), relative to national threats, whereas local threats significantly decrease them ($t = 2.03$,

Table 3. Regression Analysis of Effect of Threat Type and Threat Level on Advocacy of Violence

	Estimates	Robust standard errors
Threat type		
Interracial marriage	1.09**	.41
In-migration	.32	.29
Threat level		
Personal	.91*	.41
Local	−.61*	.30
Constant	.14	.25

Note. Threat types include interracial marriage, minority in-migration, and job competition. Threat levels include personal, local, and national. Job competition and the national threat level serve as omitted categories and can be considered the neutral (zero) reference point against which to compare the other parameter estimates. One hundred fifty random replications were conducted to generate robust standard errors in order to allow for the nonindependence of the conditions (i.e., that each respondent was in conditions at multiple, but not all, levels of both variables) and uneven sample sizes across conditions. Adjusted $R^2 = .20$, $N = 107$. Asterisks indicate that the estimate differs significantly from the neutral (zero) reference point for that variable (i.e., *job competition* for threat type, *national* for threat level) as follows: * $p < .05$, two-tailed; ** $p < .01$, two-tailed.

$p < .05$, two-sided). No significant interactions between the level and type of threat emerge, using two-sided tests.

Discussion

"The greatest existing cause of lynching is the perpetration, especially by black men, of the heinous crime of rape..."

—Theodore Roosevelt (cf. Wright, 1990, p. 77)

The thousands of lynchings of Southern Blacks, often on trumped up charges, during the post-Reconstruction period represent an early form of what we now might call "hate crime." President Roosevelt's take on the cause of lynching about a century ago must be considered within the historical context of the time. Accounts of lynchings often involved the accusation of the rape of a White woman by a Black man. Although Roosevelt's conclusion, influenced by the propaganda of the time, was almost certainly misguided, it nevertheless may offer a valuable insight into the mind of the hate crime perpetrator: that violence against members of other races may be particularly linked to concerns over interracial mixing.

Indeed, it is clear from the present study that interracial marriage is the idea that most upsets racists on the Internet and is likely to drive them to advocate anti-Black hate crime. Consistent with Green, Strolovitch, and Wong (1998) and Green et al. (1999), there is also some response to territorial incursion, but only at the personal level. In keeping with the findings of Green, Glaser, and Rich (1998) as well as Green et al. (1999), but inconsistent with Hovland and Sears (1940) and studies that followed, job competition, an economic variable, inspired very little advocacy of violence against Blacks at any level. The propensity for interracial marriage and minority in-migration to evoke extreme responses among White racists on the Internet is perhaps exemplified in the frequent, spontaneous invocations of the expression "14 words." This is White separatist code for, "We must secure the existence of our people and a future for White children," and it serves as a rallying cry of sorts, but clearly reflects concerns about race mixing.

The effect of threat level, although of less theoretical interest than threat type, was fairly clear. Scenarios posed at the personal level were by far the most evocative. This may be the case because scenarios of this sort are the most concrete and conducive to giving advice. Specifically, it seems more likely that one would advocate some form of action to someone who faces a "problem" personally and so, in this respect, this variable is not very informative or interesting. However, this was not equally true across types of threat. Job competition had the same small effect at the national and personal levels, where responses often indicated that such threats either were beyond one's control or would work themselves out, this based on the belief that Blacks are inferior and will not be able to retain such jobs.

We must also consider why the national level evoked some advocacy of violence but the local level had no effect whatsoever. The most plausible explanation for this is probably that threats posed at the national level triggered thoughts tied to the rhetoric of hate groups who tend to speak nationalistically and lament the declining state of the country, which they often attribute to "lazy" and criminal minorities and immigrants. The local threat level, on the other hand, may have been too abstract, tapping neither the empathic response of the personal level nor nationalist dogma. It is nevertheless surprising that this level evoked virtually no advocacy of violence, especially with regard to minority in-migration, which is often a community concern, or at least perceived to be.

Impact of the Internet on Race Relations

The utility of the Internet as a venue for studying racist extremists is a derivative of a potentially troubling reality: that such groups are prevalent in cyberspace. Although their prevalence is undisputed, there is some debate over whether or not the Internet has been a boon for racist groups. In fact, a Web site called Hatewatch that had functioned to list and monitor Web-based hate groups since 1995 recently shut itself down, offering the explanation that it had completed its mission and concluding that the Internet has had a negative impact on hate (Dixit, 2001). Although White racist groups have proliferated on the Internet in recent years, there appears to have been no corresponding increase in membership in these groups or in hate crime rates. In fact, one might argue that the prevalence of racist groups on the Internet works to reduce hate crime, perhaps by providing less physical, more rhetorical outlets for hate. Furthermore, the presence of hate groups on the Internet has in many ways made them more transparent to the public, which in turn facilitates monitoring by watchdog groups, government and private alike, not to mention social scientists. Nevertheless, perhaps in part because of the inherently underground nature of White separatist groups, extending back to the days of the hooded Ku Klux Klan, there is no direct evidence available that the Internet has not helped to proliferate hate groups. Furthermore, the potential of the Internet as a tool for communication, organization, and information dissemination among extremist groups is undeniable, and although it may have its incidental benefits (e.g., transparency), it clearly warrants scrutiny.

Methodological Considerations

In addition to providing insight into the mentality of White separatists and perhaps the antecedents of hate crime, the present study offers a methodological innovation that should generalize to other research questions and prove useful in the future. Specifically, by unobtrusively surveying people on the highly anonymous, yet public, forum of the Internet, and specifically in chat rooms, we are able to open up avenues of research not previously available to most researchers. There are numerous groups that are difficult to gain access to, either because of their marginality or because of illicit aspects of their behaviors that make self-disclosure potentially costly. McKenna and Bargh (1998, 2000) have also successfully employed Internet-based research to reach populations that would be difficult to access. The present study adopted a more surreptitious approach, perhaps more appropriate when measuring variables relating to illegal behavior such as hate crime and when dealing with populations that are suspicious of researchers and other outsiders. This approach could be adopted for other populations, such as terrorist or militia groups, child pornographers, and illegal weapons traders, whose members would also be unlikely to respond candidly to explicit survey questions, and the potential is clear for public good arising from greater understanding of such groups.

In order to carry out such research, however, we must consider the thorny issues of deceit and informed consent. As noted above, deceit with regard to the identity of the interviewer (and, in fact, that he was an interviewer at all) was essential for the success of the study. Otherwise, respondents would have been very unlikely to participate, or to respond candidly if they did. For the same reasons, obtaining informed consent was impossible. Fortunately, the use of the Internet had the added advantage of ensuring the anonymity of our respondents, all of whom use pseudonyms in the chat rooms. We further promoted their anonymity and confidentiality by separating even their pseudonyms from their data, assigning random numerical codes. Additionally, the public forum nature of the chat rooms mitigates the need for informed consent. Nevertheless, such research should always be carried out with the utmost regard for the confidentiality and safety of the sample.

Limitations

Despite the seeming clarity of the results, there are several limitations of the study that should be acknowledged. First, this study was conducted at one moment in time, and only through replication can one ascertain whether, for example, the motive power of economic threat was undermined by the generally favorable economic conditions that prevailed at the time of our study. This investigation is also limited by the relatively small size of the sample, which was compromised in part by rising suspicion among potential respondents. McKenna and Bargh (1998) faced similar problems in their e-mail survey of posters on White supremacist (and other ideologically extreme) newsgroups, where some posters were warning others to not respond to the survey and generating rumors about its being conducted by government agencies like the FBI. This may prove to be a chronic problem with research on this population, which appears to have limited numbers participating in chat rooms at any given time. However, incremental replications over time, as new cohorts join and grow tired of the chat rooms, could ultimately yield a substantial database of knowledge. Furthermore, we would recommend that future studies of this sort employ a purely between-participants design to minimize the appearance of inquisitiveness on the part of the ostensive neophyte (i.e., the interviewer).

We are somewhat more sanguine about other aspects of the study, in particular the sincerity with which respondents expressed their views. One respondent went so far as to reveal the types of code words that are used over ham radios to form posses and plan hate crimes. Of greater concern than the sincerity of the responses is the possibility that, because of the anonymity of the Internet and the culture of the chat rooms, responses reflected a *greater* level of endorsement of violence than respondents actually felt. Nevertheless, as far as we can tell, there is little cause for concern that respondents were not genuine. We must also consider the possibility that the very presence of the interviewer, as a curious neophyte, influenced the responses, perhaps invoking more bravado. Although we made every effort to be nondescript, this possibility is still real, but it should not represent a confound in the design and results with regard to relative differences in advocacy of violence as a function of threat type and level.

Perhaps more complex is the issue of how advocacy of violence relates to actual illegal conduct. It is telling that several respondents, but by no means a majority, indicated that they had, indeed, themselves committed violent hate crimes in the past and provided some detail of them. Needless to say, we cannot be sure that such statements are true. They could simply reflect a certain form of false bravado, even under conditions of anonymity. The possibility remains, however, that some overlap exists between racist ideology and racist action (Green et al., 1999). Consequently, variables that are diagnostic for this group may be important in predicting hate crime.

Conclusion

In sum, because of the nature of Internet-based communication, particularly chat rooms, we were able to observe a group and form of behavior that would otherwise be difficult for scientists to study. By assessing their responses to various types of threat, we develop a better understanding of the motives and beliefs that animate those who advocate and perhaps commit hate crimes. These results are consistent with our past findings that economic threat, whether in the form of declining cotton prices, increases in unemployment, or heightened job competition, does not in itself trigger violent ideation. Rather, perceived threats to White hegemony and separateness, via in-migration and especially interracial sex and marriage, generate a visceral reaction against outgroups. These findings are important insofar as they shed light on the parlance used to incite fear by racist ideologues, both past and present.

Although further research is clearly warranted, the present study has some important policy implications. First, it offers a methodological approach that policy analysts can employ to survey otherwise inaccessible groups (e.g., separatists, child pornographers, weapons traders) to better understand their motivations and behaviors. Second, as noted above, the findings, in conjunction with past research, challenge the presumption that economic conditions are direct determinants of intergroup violence. Those concerned with reducing such socially destabilizing phenomena should look to other factors, including extremist group belief systems, which may prove more worthwhile targets of change. Similarly, it is questionable as to whether the Internet itself serves to promote racial violence, but clearly it can be employed as a means to understanding, and perhaps reducing, such bigotry and conflict.

References

Anti-Defamation League. (1999). *Poisoning the Web: Hatred online.* Washington, DC: Author.
Bobo, L. (1988). Group conflict, prejudice, and the paradox of contemporary racial attitudes. In P. A. Katz & D. A. Taylor (Eds.), *Eliminating racism* (pp. 85–114). New York: Plenum.
Cole, J. I., Suman, M., Schramm, P, van Bel, D., Lunn, B., Maguire, P., Hanson, K., Singh, R., Aquino, J., & Lebo, H. (2000). *The UCLA Internet report: Surveying the digital future.* Los Angeles: University of California at Los Angeles, Center for Communication Policy.
Crosby, F., Bromley, S., & Saxe, L. (1980). Recent unobtrusive studies of Black and White discrimination and prejudice: A literature review. *Psychological Bulletin, 87,* 546–563.
Dixit, J. (2001, May 9). A banner day for neo-Nazis [On-line]. Available: www.salon.com/tech/feature/2001/05/09/hatewatch/index.html
Dollard, J., Doob, L. W., Miller, N. E., Mowrer, O. H., & Sears, R. R. (1939). *Frustration and aggression.* New Haven, CT: Yale University Press.
Eberhard, K. (1988). *The Weimar Republic.* Boston, MA: Unwin Hyman.
Ezekiel, R. S. (1995). *The racist mind: Portraits of American neo-Nazis and Klansmen.* New York: Viking.
Franklin, R. A. (2000). *The hate directory* [Internet Website]. Available: www.hatedirectory.com
Green, D. P., Abelson, R. P., & Garnett, M. (1999). The distinctive political views of hate-crime perpetrators and White supremacists. In D. A. Prentice & D. T. Miller (Eds.), *Cultural divides: Understanding and overcoming group conflict* (pp. 429–464). New York: Russell Sage Foundation.
Green, D. P., Glaser, J., & Rich, A. O. (1998). From lynching to gay-bashing: The elusive connection between economic conditions and hate crime. *Journal of Personality and Social Psychology, 75,* 82–92.
Green, D. P., Strolovitch, D., & Wong, J. (1998). Defended neighborhoods, integration, and racially motivated crime. *American Journal of Sociology, 104,* 372–403.
Hodes, M. E. (1997). *White women, Black men: Illicit sex in the nineteenth-century South.* New Haven, CT: Yale University Press.
Horowitz, D. (1985). *Ethnic groups in conflict.* Berkeley and Los Angeles: University of California Press.
Hovland, C. I., & Sears, R. R. (1940). Minor studies of aggression: VI. Correlation of lynchings with economic indices. *Journal of Psychology, 9,* 301–310.
Klanwatch. (1998). 474 hate groups blanket America: God, rock 'n' roll and the Net fuel the rage. *Intelligence Report Special Issue: 1997, the Year in Hate, Winter, 1998,* 89.
McKenna, K. Y. A., & Bargh, J. A. (1998). Coming out in the age of the Internet: Identity "demarginalization" through virtual group participation. *Journal of Personality and Social Psychology, 75,* 681–694.

McKenna, K. Y. A., & Bargh, J. A. (2000). Plan 9 from cyberspace: The implications of the Internet for personality and social psychology. *Personality and Social Psychology Review, 4*, 57–75.

Myrdal, G. (1944). *An American dilemma: The Negro problem and modern democracy.* New York: Harper.

Olzak, S. (1990). The political context of competition: Lynching and urban racial violence, 1882–1914. *Social Forces, 69*, 395–421.

Pinderhughes, H. (1993). The anatomy of racially motivated violence in New York City: A case study of youth in Southern Brooklyn. *Social Problems, 40*, 478–492.

Smith, J. A., Harre, R., & Von Langenhove, L. (1995). *Rethinking methods in psychology.* New York: Sage.

Tolnay, S. E., & Beck, E. M. (1995). *A festival of violence: An analysis of Southern lynchings, 1882–1930.* Urbana, IL: University of Illinois Press.

Turner, H. A. (1996). *Hitler's thirty days to power: January 1933.* Reading, PA: Addison-Wesley.

U.S. Department of Justice. (1997). *Hate crime statistics 1997.* Washington, D.C.: U.S. Department of Justice, FBI Criminal Justice Information Services Division.

Whine, M. (1999). *The use of the Internet by far right extremists* [On-line]. Available: http://www.ict.org.il/articles/right-wing-net.htm

Wright, G. C. (1990). *Racial violence in Kentucky, 1865–1940: Lynchings, mob rule, and "legal lynchings."* Baton Rouge, LA: Louisiana State University Press.

JACK GLASER is an Assistant Professor in the Goldman School of Public Policy at the University of California, Berkeley. After earning his PhD in psychology from Yale University in 1999 he received a National Institute of Mental Health National Research Service Award to serve as a postdoctoral fellow at UC Berkeley's Institute of Personality and Social Research. Glaser studies intergroup bias at multiple levels of analysis and manifestations, including implicit stereotyping and prejudice, racial profiling, and hate crime, and has interests in the psychology of electoral politics and political ideology.

JAY DIXIT is a prize-winning New York City–based freelance writer. His work has appeared in *Rolling Stone, The Village Voice, Salon.com,* and *Psychology Today.* He received his bachelor's degree, cum laude, in psychology, with distinction in the major, from Yale University in 1998, where he wrote for *The New Journal,* including an article about White supremacists on the Internet.

DONALD P. GREEN is A. Whitney Griswold Professor of Political Science at Yale University, where he has taught since receiving his PhD from UC Berkeley in 1988. Since 1996, he has served as Director of the Institution for Social and Policy Studies, an interdisciplinary research unit at Yale. His scholarly interests include hate crime, political behavior, public opinion, campaign finance, and research methodology.

Journal of Social Issues, Vol. 58, No. 1, 2002, pp. 195-205

Is the Internet Changing Social Life? It Seems the More Things Change, the More They Stay the Same

Tom R. Tyler*

New York University

Although there has been a tremendous amount of discussion in the popular press about how the Internet is changing all facets of social life, research on the impact of the Internet is only beginning to emerge. A review of the studies reported in this issue suggests that the Internet may have had less impact on many aspects of social life than is frequently supposed. In many cases, the Internet seems to have created a new way of doing old things, rather than being a technology that changes the manner in which people live their lives. As a consequence, the policy implications of increasing Internet use may be less than is often believed.

There is no question that easy access to the Internet, like the introduction of reliable mail service and the invention of the telephone, has changed the nature of people's connection to others in their social world. Mail made possible connections among people without physical proximity, and the telephone facilitated communication among distant people, making rapid connections possible across long distances. The Internet has created an electronic mail system, merging the speed and flexibility of the telephone with the written character of the mail. People can now write letters that are transmitted virtually immediately throughout the globe.

But has this communication revolution changed the nature of interpersonal and group processes? The research reviewed in this issue makes it clear that the basic nature of people's relationships with others may have changed less because of the Internet than is often suggested. On the contrary, there are suggestions that the Internet may be a new way for people to do old things. That is, there may be new and useful capabilities associated with electronic communication, and those may have led to changes in patterns of life, but the basic social patterns of

---

*Correspondence concerning this article should be addressed to Tom R. Tyler, Department of Psychology, New York University, 6 Washington Place, Room 550, New York, NY 10003 [e-mail: tom.tyler@nyu.edu].

social life have remained very much the same in spite of these Internet-induced changes. The Internet seems more like a new way to manage long-standing social problems and meet long-time social needs than a transformative technology that has fundamentally changed patterns of either interpersonal or group processes.

Do People Benefit From Internet Use?

Since the primary use of the Internet is communication, we might speculate that the Internet will have positive social consequences in people's everyday lives, because it increases the frequency and quality of interpersonal communications among people. People with easy access to others ought to feel better connected and more strongly supported by others, leading to happiness and engagement in families, organizations, communities, and society more generally.

On the other hand, the ease of electronic communication may lead to weaker social ties, because people have less reason to leave their homes and actually interact face to face with other people. The Internet allows people to more easily work from their home, to form and sustain friendships and even romantic attachments from their home, to bank from their home, to vote and engage in political and social-issue-based discussions with others in their communities from home, and to pursue other social connections from their home. In this wide variety of ways, Internet communications can potentially displace face-to-face and telephone communications. This is important because psychologists have often described such face-to-face and telephone connections as being of higher quality, when viewed in terms of their contribution to satisfaction and well-being.

These two views describe the potential for gain and loss as the Internet becomes more and more central to the fabric of our society. But which view is correct? An early study by Kraut et al. (1998) articulated the case for concern when it portrayed Internet users as less socially involved and more lonely and depressed. This negative image of the consequences of Internet use is more broadly tested in the articles reported in this issue.

Kraut et al. (this issue) expand upon their own initial sample, as well as considering new subsequently collected longitudinal data, in an effort to explore the social consequences of Internet use. Interestingly, the expanded longitudinal data for their original sample suggest that Internet use has fewer negative consequences than were suggested in their initial presentation, when Internet impact is considered over time. At later time points in an ongoing interaction, they find no negative effects, suggesting that such negative effects disappeared after people's use of the Internet became far more sophisticated. A second study that also examined the influence of Internet use was more positive in its findings, suggesting that there were small but positive effects of using the Internet on social involvement and psychological well-being. In the current article, Kraut et al. present a more positive image of Internet use than in their earlier work.

The influence of the Internet on interpersonal relations is further examined by McKenna, Green, and Gleason (this issue) and by Bargh, McKenna, and Fitzsimons (this issue), who articulate and test a theory of relationship formation on the Internet. In a series of longitudinal and experimental studies, these researchers directly address the argument that the psychological quality of Internet social interaction is lower than is the psychological quality of traditional face-to-face interaction. They find that relationships that develop through the Internet are close, meaningful, and long lasting, suggesting that many of the concerns expressed about the quality and meaningfulness of Internet interactions are unfounded. Further, they find that people bring relationships formed on the Internet into the real world by meeting, talking with, and otherwise connecting with others in other ways and show how the self-concept and social identity play a crucial role in this process.

Perhaps the strongest test of the beneficial or harmful character of Internet communication occurs in the case of adolescent communication, which is studied by Gross, Juvonen, and Gable (this issue). The most striking finding of their study is that adolescents use the Internet like a telephone, rather than as an opportunity to try different personalities and identities. Their study finds that Internet communication is very similar to "traditional means of youth social interaction" (p. 86). As a result, the use of the Internet does not shape psychological well-being in any way that is different from the influence of social interaction via other modalities.

Spears, Postmes, Lea, and Wolbert (this issue) raise fundamental questions about the assumption that there is something "less social" about electronic communications. That view develops from the important "reduced social cues" model (Kiesler, 1986), which labels Internet communication less complete because it lacks important social information. This more anonymous communication is deindividuated. However, the authors suggest that, far from the image of deindividuation often presented in social psychology, a social identity perspective would argue that deindividuating, anonymous communications are likely to be governed by group norms. With the individual less salient, the group becomes more central to decisions about behavior. In other words, the impact of the Internet is likely to be to remove the element of reactions that is keyed to specific others—for example, the self. Ironically, Spears et al. argue that people will be more socially responsive in such situations, not less. In sum, the conditions of electronic communication may in fact enhance the influence of group norms on individuals' behavior.

Taken together, the findings of these studies support the suggestion of McKenna and Bargh (2000) that "there is no simple main effect of the Internet on the average person" (p. 59). The Internet seems to have value as a tool used by people to overcome particular problems, like social anxiety, but overall patterns of Internet impact emphasize how little long-term impact Internet use, per se, has upon the person, his or her relationships, or psychological well-being. This change in technology, with its resulting changes in the way people live their lives, has not led to changes in well-being or the quality of people's social relationships. Instead, it has given people new ways to approach traditional concerns about how to initiate and develop relationships.

These studies do not suggest that the availability of the Internet changes the character or quality of people's interpersonal lives. However, they raise a deeper and more fundamental question, one that is also raised in McKenna and Bargh's Real Me model of relationship formation on the Internet. As psychologists, historians, and political scientists, we need to develop and articulate a model within which we can understand the parameters that shape the quality of interpersonal experience. The existence of written mail, the telephone, the Internet, and video conferencing provides a wide variety of alternative interaction modalities to simple face-to-face communication. How does the modality of interaction shape the nature and quality of people's social relationships, as well as their feelings of happiness, satisfaction, and well-being? And most importantly, what are the elements of interaction that mediate this impact? Is it, for example, the physical proximity of face-to-face communication that matters, or is it the immediacy of the other person's response? The studies reported in this issue suggest that there is no general impact of Internet vs. face-to-face communication on overall well-being, but they do not provide us with a broader model linking the modality of communication to its social and psychological impact. They do, however, make it clear that such a model is needed to help us talk effectively about the potential social and psychological influence of new technologies.

If we understood the qualities of face-to-face communication that influence the impact of such communication on people and on their social interaction, we would be able to predict in advance the probable influence of any new communication technology. Of course, as the research reported suggests, people make creative use of technology, and that use blunts any simple statements about modality effects. As an example, the McKenna et al. (this issue) research suggests that socially anxious people use the Internet as a way to make initial contact with others. However, they then convert that contact into more traditional face-to-face relationships. They use the Internet, in other words, to deal with specific social deficits, and they incorporate its use into a complex sequence of modalities of interaction. Human creativity defies a simple model of technological influence, because people adapt technologies to help them achieve their goals. Rather than technology's changing people's social and psychological reality, in other words, people change their use of technology to facilitate their creation of a desired social and psychological reality. This suggests that efforts to understand the influence of new technologies must view those technologies as means that people can use to achieve their social goals.

Negotiation and the Internet

Unlike the literature on social relations and psychological well-being, the article by Thompson and Nadler (this issue) suggests that Internet negotiations conducted primarily in business environments may present greater difficulties than are found in face-to-face negotiations. Reporting on a broad-ranging program of research, the authors suggest that there are a number of problems when strangers negotiate with each other electronically. To some extent, these problems are linked to the lack of a person relationship with others. For example, people feel less accountability and connection to the other party in the negotiations and are more likely to engage in actions that burn bridges, to be more emotionally aversive ("squeaky wheel"), and to be more mistrusting of the other party's motives.

Interestingly, however, the biases identified seem to be broader in scope. They are not just linked to the lack of a personal relationship with the other party. Temporal synchrony, for example, is linked to coordination problems associated with the nature of e-mail communication. Temporal synchrony refers to the relationship between the timing of expected responses from others and that of the actual responses. It is of particular importance because it is a true modality effect and reflects something unique about the pattern of communication when enacted electronically. Temporal synchrony is not an issue when people negotiate about the same issues face to face.

This problem with the timeline between communications occurring in an on-line interaction helps to explain why e-commerce has had trouble and why customer service is such an issue for on-line businesses. It also helps to explain why purely on-line business efforts may backfire whereas purely social sites, such as clubs and chat rooms, are doing well. Often, e-retailers are modeling themselves after off-line customer relationships ("traditional businesses") instead of embracing the claim that the face of business is changing and producing a truly new way of interacting facilitated by the new technology of the Internet. Success rates suggest that on-line companies that have brick-and-mortar counterparts are enjoying greater success than are solely on-line companies. This may be because people's interactions with businesses are not changing, so companies are forced to incorporate traditional off-line models of customer relationships. The issue is whether the limited change in the form of interaction found with e-commerce occurs because companies cannot think of new ways to relate to people through e-commerce or because people are resistant to changes in their traditional way of doing business and reward companies that have a traditional look with which they are familiar.

How can we reconcile the findings reported by Thompson and Nadler with those described in the other studies in this collection? We can do this primarily by distinguishing the situations studied. The individuals Thompson and Nadler studied were asked to remain strangers who interacted only electronically, whereas studies of relationships find that people develop nonelectronic elements to relationships that they begin electronically or develop electronic elements to supplement real-world relationships. It is unusual for personal relationships to begin or remain solely electronic in nature. As a result, the bulk of the biases discussed in Thompson and Nadler's research, which are linked to the lack of a real-world relationship, would be minimized or eliminated in personal relationships. What remains to be seen is whether, in business relationships, people have the same natural tendency to make Internet relationships real by telephoning, or having face-to-face communications, with others. If so, then people have a natural method for counteracting many of the identified biases.

These caveats aside, the findings that Thompson and Nadler report are important because they provide a needed cautionary note to the generally optimistic findings of the studies of relationship development on the Internet. It may be the case that there are arenas—in particular, situations in which people are more task oriented or interests are more in conflict—in which the less social nature of electronic communication may introduce problems or undermine productive interaction. If so, then mechanisms need to be developed to combat such problems.

The Internet as a Social Equalizer

Beyond the question of whether the Internet has a generally positive or negative impact upon users is the issue of whether the Internet diminishes or enhances personal or social inequalities. In the case of personal inequalities, the question is whether people can use the Internet to compensate for social skill deficits, such as feeling greater social anxiety or having smaller social networks.

The personal compensation question is addressed by Kraut et al. (this issue) when they consider who benefits from the Internet. Kraut et al. ask whether introverted people use it to compensate for their weaknesses or extraverts use it to magnify their already superior networking efforts and skills. Their findings suggest that it is those who already have strong social networks and skills who benefit the most from the Internet. So Internet access amplifies existing differences in the ability to use social resources, rather than dampening those differences, with "those who are already effective in using social resources in the world" being "well positioned to take advantage of a powerful new technology like the Internet" (p. 69).

The work of McKenna et al. (this issue) suggests the contrary conclusion that Internet connections may facilitate the initial contact among those with social anxiety, with people beginning by investing their sense of "true self" in Internet interactions. In other words, the Internet may help people to compensate for weaknesses in the short term. However, over time relationships formed over the Internet become very close, of high quality, and rooted in real-world connections. Hence, the Internet may facilitate the creation of relationships among the anxious that might not otherwise have occurred because of their lack of comfort with interpersonal situations, but that emerge to look very much like other real-world relationships. The authors conclude that, rather than turning to the Internet as a way of hiding from real life, those who are socially anxious and those who are lonely turn to the Internet as a means of forming close and meaningful relationships with others in a nonthreatening environment. They then bring these relationships into their traditional, face-to-face, circle of friends and intimates. In this case, the existence of the Internet does provide an avenue for compensatory strategies among the socially anxious.

The findings outlined do not speak to whether the Internet helps socially anxious people learn to be less anxious over time and more able to be social and begin and develop their future relationships off-line initially. In other words, the study does not look at whether, in future interactions, people who have used the Internet to develop relationships are less dependent upon the Internet for the initial stages of their future interactions. But this is a key question for future research. Although the Internet may be a facilitative tool, it may also be a tool that fundamentally changes the way that socially anxious or shy individuals interact in their daily lives. We do not currently know whether people outgrow the Internet and move on to "real" interactions in initial meetings in which they formerly would have shunned direct connections, or whether they continue a pattern of using the Internet to facilitate initial communication in situations in which they feel shy or anxious if they are involved in a "real" interaction.

Other forms of social equalization focus more directly on the equalization of access to resources and information via the Internet. For example, the Internet potentially gives people in remote areas access to otherwise unobtainable resources and to easier communication with others in their community, thus reducing inequalities. Here the Internet may have an equalizing role at the community level. In the past the availability of community resources has been key to having access to information through libraries and local government services. Now people have the ability to bypass local communities and governments and gain access to resources world wide. People can also be involved in discussions and can influence others, even when they are limited by geographical isolation. Internet access can minimize the impact of geography.

As Borgida et al. (this issue) suggest, the degree to which the Internet actually functions as a leveling force depends upon the manner in which it is implemented. If people must buy computers and pay for Internet access, then those who are initially advantaged are able to gain further advantage. If Internet access is viewed as a public resource, and the government implements it, then Internet access diminishes the impact of differences in wealth, skills, and geography.

As the Borgida et al. analysis reminds us, there is nothing automatic or inevitable about the social gains of a new technology. The social consequences of technology depend upon the social context within which the technology is utilized. Just as with earlier communication modalities—the mail, the telephone—impact depends upon implementation. When the American government decided to subsidize mail to remote locations as part of an effort to unite the population, mail then served to provide access to resources for the disadvantaged and the remote. On the other hand, it is the wealthy and already skilled who have most rapidly bought and taken advantage of the availability of personal computers. Whether the Internet is, in fact, a social-leveling technology depends not upon the technology itself, but upon the political and social framework within which it is implemented.

Why might a government resist the implementation and availability of new technologies? Deibert's (this issue) discussion of the Internet in China outlines the conflicting feelings that govern the way that a political and social hierarchy deals with Internet issues. On the one hand, the Internet is a potentially powerful engine of growth and education. On the other hand, the heightened access to information and communication with others that the Internet provides empowers people and, as a result, potentially undermines government stability and control. The Internet, from a "cyber-libertarian" perspective, as Deibert writes, will "inevitably stifle government restrictions, destroy hierarchical forms of authority, and free up the exchange of information and ideas worldwide" (p. 143). Deibert recognizes that this is only one possible perspective and that the degree to which effective surveillance and control of the Internet is possible is an evolving issue.

Through the examples Deibert presents, it is clear that the Chinese government is motivated by both views, resulting in an ambivalent and inconsistent attitude toward the Internet. As Deibert points out, "China wants to be able to reap the benefits of new information technology" (p. 145). It also wants to be able to control its use. Of course, this ambivalence is not uniquely focused upon the Internet. The widespread availability of television and cell phones, as well as open and free access to newspapers and books, also potentially pose threats to social and political hierarchies.

As with the communities studied by Borgida and colleagues, the Chinese communities studied by Deibert suggest that the Internet itself is not necessarily a politically empowering technology that lessens differences among people. Whether the Internet has such an impact depends strongly on how it is implemented and controlled by government. In this respect, the Internet joins other technologies ranging from newspapers to cell phones. These technologies hold out the possibility of social leveling but do not automatically have that consequence. If a government is motivated toward social change, it can utilize many technologies in that effort. If it opposes social change, it can implement those same technologies in ways that lessen and even eliminate their transformative potential.

The Internet as a Facilitator of Pathology

The converse of the image of Internet communication as a social-leveling force is presented in the work of Glaser, Dixit, and Green (this issue), who explore the use of the Internet to spread racism and hatred. Their research suggests that people might be less willing or able to exercise restraint and therefore act less morally in what they view as the anonymous circumstances of the Internet. Similar concerns have been raised in a variety of other arenas, ranging from on-line gambling to the exchange of child pornography (see Fisher & Barak, in press; King & Barak, 1999). In these cases, as well, it has been argued that people are using the Internet to engage in behavior that they would be less willing to engage in if they had to be less anonymous (United Kingdom Department of Trade & Industry, 1997; UNESCO, 1999).

The key question is whether the Internet facilitates such behavior. After all, it occurs often enough outside of the context of the Internet. A typical argument has been made concerning pornography on the Internet, which led the U.S. Congress to pass the Communications Decency Act in 1996. That argument is that the Internet provides access, affordability, and anonymity for those interested in sexual materials. The question is whether these factors contribute to the development of pathological control problems. It is those "out of control" problems that are most clearly psychological problems for the individual seeking access—who loses control over his or her life. They can be distinguished from enhanced access to erotica, which may or may not be a harm to the individual seeking access or for society more generally, even when people pay for sexual material (see Barak, Fisher, Belfry, & Lashambe, 1999).

Glaser et al. (this issue) extend this analysis into the area of hate speech. They do so by studying the members of White racist hate groups. Using a creative experimental methodology, members of the groups were engaged via the Internet in a discussion of a controversial topic, such as interracial marriage. Their comments were later content-analyzed. It was clear that these people were upset by phenomena such as interracial marriage and responded with suggestions that they would engage in violent behavior if they were actually in such situations.

What is missing from concerns about pornography and gambling and Internet addiction and the Glaser et al. (this issue) focus on hate groups is evidence that the Internet is facilitative of pathology (for a similar argument see Grohol, 1999). Clearly people gamble, they look at and read pornography, and at least racists threaten violence when sensitive topics are raised. But is this behavior facilitated by the context of the Internet? What is needed, and in fact called for by Glaser and his colleagues, is an effort to better understand whether and in what way the Internet facilitates pathology.

The Expression of Taboo Perspectives

A second potential group of people whose life might be changed by the Internet are those who have some taboo aspect of their identity, whether the desire to engage in socially frowned-upon practices, the desire to express extreme views, or some other issue. Here the anonymous and impersonal elements of Internet communication might encourage people to live a secret life via the Internet.

Interestingly in this regard, McKenna and Bargh (1998; see McKenna et al., this issue) found that people who initially communicate a taboo identity on the Internet are subsequently likely to both incorporate that identity into their sense of self and to disclose it to real-life friends. This suggests, as Bargh et al. (this issue) argue, that the Internet is a kind of "social laboratory" in which people test their identities before embracing them, instead of being a place to hide from taboo or hidden aspects of the self. If so, this also supports the general argument that the Internet may be important in initial interactions that are then transformed into real-world interactions. In this case people may try out taboo identities on strangers and then later on their friends and family.

Overall

All of the authors in this issue agree that the Internet is changing the nature of work, government, and social relationships. The key question is whether the availability of the new modality of communication represented by the Internet leads to fundamental changes in personal and social life. The findings of the various articles in this issue generally argue that it does not. The Internet provides people with a technology that allows them to engage in activities that they have already had ways to engage in but provides them with some added efficiencies and opportunities to tailor their interactions to better meet their needs. However, there is nothing fundamentally different about the Internet that transforms basic psychological or social life.

In fact, the research presented in this issue suggests that people generally incorporate the Internet into their social "toolkit" and use it in conjunction with face-to-face, telephone, and mail communication to deal with personal and inter-personal issues in their lives. When seeking to begin relationships, socially anxious people use the Internet to lessen the anxiety associated with initial meetings. But as relationships develop they bring them into the real world. When trying out new identities people initially express those identities over the more anonymous Internet and then embrace them and bring them into their real world by telling their friends about them. And in work settings, people naturally supplement electronic connections with the type of personal communications that minimize or eliminate the biases associated with electronic negotiations.

These findings do not minimize the potential impact of the Internet. Rather, they suggest that people are proactive and adaptive with respect to new technologies. They seek ways to use those technologies to more effectively manage their personal and interpersonal concerns. Like other modalities of communication, the Internet offers many such opportunities. The findings outlined in the articles in this issue suggest that people are actively seeking to find and make use of the possibilities offered by the Internet, just as they have embraced telephones, television, cell phones, and the blizzard of new technologies that accompany modern life. While the modalities of life rapidly evolve, the fundamental issues of life that people are seeking to address remain more constant, with people seeking tools to better live their lives.

References

Barak, A., Fisher, W. A., Belfry, S., & Lashambe, D. R. (1999). Sex, guys, and cyberspace: Effects of Internet pornography and individual differences on men's attitudes toward women. *Journal of Psychology and Human Sexuality, 11*, 63–92.

Fisher, W. A., & Barak, A. (in press). Internet pornography: A social psychological perspective on Internet sexuality. *Journal of Sex Research.*

Grohol, J. M. (1999). *Internet addiction guide* [On-line]. Available: http://psychcentral.com/ netaddiction/.

Kiesler, S. (1986). The hidden messages in computer networks. *Harvard Business Review* (January–February).

King, S. A., & Barak, A. (1999). Compulsive Internet gambling: A new form of an old clinical pathology. *CyberPsychology & Behavior, 2,* 441–456.

Kraut, R. E., Patterson, M., Lundmark, V., Kiesler, S., Mukhopadhyay, T., & Scherlis, W. (1998). Internet paradox: A social technology that reduces social involvement and psychological well-being? *American Psychologist, 53,* 1017–1032.

McKenna, K. Y. A., & Bargh, J. A. (1998). Coming out in the age of the Internet: Identity "de-marginalization" through virtual group participation. *Journal of Personality and Social Psychology, 75,* 681–694.

McKenna, K .Y. A., & Bargh, J. A. (2000). Plan 9 from cyberspace: The implications of the Internet for personality and social psychology. *Personality and Social Psychology Review, 4,* 57–75.

United Nations Educational, Scientific, and Cultural Organization (UNESCO). (1999). *Sexual abuse of children, child pornography and paedophilia on the Internet* [On-line]. Available: http://www.unesco.org/webworld/child_screen/conf_index_2.html

United Kingdom Department of Trade and Industry. (1997). *Rating, reporting, responsibility for child pornography and illegal material on the Internet* [On-line]. Available: http://www. dti.gov.uk/safety-net/r3.htm

TOM R. TYLER is a Professor of Psychology at New York University. His research examines the dynamics of authority in groups. In particular, he explores the role of justice in creating and facilitating the management of conflict. His books include *The Social Psychology of Procedural Justice* (Plenum, 1988), *Why People Obey the Law* (Yale, 1990), *Trust in Organizations* (Sage, 1996), *Social Justice in a Diverse Society* (Westview, 1997), and *Cooperation in Groups* (Psychology Press, 2000).

SOCIOLOGICAL INQUIRY

Editor: CHARLES E. FAUPEL

Published on behalf of Alpha Kappa Delta, the International Sociology Honor Society

Published by Blackwell Publishing from 2002!

SOCIOLOGICAL INQUIRY (SI) maintains a tradition of providing insight into the human condition by publishing leading theoretical and empirical research in sociology. *SI* is the journal of *Alpha Kappa Delta,* the *International Sociology Honor Society.*

ISSN: 0038-0245

Volume 72, 2002

4 issues per year

SAMPLE CONTENTS

Printed and bound by CPI Group (UK) Ltd, Croydon, CR0 4YY

09/06/2025

14685984-0001